DEADHEADS

Stories from Fellow Artists,
Friends, and Followers of the

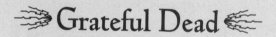 Grateful Dead

LINDA KELLY

CITADEL UNDERGROUND

A CITADEL PRESS BOOK
Published by Carol Publishing Group

CITADEL UNDERGROUND

A Citadel Press Book
Published by Carol Publishing Group
Citadel Press is a registered trademark of Carol Communications,
Inc.
Editorial Offices: 600 Madison Avenue, New York, N.Y. 10022
Sales and Distribution Offices: 120 Enterprise Avenue, Secaucus,
N.J. 07094
In Canada: Canadian Manda Group, One Atlantic Avenue, Suite 105,
Toronto, Ontario M6K 3E7
Queries regarding rights and permissions should be addressed to
Carol Publishing Group, 600 Madison Avenue, New York, N.Y. 10022

Carol Publishing Books are available at special discounts for
bulk purchases, sales promotion, fund-raising, or educational
purposes. Special editions can be created to specifications. For
details, contact: Special Sales Department, Carol Publishing
Group, 120 Enterprise Avenue, Secaucus, NJ 07094.

MANUFACTURED IN THE UNITED STATES OF AMERICA

10 9 8 7 6 5 4 3 2 1

Designed by Jessica Shatan

Library of Congress Cataloging-in-Publication Data

Kelly, Linda.
    Deadheads : behind the scenes with the family, friends, and
followers of the Grateful Dead / Linda Kelly.
        p.   cm.
    "A Citadel Press book."
    "Citadel underground"
    ISBN 0-8065-1687-9 (pbk.)
    1. Grateful Dead (Musical Group)   I. Title.
ML421.G72K45   1995
782.42166'092'2—dc20
[B]   95-217
                                                       CIP
                                                       MN

For the dear souls who have left me in this lifetime:

My mother, Patricia, who once told me, "Angels fly because they take themselves lightly"; my agent Tony Secunda, whose encouragement and faith in me blessed my spirit with newfound inspiration and confidence; and to my horse, Ben, my best friend throughout my youth.

Fly on my sweet angels.

CONTENTS

ACKNOWLEDGMENTS

My gratitude and appreciation goes to all the people who stood by me throughout this project. Their support and faith helped me make my way through the whole experience.

In particular, I would like to thank Franki Secunda for her encouragement and laughter; Charlie Ordonez, my "landlord," for his generosity—the use of his wonderful house and sweet '78 Ford pickup truck helped make this book a reality.

Special thanks also to the various people whose presence in my life influenced this work: John Burks and Ben Fong-Torres—original staff members at *Rolling Stone* who were very supportive as my teachers in college; all the musicians in my life, too numerous to name, who turned me on to the magic of music; Steve Brown; Cynthia Johnston; HA Kelly Esley, Frisco who taught me that pressure makes diamonds; Cree McCree and Donald Miller; David Godfrey; Crisco Janda and friends; Astra Esley; D.J. and everyone in my family especially my father, Bud Johnson, who always believed in me. My love, respect, and admiration to Eric Schenkman, an infinitely-talented and passionate musician as well as an excellent human being.

I am grateful to all the folks who participated in this project for their help, enthusiasm, and willingness to share. And, of course, to the Grateful Dead, who are the fire around which the people in this book dance, and without whom none of the stories herein would ever have occurred.

Last, and most certainly not least, I'd especially like to thank Jerry Garcia and Bobby Weir, who, through their radiant spirits and kind words, showed me the light in a time of confusion and helped guide me back home.

Because I finished this book just a few days before Jerry died,

PHOTO BY JANICE BELSON

everyone in it talks about Jerry and the Grateful Dead in the present tense even though he's gone now—wherever it was he went. I wondered how I should deal with this issue and decided to leave everything the way it is because I believe—and I reckon I'm not alone on this—that Jerry is still very much "present" in our hearts, and always will be.

In "Afterwards," you will find some feelings, thoughts, and photos from just a few of the hundreds of thousands of people out there who experienced Jerry's magic and who are now left to pick up the torch and carry on.

FORWARD THOUGHTS

Something I wrote caught the attention of my college professor. The story interested him, and he wanted to hear more.

I'd been writing down the ideas flying around in my head ever since I was a little girl, but having an outsider walk into that world with me that day thirteen years ago made me realize that I was the only one who knew the territory, who could navigate the way around this otherwise hidden place—my mind. This was my creation, and now someone wanted to visit. My soul was filled with a soothing feeling of hope, inspiration, and optimism.

I grew up with a big creek running through my yard, and I spent many long days down there by myself, digging in the dirt, looking for frogs, racing leaves downstream—curiosity guiding me. Something always happened, a story always unfolded right before my eyes, keeping my imagination fresh because I never knew what to expect. I never knew what I would find. That voice of "wondering" lures my soul to this day, and hundreds of collected memories run through my head like water rushing down that creek out back. I continue to gather as many as I possibly can. There's always something just around the bend, something new always on its way.

Magic'll come at ya if you're open to it. As did this book. Out of nowhere.

So many stories came at me from so many people for this project, there are thousands more I didn't get to hear due to time restraints. I connected with a variety of people, gave them an idea of what I was curious about, then let them lead the way. I merely followed them, recording the memories as we went along, gathering experiences inspired by this band called the Grateful Dead, whose music weaves the road the whole way there.

ABOUT THE AUTHOR

Linda Kelly experienced her first rock 'n' roll concert when she was twelve, and has been a great lover of music ever since. She majored in journalism from San Francisco State University in 1984, and since then has interviewed, researched, and profiled musicians, artists, and actors for such publications as *Spin*, *Mix Magazine*, *The Quake*, and *San Francisco Calendar*. After seven years in New York City, she now lives in her native San Francisco Bay Area.

1

Getting Turned On

Stuart Wax, 37, music manager, Los Angeles:

I was twelve years old at my first Dead show. It was at the Felt Forum in New York in 1971 with the New Riders of the Purple Sage. My brother took me. It was great.

I was in sixth grade, and I had a reading teacher who was getting rid of his albums, so I bought *Anthem of the Sun* and *Aoxomoxoa*, which are two way-out albums for a sixth grader to have. That was my beginning. My brother, who was already seeing them at the Fillmore East, came home from college and said, "What are you doing with *these* albums!"

Kim Weiskopf, 48, TV writer/producer: *Married . . . With Children*, Los Angeles:

My very first Grateful Dead show was at San Francisco State University in 1965. I was taken there, completely impromptu. I didn't know what to expect. To me, it was like "Jeez, does anybody have ID? Maybe I can get a beer or something." That was about as basic and as simple as I was at that time.

Jerry Garcia playing at the Electric on the Eel River, Northern California, 1992 (PHOTO BY CHRIS FLUM)

It was a seminal experience. It was as if the oranges tasted like they'd never tasted before. The sound of the band! I was about eighteen. I was a pretty straight kid from the suburbs—San Fernando Valley—trying to figure out how to get laid. After this event, which is still *very* clear in my mind, having listened to them play for what seemed like many hours and very likely was—and that was just one of Jerry's solos!—I didn't feel so out of it. I felt like part of a tribe. I really felt like I wasn't so alone in some of the feelings I was feeling. Their music brought to life some of the things inside of me. It was a real coming-of-age sort of sensation. I'm sure the pot didn't hurt!

I remember it like it was yesterday because it was the first time in my life I didn't feel as if I had to hide anything. I could be completely candid with total strangers. Again, that might have been the pot talking, and probably was, but . . .

The Dead were playing in the college cafeteria. I'd been in there before but only with my schoolbooks, getting something to eat. The tables were cleared away, and people were either standing, sitting, or dancing. And there was a light show—guys with eyedroppers and oil, colors projected on the wall.

The thing I connected with on Jerry was that he . . . other musicians to me made a *huge* show out of playing. He didn't. In other words, he was compact, like he still is today. Everything is kind of self-contained. I was watching his hands and thought, "Man, all of this sound is coming from this one guy." Well, not all of the sound, but he was the lead, and he had several of the longest solos that I can recall ever hearing. I was just starting to listen to music at the time. This really was like my first baby step.

At that time, you put on the Dead, you played them loud, and you were transported somewhere else. If you asked me now to recite Dead lyrics, I couldn't do it. That show at SF State was the first time I ever experienced white noise. I remember actually moving closer to the speakers. It was the first live, loud, San Francisco music I'd ever heard, and another week didn't go by before I actively went out seeking these concerts, most of which were free so you could get to them. I was at the Human Be-In, and I was at Monterey [Pop Festival]. I kind of structured my life around the music.

That time of my life actually became part of my being and still is. I was lucky to be where I was geographically when I was coming of age. I'm indebted to all kinds of people. Certain professors at school, certain friends I met, were really instrumental in my coming of age. When you're seventeen or eighteen years old, your footsteps kind of start being in cement, and it just so happened that I was that age in the mid to late sixties, right when the best party ever was going on. I wonder how I could be who I am now having been at that party! I'm just glad I got to go. It was a lot of fun. And I'd say that the Grateful Dead were the very first ones. Absolutely. They popped my cherry.

Dan Wilson, 49, street artist, Sacramento, CA:

When I first saw the Grateful Dead, I didn't know where I was going. I'd heard there was gonna be a band, some music at San Francisco State College where I was studying radio, television, and film. This was 1965—somewhere back in there. I must've been about seventeen. I got out of there with a BA in 1967 with the draft board breathin' heavy on me all four years. I ended up finally refusing the draft—that's where that went. But anyway . . .

Here came the Grateful Dead! I'd never heard of the Warlocks or anybody like that before, so this was brand-new to me. When I walked into the cafeteria, they had just started. They were standin' on the tables playing their music. I'll always remember Jerry Garcia saying, "Turn the bass up! Turn it up till it pops when he touches it!" I thought, "Oh, man! This is gonna be great!" I like a loud bass. And it *was* great. They had the place just dancing like crazy. All these college kids, clean-cut, and here's the Grateful Dead, the most

Baby BA for the GD, Cal Expo, 1985

(PHOTO BY DAN WILSON)

unusual and different-looking people I think I'd ever seen in my life at that point. They stood out. I mean, they had stage presence—as well as *world* presence!

I really enjoyed hearin' that first time, and I decided right then and there, "This is my band!" The music they played was so full of fun—*life!* And I was worried already about the army and the Vietnam war, and that was so dreary—it's death. And here was the Grateful Dead, just the opposite. I've never played a musical instrument, but I really do listen to music and I really loved this band. I started looking for them after that first show. I saw them quite a bit during their first few years. I remember the next time I saw them was over at Longshoremen's Hall. Owsley had his sugar cubes out near the door in the lobby. I passed on that, not really wantin' to get involved right then in what that was. But I was watching other people and they seemed to be doing all right! And the music was cool. My college roommate knew a guy in a band, so he wanted to see them, and the Grateful Dead just happened to be there too. So that was my second time.

Then I saw them again over at the Matrix—a little tiny club down on lower Fillmore. They put the whole band up there on this tiny stage. I remember "Viola Lee Blues" that night was outstanding! They played it for everything it was worth. Bob Weir was outstanding. The music just finally got through to me, to where I was right with what they were doing up onstage, really not aware of my own surroundings. I was going with 'em!

Then I saw them . . . gosh, I guess probably at California Hall— that was a memorable gig. I think they put that on with Big Brother, and the Hell's Angels were involved too. That was a big party. My sister Suzanna came out from New York. She's a bit older than me. She'd heard about the Grateful Dead, and I told her, "You gotta see them if you're out here." So, I took her to this show and I remember watching her dancing down on the floor. They played "Midnight Hour" for about forty-five minutes. She was just loving this music. She was just really gassed by the whole thing. I was happy to get her acquainted with the Dead.

Sheila Rene, 56, music anthropologist, Texas via San Francisco:

I have a list of every show beginning in 1966 to 1993, every year, every show, who opened, if it was a benefit or not . . . the whole bloody history. The first time that the Grateful Dead played for Bill Graham, according to his own records, was in June of 1967, opening for the Jefferson Airplane at the Fillmore Auditorium. My first show was at the Fillmore in 1967, but probably the best Dead show I ever saw, bar none, just because of the acts involved, was at the Santa Clara Fairgrounds. It was the Grateful Dead, Janis Joplin, Jim Morrison, Airplane, Big Brother, Santana, In Cold Blood . . .

My very first Dead show was very spiritual. I felt safe, like it was a good place to be, I felt taken care of, and moist and warm. Because of that I went back to see them many, many times.

David Gans, 41, radio producer: *Grateful Dead Hour;* **author:** *Playing in the Band* **and** *Conversations With the Dead,* **San Francisco:**

I've been seeing the Dead for twenty-three years. My first show was in 1972. I was eighteen, living in San Jose. My friends had been bugging me for months to check out the Grateful Dead. I was into the wimpy singer/songwriters of the time, playing my guitar and singing for fun and sort of a living, doing Elton John, Cat Stevens, and things like that. It was kind of a leap for me, but my songwriting partner and best friend, Steve Donnelly, persuaded me to take some acid and go see the Grateful Dead. I had been to concerts before—I'd seen the Doors—but not many. I didn't have a car and a lot of bucks, so it wasn't that easy for me to get around. Plus, I lived in San Jose. I wasn't a guy who frequented the Fillmore or anything like that.

So, we got our friend Dennis to be our designated driver, we took some Windowpane, and we hit the road. By the time we got to San Francisco, we were completely out of our skulls, and there was something wrong with the car. The throttle was stuck all the way open, so we had blazed up Highway 280 at about eighty miles an hour! We were determined to get to the show and not deal with the car thing. It was a VW 1500, and Dennis had to ride the clutch to keep it from going ninety miles an hour all the time. We got there and took the car to a service station. Something got dealt with at least enough to get us to the show.

It was completely crazed. We got there late, the place was full, and we ended up going all the way to the topmost part. This was Winterland, and the stage was on the side, which is the only time I ever saw the stage on the side. There was one balcony that went way up to the roof. Well, that's where we ended up. All the way in the last row. It was 130 degrees up there, and this is March 5, 1972. The weather inside had nothing to do with the weather outside. In fact, one thing I remember distinctly about the ride home was that we were driving through this thick fog, and then suddenly we were in this tiled tunnel, like being in the biggest fuckin' bathroom you ever saw! From this murky fog into this porcelain heaven for fifteen seconds, and then back into the fog again. Obviously, I have only fleeting impressions from this tremendously big night.

I was pretty overwhelmed by the crowd and stuff, a little bit scared. I had a hard time handling acid in those days. It was always a *big* thing. We saw the New Riders, which was pretty interesting. I enjoyed "The Last Lonely Eagle" and I think they did "Honky Tonk Women," and one or two others songs I recognized.

Then the Dead came on. I was quite impressed. It took me a long time to sort out what had happened. They started with "Bertha," and what stuck in my mind was certain things about that piece of music. My mind interpolated a musical lick that was never there. In my head, I heard this other thing that belonged in there. It took me a long time to figure out, "Ah, this is their music, and this was the thing that I contributed to it in my mind." I later figured out that another thing I was impressed with was Jerry's guitar line on "Black-Throated Wind." Everything about "Greatest Story Ever Told" knocked me out. The second set was all familiar tunes. They did "Good Lovin'" and "Not Fade Away" with Pigpen. It was the only time I ever saw Pigpen. I saw him from way the fuck up in the top of Winterland! It was not an intimate encounter at all. But he had a commanding presence, even from that distance.

I remember fleeting things from that night, and over the next few months I bought records and started to get a sense of what was what. *Ace* came out, and "Greatest Story Ever Told" was just amazing to me. Bobby's rhythm-guitar style on that record—it's quintessential Weir guitar. Everything about it caused me to revise my musical sensibility. I was immediately interested in the songwriting of the Grateful Dead as being an alternative to the commercial stuff. It was no conventional structures with hooks and choruses. Other things were going on.

One thing about the Grateful Dead was that they had a lyricist who wasn't on the stage. That was an interesting model for my partner and me because he was a lyricist and I was the performing half of the songwriting team. The Dead's songs were vastly more interesting than most of what I'd been hearing up to that time. It was engaging stuff. It engaged my own mind. It was sketchy. There were stories. It took a long time to figure out what the words were, and even then, when you thought you had a pretty good idea, it wasn't a straight narrative, it was something that required a little more imagination. It led me into a more sophisticated approach to my own songwriting. I started writing in odd time signatures, started looking at deeper themes, started working a song-cycle thing, like a rock opera kind of deal.

Over the next few years, I started to comprehend what was going on in the Dead's musical passages. At first, I didn't know what to make of those big long jams. They were just confusing. After that first show, I bought a bunch of records, and the next time I heard they were coming to town, I went to all four shows.

Cree McCree, 47, writer, New York:

So it took me a couple of decades, but I finally caught up with the Grateful Dead in 1991. Or maybe the Dead caught up with me. In any case, a conjunction occurred on the space-time continuum of Giants Stadium, where a "Picasso Moon" rose over sixty thousand Deadheads and this neophyte initiate, who was totally underwhelmed and thoroughly overwhelmed by the once-in-a-lifetime experience called My First Dead Show.

So I hooked myself a trip-tick from Captain Hook himself, T. J. Can-do, who's riding serious shotgun while his brother steers us out to New Jersey, three hours behind schedule but right on time.

Stadium shows are not my métier; I haven't been on a playing field since Shea, when I went three times in one week (but, hey, that was for the Rolling fuckin' Stones, who have always been, and will always be, My Band). So there's the usual crowd-claustrophobe disorientation, tempered by a vibe that can only be called mellow. Then the band materializes onstage.

I wait so patiently, a stranger in a strange land. Everyone else goes nuts when they pull "Bertha" out of the hat, but I don't know the

Chris Flum (far right) and friends, Shoreline Amphitheater, California, 1991 (PHOTO BY CHRIS FLUM)

material, the codes, the familial signals—and worst of all, I'm not getting off. The music isn't getting into my body, there's no vibrations I can seriously groove to. It all seems like so much psychedelic mood music, scattered to the winds. Then along comes "Red Rooster," which gives me some bearings, and even though I'm wishing it was Clapton or Mick, instead of Bob Weir, the blues inevitably draws me right up front to the stage, where things begin to change.

Up close and personal, the Dead are grittier, the sound waves more compelling as the acoustics begin to crystallize. It's an epic musical journey, the hills higher, the valleys deeper, crazy as the marching bears; as vividly close to the bone as the grinning skulls. Suddenly, it's just us and the band, Jerry's white hair flying behind him like angel wings, all of us singing "the sun's gonna shine in my back door someday" like it's the "Hallelujah Chorus."

Chris Flum, 28, "cool dude," Orinda, CA:

I know I was taken to a Grateful Dead show when I was a real little kid, but 1982 was the first Dead show that I remember. I was working at Little Winterland Studios at the time, which was derived from the original Winterland Studios, and learning all the studio business. Stephen Barsotti, who's worked with and been around the Dead a long time, happened to give me backstage passes to the Dead at Frost Amphitheater—three days in a row! I had an all-access backstage pass. Talk about cool! I got an actual laminate! I still carry it around to this day.

I thought I was the coolest cat in the world. I had passes to the Grateful Dead. Backstage. We're talking private parking and everything. Nobody could tell me what to do and what not to do. So I was dancin' around, bein' the fool that I was. The first day there, I dosed hard. That was cool. I loved that show. The Grateful Dead were the coolest people. I went everywhere. I caught the show from every angle. Nobody ever questioned me, they saw the pass on me. The Deadheads were all cool. I got to go up onto the podium in the center where the soundboard is. They had a two-story soundboard and I went up on the second story and watched half the show from there.

Familiar scene at the Dead, Squaw Valley, 1992 (PHOTO BY CHRIS FLUM)

That was the first time I ever really got *into* the Dead. I was spoiled. Which I still am. I've bought my fair share of tickets, I'm not one to always say, "I have to have a backstage pass." I buy tickets, and if I get a backstage pass, then, "Yahoo!" But if not, I still always enjoy the show. But I usually always end up getting a pass.

I was in the music industry, a wanna-be, and the next thing I know, it happened for me, and there I've been ever since— stuck to the Grateful Dead. Everybody was so nice to me at that first show. I remember the security guard at the backstage entrance—the first thing he asked me was my name. I told him it was Chris, and from then on out, and I still see the same guy to this day, he knows my name. That was something you could only find at a Dead show. You wouldn't see that at a Metallica show or any other type of show.

Bob Rupe, 38, Cracker bassist, Richmond, VA:

I think we got the gig playing with the Grateful Dead because Cracker covered "Loser" on *Kerosene Hat*. I guess it raised Garcia's eyebrows or something. I don't know. Plus, Jackson Herring, who was Cracker's business manager at the time, is pretty much a Dead fan. He's over at Bill Graham Presents now. It all lines up!

So, in 1994, we did three days with the Dead in Oregon. I was more curious than anything about that gig, because I'd never even been to a Dead show. The first time I go to a Dead show, I end up playing with 'em! That was kind of wild. And it wasn't like I was anti-Dead. I'd listened to their records, or whatever was on the radio, but it just never really connected. I thought some of the songs were good, but really that's not what the Dead are about. They're about the jam, they're not so much about the song. That's why so many live tapes circulate. I really didn't realize that until I played with them.

The first day, I was standing on the side of the stage seeing what was going on, and I began to understand what the Grateful Dead are all about. I thought, "Okay. This is why people trade tapes, because they get into the song, they work their way to the section of the song where they're gonna jam, and sometimes it happens and sometimes it doesn't. But when it happens, it's great." They really do manage to get to that next level and take everybody with them. That's why the audience is so cool too, because they're just waiting for that. They want it to happen. Garcia knows that the Grateful Dead are about getting into that jam section, and that's what makes them great.

Paul Perme, aka Trinket Guy, 31, Gila Monsters harmonicist, KY:

My first show was in 1983. I was nineteen, a freshman in college in Boston. I'd heard of the Dead, but I never really knew what they were all about. I'd heard "Truckin'" on the radio and thought they were kind of a country band or something. My friends said I had to go to a show, so we went, and of course we were in altered states. I was like, "Holy shit! Where did all these people come from? Where do they go?" It was just fascinating to me. You're driving around and there's all these people, normal, and then a Dead show happens and *boom!* A million Deadheads come out of nowhere.

I remember trying to call songs at that first show because it was the cool thing to do: hear the band tunin' up and try and call the song. Everyone was laughing at me because I didn't know any tunes except "Truckin'" and "Casey Jones." I got laughed at a lot. "Hey, it's the experimental, guinea-pig guy. It's his *first* show!" But I felt like everybody around me was so *for* me, helping me along. I wanted to go to more and more shows, because all these amazing people came out of the woodwork.

Caryn Shalita, mid-20s, actress, Los Angeles:

I 'd listened to the Dead and liked them, but for whatever reason I'd just never gone to a show. The first time I saw them
was in Albany, New York, 1990. My husband and I went on a
break from school: down to Florida for a couple days, up to New
Hampshire to go skiing a couple days, and then we detoured
through Albany on our way back to New York so we could hit the
Saturday-night Dead show.

We were supposed to meet up with a friend at that show. That's
one of the cool things about Dead shows: you always run into people you know—somehow. This happens *consistently*. You have no
plans of when to meet, where to meet, but just somehow, you will
find whoever you need to find. There's this karma that works only
at Dead shows. That's just not true anyplace else. There's this sort
of synergy of the crowd, or whatever you want to call it. So it was
fun at this show because we got to hook up with Pete, a very, very
good friend who's just nuts and is someone you'd want to hang out
with anywhere.

Paul Perme and Tracey D'Arcy, Las Vegas, 1994 (PHOTO BY KEN 4-DING)

But what made that first Dead show like no other concert I'd ever been to was that I was sitting around people I didn't know, and I was offered food by one person, and drink by another person. I thought, "This doesn't happen! This is not normal. This is great!" People just don't share like this, I mean, I wish they would, but they don't. Most people at concerts are rude, not very nice. A lot of the people are just very self-centered. They tell you to sit down when you're dancing or whatever. I tell people who like the Dead but have never been to a show that they have to see them live because they won't experience what the Grateful Dead is all about until they are at a show.

Tom Constanten, 51, pianist/composer, San Francisco:

I saw the Grateful Dead back when they were the Warlocks. They were like a lot of other garage bands, doing the pop tunes of the day. It was sort of funny seeing Jerry Garcia singing "Wooly-Booly"!

Ricky Begneaud, 37, Cajun chef/caterer, Mill Valley, CA:

I was born in Lafayette, Louisiana, and grew up there. In the early seventies, I used to go to a store called Budget Records, which was this little hippie place. I was about twelve or thirteen years old, and I'd get those original *Rolling Stone* newspapers. That's the first way I heard about the Dead. It's the only reason I ever knew about them. There wasn't a radio station where I could plug into too many different kinds of music down there. Lafayette was a little town and it wasn't hip. A few hip folks were around, but I was young and I wasn't really connected with those types of people. The hippest I got was when I would travel with my uncle (artist Robert Rauschenberg) and my mom. We'd go to concerts like Ravi Shankar in a tent in upstate New York.

The first person who ever really turned me on to the Grateful Dead was Jimmy MacDonell. Jimmy and I grew up together in Lafayette. There were no Deadheads in Lafayette. If there were, nobody knew about it. Most people didn't even know about the Grateful Dead. When we were about eighteen, Jimmy left our little Cajun domain to go to Amherst College. He started rantin' and ravin' about this band called the Grateful Dead. I remember once I was down at Rauschenberg's house in Florida, and Jimmy sent me an Easter card with this list of records to buy: *Wake of the Flood, Mars Hotel,* and some others. I got to learn the Dead's music and I fell in love with it. The more I listened to it, the more it made sense. The Easter card also had some other things in it that helped the music make more sense too! It just kept getting more and more interesting, lyrically and musically.

I'd been to *a lot* of rock concerts, but I'd never gone to a Dead show yet. I remember Jimmy brought a live tape once, and I heard a "Scarlet Begonias." I said, "Man, the stereo is messed up. It's warbling, man. It's off-sync." Jimmy said, "No, that's how it is." I was only used to studio versions of the songs, and I was listening for the first time to this live audience tape somebody had recorded in the back of a stadium. The syncopations—everything—was totally different. It totally threw me! I was used to a more consistent sound.

Then Jimmy and I went to our first show on January 8, 1979, at Madison Square Garden. We came in from Amherst, and the train station must of been underneath because we just walked up the stairs and got a ticket for the show. Then we went home, changed clothes, and went back to the concert. I remember I bought my first Dead T-shirt there that night. Some Egyptian thing, *really* ugly, but I wore it out anyway!

Anyway, we got in and got to our seats, which were eye level but way in the back. Right before the band came on, we took . . . I don't even know what it was, but it had some label of green associated to it. I remember the second set beginning and the whole building . . . Madison Square Garden is round, and everybody was little pink pyramids dancing all around me, and I didn't know how to deal with it! I couldn't navigate too well that night. I was totally out there, and finally I blasted through the roof. I said to Jimmy, "I gotta go." And Jimmy said, "You can't leave. We can't go." And I said, "You don't have to leave. I have to go." I start making my way through what seemed like catacombs, tunnels. I was trying to make my way through the hallways. Jimmy was following me because I hadn't been to New York that many times and I didn't know where I was going.

There were police slamming this guy's head in the door, all this weird shit going on, and we opened this one door out of all this

High on a mountain, Squaw Valley, 1992 (PHOTO BY TREY ALLEN)

chaos, closed it behind us, and everything was silent all of a sudden in this huge room! At the time, it seemed like ten stories high, five basketball floors wide. Two policemen with white gloves were standing there with their arms crossed, talking to each other, at the very opposite corner. They just looked at us, and we're standing there looking bewildered, like, "Where are we?" Jimmy and I looked at each other like, "Well?" We tried to walk out, but the door was locked. Finally, we got out of the place somehow, I don't quite remember how, but we got out!

We negotiated a bit, then got this bizarre Jamaican cabdriver. It was his first night ever as a cabdriver. Jimmy was at the helm. He was trying to tell the guy how to get home, but he didn't know where we were either! Buildings were bending over the road, so we just wanted to get somewhere we knew! Finally, we got to Rauschenberg's house on Lafayette Street, and I thought, "I can't even go inside." So we walked down to this little bar, and for about thirty minutes, I couldn't even talk. Jimmy was saying all this stuff, and he started getting concerned because I was just sitting there!

The show was great, but whatever we took that night was too out there for me. I mean, there were bottles flying at Madison Square Garden, and it just wasn't something I was used to. That was my first experience with the Grateful Dead. It was so overwhelming for me. It was heavy. It's what I call a "colorful blur." It changed my life for a long time.

Rachel Clein, 13, student, Marin County, CA:

I was a baby at my very first Dead show, so I don't remember it. The first show I can remember was when I was three. It was at the Greek Theater in 1985. All I remember is that it was really colorful and loud! I've seen them maybe twenty times or so. I still like seeing them now. I like their music.

Last time I saw the Dead was last year, New Year's Eve at Shoreline. It was pretty much one of their normal shows, but they played a couple of songs they don't normally do. I usually don't know the titles, but usually I can sing some or all of the words to their songs. If not, I know the tune at least. I remember the first real song that I learned was "Bertha." My parents had an anthology of their songs up to 1983, and that song was in there. My dad used to sing it, so I learned it. I don't remember all of the words anymore, but I remember the tune.

I don't have that many tapes that the Dead have put out, but my dad has tapes he's made at shows, or that his friend made in the soundbooth. I only have one actual studio Dead tape. The rest are ones we've made at shows. I think my favorite song is either "Truckin'" or "Casey Jones."

Jeff Brown, 36, landscape architect, San Francisco:

My very first show was at the Capitol Theater, New Jersey. I think it was 1977. I really didn't know much about the Dead, and I didn't know anything about tickets yet—that took a while to sink in. A friend mail-ordered the tickets. They were third row! My first show was third row, center! Right there. And I remember saying something like, "Hey, Jerry, you're putting on a bit of weight!" I have felt bad about that ever since! I mean, I was in the third row in this little theater—he *must* have heard me! Maybe he didn't. Who knows *where* Jerry is during a show! But, boy, I felt bad about that, in a friendly kind of way.

Rick Begneaud (right) with his Dead pals Michael Nash and So Young
Mac, Greek Theater, California, 1987 (PHOTO BY PHILIP GOULD)

Richard Yaker, 26, futurist engineer/visionary, Los Angeles:

y very first show was in the summer of 1987, between
my freshman and sophomore years in college. It was
Dylan and the Dead at Giants Stadium in New York.
My little brother was a Deadhead, he had extra tickets, so me and
my high school friend went.

When it came to getting high in high school, we got it in very
small quantities. But when we got to college, it was easy to get because connections were far more abundant. So, one of my friends
had gotten a "QP"—quarter pound. We had tons! We went to the
show and my friends and I decided we'd each smoke our own joint
rather than share because we had so much we didn't have to worry
about it. Here we are, these stupid, immature kids, getting really
high, and . . . I passed out! Not for the whole show, but for one section of it. I think it was part of Dylan's set, the transition. I missed
Dylan's opener!

A key part of this story is that during our freshman year, my buddies and I hung out one day and played Hendrix's *Greatest Hits*, and
my friend kept playing "All Along the Watchtower" over and over

again. So . . . here I am at my first Dead show, and this same friend
is shaking me, I'm waking up, and I'm hearing "Watchtower." It was
really weird, I was totally out of it, and my friend is going, "Dude!
They're playing 'Watchtower'! They're playing 'Watchtower'!" and
shaking me to get up. All of a sudden I woke up and I realized that
they were in the middle of the song. I'd heard Dylan's version, and
compared to Hendrix's version, it's like night and day. But this was
really weird because it was in between the Dylan version and the
Hendrix version, with Dylan singing and the Grateful Dead playing it! When you wake up, you're out of it anyway, and then on
top of that it was my first Dead show, I was wasted, and I had twenty
thousand people around me. It was totally bizarre, but really cool!

Ken Fine aka Kew, 36, organic T-shirt salesman, Liberty, ME:

R emember it well: Englishtown, New Jersey, 1977. I was
nineteen. I'd just gotten my first Grateful Dead album, Anthem of the Sun, and then my younger brother and I got a
copy of Terrapin Station and we listened to it all summer. At that
time, I'd just read the Electric Kool-Aid Acid Test, so I was really intrigued by that whole aspect, and then to go to the show—which
was 150,000 people in a big field in the middle of a racetrack—I
had a pretty amazing experience.

It was just huge. We went to the show—got a ride down in a big
Cadillac with a bunch of people. There was a huge camp-out there,
so we stayed the night before and went in the next day. The place
was mobbed, and we just "landed" with our coolers and blankets
and stuff, right in the middle of 150,000 people. And of course, drugs
were involved . . . in this case, having read the book, I was intrigued
by the whole acid thing, so when we scored acid from some guys
who couldn't even see straight, it ended up being really good stuff.

There were three bands: the New Riders were done, the Marshall
Tucker Band was done, and now it was the middle of the afternoon—really hot. They started breaking down the amps from the
Marshall Tucker Band, and the audience was just standing there,
fixated on the stage. My friend turned to me and said, "This is
ridiculous! Everybody sit down!" and he sits down on our cooler. I
sit down next to him and I look, and everyone just starts sitting

down—150,000 people just all sat down! I looked at my friend and said, "Did that really just happen? Wow! We're in sync! Everybody's in sync! This is great!"

Later in the day, we went to get some water. We gathered up a few jugs from our gang, and as we stepped over everyone's legs and tried to make our way through this huge mass of people, everyone said, "Oh! You're going to get water? Here, take my jug; if I never see you again, it's fine. If I do, that's great!" So, we ended up at the water hose with about fifteen jugs, and we filled 'em all up. I'll always remember my friend lost his shoes in the mud! Anyway, we're hiking back through the crowd, and everybody's going, "Oh! There's a guy with some water!" We were like, "Sure! Have a whole jug!" We were feeling pretty powerful, sharing all this water. We made a lot of friends on the way back. There's a fine art to stepping over three thousand people and getting anywhere! Then, of course, the band starts playing "Truckin'" and everybody's singing: "What a long, strange trip it's been!"

Oh! Someone had a baby there too. The announcer came out and said, "Congratulations. You're the second-biggest town in New Jersey right now," and he announced how many people were there. Later he came out and said, "Okay, now you people over there by that speaker know who you are, you have to make a path from there to the gate there's a lady havin' a baby"—and everybody just moved! It was just huge, massive. And I realized when they said that, that truly out of 150,000 people there probably 70,000 were on acid, so there definitely was a real shared energy on a massive scale. It was amazing. So I was hooked from then on.

Annie Myles, 24, music manager, New York:

I was sixteen years old when I went to my first show. It was New Year's Eve, 1986, at the Henry J. Kaiser in Oakland. I snuck out of my house and I flew to California without my parents knowing. Oh, no! Wait. They *did* know about that one. I flew out there and just went and checked out the shows. I'd been listening to their music for a while; I was definitely developing my own personality at the time, and it seemed to be in alignment with a lot of what I found in the Grateful Dead's lyrics and the people I met who listened to the Dead. I was totally into music at that point, absolutely.

I caught the four shows there and I came back a completely different person. I was never the same! In those four days, I had the most mind-boggling experience of my life. I met so many different people. We had a hotel room, but we got kicked out and ended up crashing with different people wherever we could. I had my first introductions to LSD, ecstasy, opium . . . hmmm, what else did I take when I was out there? . . . mushrooms. So it was a *very* expansive time for me. My mind was totally psyched to be blown, and it was. But it was blown by people who were so positive and artistic and embracing of me, and gentle towards me. They were so willing to teach and to kind of push me in a direction that was peaceful and giving towards others. I really dug that. I was into community. I was into communication amongst one another.

What the Grateful Dead did to me really was exemplify that music can unite people, no matter where they're from and no matter what their backgrounds are. For the two hours that you're in a show, music totally brings you together. There are people who you'd probably never talk to, but . . . you'll dance with them at a Dead show! You'll smoke their pipe at a Dead show! You'll give 'em a back rub or share their orange or something like that. I mean weird shit happens. The whole scene—at least it used to—transcends all social ramifications of your normal experience. I was really into that. It was a great place to stake out my own identity.

Annetta Pearson, 50, artist/homemaker, San Francisco:

My suitor, Greg, wanted to introduce me to the Dead because he wanted to marry me, but before he proposed, he wanted to make sure I could love the Dead. He didn't want to have any mixed marriages! So, on Ash Wednesday in 1986, he took me to the Henry J. Kaiser in Oakland.

It was rainy and dark, and as we got closer and closer to Kaiser, I kept noticing these *weird* people. It was like all these people had crawled out from under a rock. It was amazing. It was like a medieval fair. I remember holding Greg's hand real tight because there were lots of people and I didn't want to get lost. This was about the second concert I'd ever been to in my life. I was forty-two.

We got in, and we have a large group of friends that go to shows and they always sit in the same spot in various venues. So seats had been saved and they were excellent. The decorations were superb. There was lots of activity. Some people were playing volleyball on the downstairs floor. I was agog over all these strange people, barefoot in the middle of winter, and babies. The crowd went wild every time there was any kind of movement on the blank stage; a roadie would come out and everybody would roar.

What really caught me was when suddenly the lights went out and the Neville Brothers came on. The first thing I said was, "*Wow!*" and I was hooked from that moment on. I was totally taken. Then the Wild Tchoupitoula Indians came on. That was great. And the Dead came on and the frenzy was just incredible in the crowd. My next big impression was Brent playing "Ton of Steel," and I fell in love with Brent. That was when I really sat up. It was an amazing show.

John Popper, 27, Blues Traveler harmonicist, Princeton, NJ:

My first show was in 1986 or so. I was just starting to hang out with Bob (Blues Traveler bass player) a lot, and he was a big Deadhead since 1982. So I went to see Dylan and the Dead at JFK. I ate a whole lot of acid. I remember that, and I remember everybody knew the words, and it was like the emperor's new clothes. Everyone was asking me, "Aren't you enjoying it? Don't you like this?" That drove me nuts. It made it impossible for me to enjoy the show. If you're not having fun, it ruins their fun. I remember I was convinced at one point that they were trying to hypnotize me and control my mind. I hallucinated severely at that show. Luckily I had my harmonica and just started playing as hard as I could during the set break, and that got me back down.

The first time I actually enjoyed a show was at Madison Square Garden, I think in 1987. I snuck away from everybody and sort of lost the people I was with, so when people said, "Dude! Why aren't you dancing?" I said, "Because I don't want to!" I just sat in a chair and watched the Dead and that was really fun.

Steve Eichner, 30, R&R photographer, New York:

The very first album I bought was Led Zeppelin's *Presence*, but the very second album I bought was *Steal Your Face*. It wasn't really that I'd heard of the Grateful Dead, but I'd seen that steal-your-face around and I thought it was really cool. I was ten years old. I didn't play that album that much. I think "Truckin'" is on there, so I kind of knew that song, but I wasn't really a Deadhead. I was a Zeppelinhead in high school.

When I went to Fredonia State College, up near Buffalo, New York, that's when I got turned on to the Grateful Dead. My roommate was into them. The first song I remember hearing over and over again and really liking was "St. Stephen." My name being in it made it mean even more. Everybody was always describing to me the Grateful Dead experience and how great it was. In 1983 or 1984, there was this show near college in Niagara Falls. We all road-tripped up there with a guy named Fred Bonn, who was taking ceramics class and had been making these Grateful Dead plates and things. He called them Stonedware.

I was always a partier, but I was more like a heavy-metal guy than a Deadhead type. But I went to this show and we all dosed. It was a really nice day, Fred sold all his Stonedware, and we went into the show. We were all dosed, and we walked up on top of this really high structure, which was really amazing.

I don't remember the songs they played because I wasn't familiar with them, but apparently it was a really good show. I was really psyched because I went with people who knew it and were into it. The Deadhead experience was really cool, so I started to go to shows with all those people.

Greg Martens, 31, entrepreneur, Portland, ME:

I moved up to Maine when I was thirteen and never knew who the Grateful Dead were, didn't even know what drugs were, having been sheltered in Greenwich, Connecticut, where it's very conservative. My father worked in Manhattan for Crayola Crayons, so I always had the best crayons. One night he came home, had a couple drinks, and said, "We're moving to Maine."

Admiring one Dead T-shirt of thousands, Alpine, 1987 (PHOTO BY STEVE EICHNER)

He's an artist and he wanted to work with his hands, so we moved from Greenwich to a dirt road on a lake up in the middle of nowhere so he could do what he wanted. My neighbors grew dope and listened to the Grateful Dead, so my life changed a lot right then. If I'd stayed in Connecticut, I wouldn't be telling this story now. So I lived on a lake, hung out with my neighbors, and found out what the Grateful Dead and the whole psychedelic scene was about at a very young age.

My first show was May 13, 1979, in Portland, Maine. It was Mother's Day. I was a freshman in a private school, and my best friend, Tom, and I came up with some lame excuse so we could miss study hall on Sunday night. We hitchhiked from Hebrin, Maine, to Portland, which is about eighty miles, got dropped off in Portland at about one or two in the afternoon, and walked to the Civic Center. We got to this huge parking lot where all these Deadheads were parked with their feet hanging out the doors, cranking Grateful Dead tapes. We walked over to them and they said, "Yeah! This is last night's show!" We didn't know anything about tapers, this was in 1979, so there weren't very many people touring. Tom was so taken by these tapers that he became a taper, which led him to his profession today. He's in Hollywood doing audio for NBC movies of the week, and CBS.

As we walked over the hill to the arena, I ran into this guy who was bootlegging T-shirts. I started talking to him, and that's how I got into the T-shirt thing. Not that I bootlegged anything from the Dead, I never did. They gave us permission to sell M. C. Escher T-shirts when the whole scene broke open. We gave three hundred shirts to the band; Bobby wanted his in a different color, Mickey wanted a tank top, so we special-ordered a bunch of stuff for the band.

Anyway . . . getting there to that first show was so intense. Some lady came out from the backstage area with a purse full of— I assume it was—Owsley's paper. Dosed everybody all day long. There were probably ten thousand people at the show and everybody was on the same stuff. It was quite an experience. I'll never forget it.

Annie Harlow, 36, green grocer, New England:

I was sixteen when I went to my first show, at the Boston Garden, June 28, 1974 . . . row L. I can find out my seat number, which I'd like to, because that was my first show and it was very much *my* seat! Details, you know? I remember so much from that night.

It all kind of started out in 1972. We had just moved to the Boston area and lived in a little suburb, a regular town. My father met somebody that was walking their dog as he was walking our dog. It turned out that they had just moved to the same town, so our families became acquainted because we were all new. They had kids the same age range, and my brother became really good friends with them. I sort of did, but I was young, kind of a weenie. You're kind of in your geek stage in ninth grade.

Anyway, they had a party. Well, their *parents* went away and the *kids* had a party, as I recall. A lot of people there were older than me, and when you're fourteen and see people eighteen and nineteen, at least for me, I was hanging with the "older group." There was music playing, and I saw this one guy dancing to this music and

Another day at the parking lot, Buffalo, New York, 1992 (PHOTO BY TREY ALLEN)

he was fluidity defined. He was beautiful! If you looked at the guy himself you might go, "Who is this gangly guy? Fit into your body, will ya, buddy!" But he was dancing to *Europe '72*, which was a new album, because this is 1972. The song was "Brown-Eyed Women" and I remember hearing the song, I remember seeing this guy dance. I'm listening to the music going, "Wow. What is this? What is this music? How can this person be dancing to this kind of music in such an incredibly beautiful way?"

I leave the party and I go on my merry way. The next year, *Wake of the Flood* comes out, and I'm upstairs on the third floor of our house. My parents never came up there because it was my brother Teddy's area. He puts on *Wake of the Flood* and says, "Listen to this, Annie. Listen to this music." Jerry's doing his great guitar stuff, which at the time I didn't know was that great. Teddy says, "Listen to this lead guitar!" I said, "Teddy, what's the lead guitar?" And he starts imitating Jerry on "Eyes of the World," and I was like, "Okay, I get it, I get it." Shortly thereafter, I realized that *Wake of the Flood* was by the same band that did the song that I saw that guy dancing to the year before. I put two and two together and said, "Wow. This is it!"

In 1974, the Dead played the Boston Garden, and Teddy got me a ticket. I went with all his friends, who were now becoming my friends, but I was still the proverbial geeky little sister. But they welcomed me into their world, and I went to my first show with this whole herd of people. There must have been twelve of us in one row. It was great. It was the wall of sound. We had great seats, this whole herd of us together getting stoned. It kind of finalized that feeling from seeing one person dance to their music in a suburban Boston home at the age of fourteen to being in this arena and really getting it. I knew then that I was into them.

Trey Allen, 27, R&R caterer, Nashville, TN:

I tapped into the weird zone at my first show. It was in the spring of 1987 at the Hampton Coliseum in Virginia. I was a freshman at the University of Tennessee, on spring break. My best friend and his friend Jody and I were looking for something to do, and we found out about these Dead tickets going on sale. I'd heard Grateful Dead music maybe a handful of times, the idea was brought on to me, and I said, "Sure! Let's go." We had to camp out and buy the tickets when they went on sale the next morning. I'd done this for other concerts; when I was in high school, I was a big Bruce Springsteen fan actually, so I camped out for the *River* tour and the *Born in the USA* tour. But my whole Dead experience caused me to drop everything spontaneously and decide, "Let's go!"

It was hard getting the tickets; we only got tickets to two out of the three shows. Then we hopped into Jody's car, drove an hour eastward, and we'd forgotten the tickets. So we turned around to get them. It was a sign as to the way the rest of the trip was going to be. It was a wing-and-a-prayer kind of thing. We got to the show really early, way before any scene of any kind had ever started. We stayed in some hotel filled with Deadheads where you pay about $200 for a one-bedroom shack that's normally twenty bucks a night, but since the Dead have rolled into town, the city lives for it.

I was completely blown away by the whole scene and all the ideas flying around, the openness of it. People my age had this whole other life that I'd never been turned on to. At first it was a bit intense, and I was a little wary of it—especially after getting really, really high. As it turns out, Jody had bitten off more than he could chew, and he began a downward spiral. My friend and I were really into the show, so we sort of got away from Jody because he was bringing us down.

After the show, we went back to the car and Jody wasn't there—the car was gone. It was interesting. We were high as shit, and now we had to "deal." We began to look around and notice all the people and decided we had to get a sign together saying, "To Hampton Beach." We just continued on. We met people, and eventually we got a ride to the beach and hung out all night.

We went back to the show the next day, though we still hadn't located Jody, and he was our ride back. We finally found him, and he was very agitated. He's been tripping for about three days with no sleep. He took us to the show, but he wanted to get back to Knoxville. So we decided to just dump our tickets. We went to get gas and looked for people to buy our tickets. When we came back to the car where Jody was filling it up with gas, he was gone! So it's just my friend and me now, with no way back to Knoxville.

Turns out Jody was going through a lot of heavy problems, of which I had no idea existed until then. He actually tried to come back and get us, but the cops grabbed him and put him in some home for a while, and that's the last I've seen him. So that was that . . . . I don't know how much fun you're gonna be able to make out of that one. And the whole Dead vibe actually didn't really help me get through all this shit because at that point, I'd been up for a couple days and it was just too much for me to deal with. Here I am, I have no ride back, I need to get back. I wished I'd never come. But then just by the networking of Deadheads, we found a ride back.

What my friend and I went through, looking for a ride back, the openness amongst all the Deadheads, made it not quite as bad as it could've been. After that, I continued to go to more Dead shows, but I think every Deadhead has a horrible story, and it's funny that my mind opened up with this horrible story. As bad as things have gotten, as mentally off as you are at certain times, it's never gotten that bad! This was my whole introduction to something so bizarre that I hadn't realized went on. To get there and have things fall apart, in the long run, they stayed together. It was a very exhilarating experience. For a while I thought, "The Dead sucks and I never want to see another show. I wish I was back at my favorite bar in Knoxville, and that I'd never left."

But after I'd digested the whole experience, it was like, "What a long, strange trip it's been." That was when I really started questioning things. What being a Deadhead provided for me was being able to just say, "Go. Let's just drop it, and we'll just see where we end up." Before long, you're just doing tours like that. That summer I was doing tours.

Jerry Miller, 51, Moby Grape/Jerry Miller Band guitarist, San Francisco:

I'm from Seattle. Jimi Hendrix and Larry Coryell, were from up there, and we all used to hang out at the Spanish Castle. It burned down, but that's where we'd go to see Gene Vincent, Chuck Berry, Jimi Hendrix. Yeah, Jimi was magic. He was really strong, he played hard.

I came to San Francisco in 1964. The first time I played with the Dead, they were the Warlocks. It was down in Belmont at the Anteroom. This was right about when they were changing their name to the Grateful Dead, back in '64 or '65. My first impression was, "These guys are pretty radical." They had great people working with them. They were a little different. Half the time pretty sour, and half the time genius. At that time, that was the way it went. There was much in between. I heard them a few more times, they were a bit sour, and then I heard them in Pescadero. There wasn't hardly anyone there, maybe three or four kids slidin' back and forth in their stocking feet. That was a day when the band was firing good. They were really playing nicely. It was really cool.

At that point, we were just starting to get Moby Grape going. We were playing the same gigs as the Dead. That's about when we got Bob Mosley in Moby Grape. All the people were around, they just weren't in the same band. Lee Michaels was showing up. Things were starting to cook pretty good. They had the acid tests and everything going on then. New bands forming. That's the early experiences when I first started checking out the Dead. They were nice. Good folks. Down-to-earth people. They had quite a following even then. They had a lot of friends.

John Perry Barlow, 47, Dead lyricist/cyberspace pioneer, WY:

In June of 1967, I found out that the Grateful Dead were going to be in New York, so I could see them for the first time—finally. That would be my first opportunity to see Bobby in three years, since I'd seen him at my ranch.

I think they played at a place called the Champagne A Go-Go in Manhattan. I can't really remember where the hell this place was. It was down in the Village somewhere. I went to the concert but I can't really remember that much about it. I thought my buddy Bobby was in a pretty hot band. I liked a lot of the stuff they were doing. There was a lot of press like, "Something weird is happening in California, folks. Put up your early-warning flag because we've got something strange in town." There was a fair amount of attention for something that was basically small potatoes showbizwise. I had a good time.

Timothy Leary, 74, chaos engineer, Los Angeles:

The Grateful Dead came up to Millbrook several times. I'd known them in San Francisco. I first met them at the Avalon, Chet Helm's place. They were great.

I remember another time coming home late one night down Market Street after flying around San Francisco, and I ran into Jack Cassady. We all went into someone's apartment and they were all just jamming away. I used to hang out with the Dead a lot at their apartment on Ashbury. I also used to meet them all the time at the Chelsea Hotel. We were always partying! Sometimes they played up at Billy Hitchcock's big mansion. They were just hanging out. They were part of the gang. They were part of the music team.

There was a small culture, and we all knew each other, and we'd all meet and hang out. I had a house in Berkeley, and I went out to see music a lot. San Francisco was just a great, great cultural scene. Wow!

Bill Cutler, 47, musician/producer, San Francisco:

I 'm from New York City originally. I grew up on Fifty-second Street, between Third and Lexington. That's where all the jazz clubs were, Billie Holiday played around the corner, all that stuff. I first picked up a guitar when I was about eleven or twelve, and that's what I still do. I started writing songs when I was about sixteen. I first started gigging as a folksinger in New York, with a fake ID, down at the Gaslight Cafe, opening shows for Eric Andersen, David Blue, Tom Ghent, all of whom were the local stars. I saw Dylan at the Gaslight Cafe.

My life's always involved music. When I heard people like Dylan going electric, it excited me. Then I got into the Dead, and I began to realize they were writing—especially around *Workingman's Dead*—songs that were very much Americana songs. That was important to me.

At the University of Connecticut, I got involved in the antiwar movement, which was just starting at the time. I went to some of the first Vietnam marches in Washington, dropped out of college, and put together my first rock band.

I can hardly remember which was the first one, but I saw the Grateful Dead at the Fillmore East in 1966 or 1967, right after it opened. Then I went to Woodstock, and I saw the Grateful Dead there, along with everybody else. That's when I decided that I had to move to California, between the Airplane and the Dead and the whole thing.

Then I started getting hassled by the draft board. I didn't want to go to Vietnam, I had a long record of protests, so I ran out to California because I'd heard about this great scene out here in San Francisco. This was about the time of the Summer of Love, 1967. I came out here and I jammed around with a lot of different musicians on my own and decided I wanted to live here.

My first impression of Haight Street was unbelievable. It was so crowded and rich as a tapestry of color and the senses! Everything smelt like incense and patchouli, everybody was dressed in wild colors; coming from the East Coast, which is such a drab place comparatively, I was blown away! What I found was so much more exciting than what I'd heard about. Also, people were so generous! I came from that New York thing where you have four police locks

Phillin' all right, Cal Expo, 1985 (PHOTO BY DAN WILSON)

on your door, and I came out there and people were crashing at each other's house.

At the same time, I was like a fish out of water, and I really wanted to find my way in. But I didn't have any way to support myself, and I went back to the East Coast. I went through my big fight to get out of the draft, won that fight—eventually—as a noncooperator. Then I moved to California finally in 1970.

When I came out here, I had heard a couple of records I really liked that a guy named Steven Barncard engineered. I liked the sound of his stuff. He wound up doing *American Beauty* for the Dead, he did David Crosby's solo record *If I Could Only Remember My Name*, and I think he'd done some Joni Mitchell stuff. Anyway, out of the blue, I called him and said, "I really like your sound. I want to make a tape." He was like, "Who are you?" I told him I was Bill Cutler, a songwriter, and that I wanted to make a tape. So we got together and he liked the sound of my tunes and said okay. I put some of my friends together as a little backup group, and we went in and recorded it at Funky Jack's Recording in the Haight.

Herbie Greene, 52, R&R photographer, San Francisco:

I moved to San Francisco in 1960 to study photography and be a beatnik. That year, I wandered around North Beach looking for beatniks. The beatniks were all gone, but the folk thing lingered on. I was walking down Columbus Street when I heard this amazing fiddle music coming out of this cafe called Coffee and Confusion. I went in, and there was Garcia. I walked up after he played and introduced myself. I just took an immediate shine to the guy. I knew right when I met him we'd be friends.

A little bit later, everybody was practicing rock, learning how to play rock and roll, and I ran into Jerry and the band again and struck up a relationship that's lasted ever since. They were still the Warlocks when I first started seeing them. I hung out with them a lot. I was taking pictures back then—not of bands, I was taking pictures of banjos leaning on trees and stuff like that. Then, as it turned out, as I was wanting to do that stuff, the scene was just sort of built for me right there! I loved the folk music and these guys were playing it. I loved the music so much that's what I wanted to photograph, and the opportunity to do that was pretty remarkable—having it built into the people that I knew. In about a ninety-day period there, all the bands formed. I was there. I photographed it. And I'm so glad!

Gina, 31, Blues Traveler's personal assistant, New York:

My first Dead show was in Detroit, 1981. I was seventeen. My sister and brother were into the Dead and turned me on to them. They were older and had been taking me to rock-and-roll shows since I was about eight. It was like, "You gotta take care of Gina," and they'd say, "Okay, we're gonna go see J. Geils." I was really into J. Geils. That was my big band. I was into the Detroit-sound bands.

I wasn't really into the Grateful Dead when I first saw them. I thought it was really silly. Then I met a guy in college who was way into them, and I started going with him all the time to Red Rocks, Colorado, Wisconsin—all over. We'd go on the road and sell jewelry and T-shirts. He was into making stickers. We'd make something every time we went out. We'd have a big tie-dye party and make tie-dyes and we'd sell those. We went and got these little plastic babies once and we sold those. Just really weird stuff. That was back in '82, when you could just walk in and buy a ticket. It was really easy to get a ticket, and it was much easier to move around then too.

PHOTO BY JANICE BELSON

2

Getting Tickets

Jeff Brown, 36, landscape architect, San Francisco:

Getting tickets is like this train is just roaring down the track—the Grateful Dead train—and you jump on the tracks in front of the train and it stops, and you get on! It doesn't run you over or ignore you or anything. Just sorta somehow you get scooped up by it. The norm is that you get in.

I think I've definitely shifted. The days, back in the early seventies, when I would just sorta get out there and get in are less now. I've got my shit together now: I send my money into mail order and now I get to give away tickets! It's nice because so many people have given me tickets in the past. It's really beautiful. Sometimes you give tickets away to just the first person you see, and other times, I don't know, it's tough. I've traded tickets—that's easier because you see which vendor has what you would like and trade for it. Once in a while it has to do with attitude. If somebody is whining about wanting a ticket, I'm a little reluctant to give it to them.

My girlfriend and I always got by, although I remember selling my record collection to have enough cash. I would go down to Winterland and spare-change for tickets, which were maybe six or seven bucks back then. So it wasn't that tough, and once you had the change, you could find a ticket pretty easily. It was a really different scene. I remember one night, I spare-changed my ticket, but my girlfriend was really bad at it. I went over to see if she'd gotten enough yet, and she hadn't gotten any. So I went back to where I was before and I found a ten-dollar bill on the ground . . . just like that!

Then there was the time my friend Linda visited from Santa Fe and we were really nonchalant about going to the show at the Greek Theater in Berkeley—back in the days when they set up speakers on the soccer field next door. We were so nonchalant! We were at home, listening to it on the radio, and we decided to go. It had already started, we went without any tickets, and it was sold-out. Linda kept saying, "Hey, we're gonna find some tickets on the floor. I know. It's gonna happen. It's gonna be great. Some unfortunate souls dropped their tickets and we're gonna find them."

So, we're in BART (subway), and we're looking all over for tickets. We get to Berkeley, and all the way up University Avenue we're looking on the ground for tickets. We walk all the way up to the turnstile at the Greek, and we still haven't found the tickets. I look at the guy at the turnstile and say, "How do we get in?" and he says, "Sorry, the show is sold-out." And I'm thinking, "Well, that's not what I asked. I asked, 'How do we get in?'" And with that, some guy on the inside says, "Do you wanna get in?" He reaches through the fence, hands a couple of tickets to us, and we went in. He was a nice guy. The next day we came back and gave him a bag of chocolate chip cookies that we'd baked up. And then we danced the show away. That was a good one.

One time I was at a show in San Jose and I didn't have a ticket. I got there early, and I was spare-changing. I almost had enough money when somebody hands me a ticket! It was like, "Uh-oh! I've got all this money *and* a ticket! Now what do I do!" If there are rules or laws about how things happen at shows . . . I'm not quite sure what they are because the weirdest stuff can happen. But if the law is that everything balances out, that there's some reason things go down the way they do, that scares me a little because I'm sure I've got something back there somewhere coming back at me!

One year, all these people came all the way out from the East Coast to have a holiday and see the Dead. Everybody's psyched, we're gonna get into all the shows, we're gonna have a great time, we send away all these mail orders, but we end up with only, like, two New Year's tickets! There were about seven of us, and we only had two tickets for the New Year's show. So, I called Marie, the Balloon Lady. She puts together a big crew of Deadheads for New Year's—or at least she used to, now that you can't just trade off tickets in exchange for labor since Bill Graham died. Marie and Bill go back a long way. She knew bill from Kezar Stadium when she had a popcorn and candy cart in the lobby and Bill was ripping tickets at the door!

Anyway . . . it turned out Marie and I knew a bunch of people in common, so she said, "Sure! How many tickets do you need?" My friends and I worked three eight-hour days, blowing up balloons for her, and she gave us tickets to that last New Year's before Bill died. We all got in. It was really nice. It was so beautiful to watch these balloons come down on New Year's and be able to say, "Hey, I blew up that one!"

David Gans, 41, radio producer: *Grateful Dead Hour;* author: *Playing in the Band* and *Conversations With the Dead,* San Francisco:

My experience of Grateful Dead concert-going changed dramatically in 1977 when I got involved as a press person. I was working for BASS Tickets too, so my access to tickets was always there. I don't have the typical Deadhead stories. I've never mail-ordered, ever.

Lauren Astra Esley, 20, writer, San Francisco:

I arrived at the Oakland Coliseum parking lot and set out to find friends of mine who toured a lot, following the Dead. I found one of my best friends and we rekindled our friendship in a matter of minutes. The lot was filled with tons of buses and cars, and many people were trying to get into the show. I went to one of the portables to urinate and accidentally dropped the top of my overalls to my feet—into a basin filled with pee.

That's how that night began.

My friend and I were trying to find a ticket or two to get into the show. The night was cold, but it didn't seem to stop me from having a good time. As we were looking for people with extra

Shakin' some bones, Cal Expo, 1985
(PHOTO BY DAN WILSON)

tickets, I noticed this man standing there with an expressionless look on his face. He was holding his finger up in the air (translation: "I need a miracle. Give me your extra ticket"). I saw him again five more times in the lot, and he would just stare at me strangely. He was in all white clothes and brown shoes, and let's just say he didn't look as if he were on the "reality trip."

We never did find tickets, but we had a great time just wandering around the parking lot with all these weird strangers.

Paul Perme, aka Trinket Guy, 31, Gila Monsters harmonicist, KY:

I see the Dead whenever they come around. It's funny because I happen to be places coincidentally that they're at. Like I'll be here in Los Angeles, then I'll go to New York to see my friends, and they'll say, "Oh, the Dead's here." And I always get a ticket somehow. I order for the Vegas shows because those are tough.

I'll tell ya, there's a bunch of times in the old Irvine Meadows days that the parking-lot scene was so much fun I just gave my ticket away because I was having such a great time out there. It's like a Renaissance fair. Whether the Dead play or not, that's cool. I love them, but sometimes I wish I could go in for one set and then come back out, but nowadays they're clearing the parking lot and it's not as fun anymore. But in the old days in the parking lot there used to be bands, people playin' congas, dancin', doin' all kinds of stuff for hours and hours even after the show, and then they'd let you spend the night in the parking lot. You didn't even have to go home.

Chris Flum, 28, "cool dude," Orinda, CA:

After seeing the Dead for the first time in 1982, I knew I was going back, and I went as often as I could. I bought tickets, I bought tickets, and I bought tickets. I went as a regular fan, and every once in a while, I'd see Stephen Barsotti, who'd kick me down special seating tickets and backstage passes, and before I knew it, I had met people back there. Years went by, and I'd met a lot of people.

Then I went away to school in Russia, and when I came back, I met Rutson Shurtliff, whose father is Ramrod, the oldest, very first paid employee of the Grateful Dead. Ramrod was very nice and he kicked me down passes. I helped him do some work around his house, then in turn he'd help me out. It's always nice to get known and be known. I want to work. I don't just want passes, I want to help out and work to deserve them. Some people want something for nothing, but I want to work for it.

There's no way I could give every Deadhead that's ever asked me for one a miracle ticket. I've given away miracle tickets a lot, at least fifty times. If a comp ticket comes to me and it says "$000" on the price, then I cannot let myself sell it for profit because that's not the way things happen. I'll give it to somebody, but I'll walk them all the way up to the entrance and make sure they use that ticket.

One time I was at the Oakland Coliseum and this girl said, "I have a ticket, but my friend needs one." I said, "I'll tell you what. I'll give you this ticket, but I'm gonna walk you up there." They knew that their other ticket was counterfeit, they just wanted to get a miracle ticket so they could sell it and make some money. I walked them up to the entrance, and I handed the ticket to the security guard like I always do, and I said, "This is for this girl right here." So immediately, they grabbed the other girl as she was trying to go through. They said, "You don't have a ticket. This is a bogus ticket." This girl said, "Oh. Well, *he* gave it me." I turned around to the security guard and luckily I had an all-access laminate on. I said, "If I had given that to her, do you think I would've walked all the way up here?" Here these guys were questioning *my integrity* when I was trying to be kind to this girl, and I got treated like shit. That was the worst thing that's ever happened to me at a Dead show.

Almost everybody wants a free ticket. Everybody wants their miracle tickets, and I'm always willing to trade. I'd rather trade a ticket than go out and give one away or sell it for the same amount of money I paid. I'd rather have a really nice warm, wool sweater like they sell at shows. They have some of the best stuff at Dead shows, so I'd rather trade.

Sometimes there's this flakiness factor at Dead shows. I've mail-ordered tickets a lot of times, and in my mail order I ask for taper tickets. Well, a few times, I got taper tickets and I give these taper tickets away at face value. I don't try and scalp them and make a ton of money. There are people out there who do that. But what I do is go to the tapers who don't have a ticket and say, "I've got a taper ticket. I'll sell it to you for face value. All I want you do to is send me a copy of tonight's show. Here's my name, address, phone number. Here's a blank cassette tape." I've *never* gotten it! I've done that six times! Six out of six times I've never gotten a copy!

Gina, 31, Blues Traveler's personal assistant, New York:

I was looking for a ticket at a show in Ohio because it was a really hard one to get, and I was freezing cold. I'd been looking for a ticket since the morning, and the sun was going down. I was so cold my hands were purple. Here's a coincidence with the whole Grateful Dead/Blues Traveler thing for me: I met Dave Prushur (Blues Traveler's manager) as a Deadhead way before I worked for Blues Traveler. I barely knew him. I was like, "Hi, Dave. Remember me? Gina?" He gave me the keys to his rent-a-car to hang out until the show was over.

I was so high, I lost his keys! I was freaking out—really high, and really freaking out. I'm looking for them everywhere, the show's gonna let out any minute, and I can't find Dave's keys. Then, at the last minute, I find them on the ground, and Dave comes walking up and I say, "Hi, Dave, thanks! Here's your keys!" I didn't tell him that story until years later, and he laughed so hard!

With tickets, the harder you try, the more you won't get them. When you stop trying, that's when you get your ticket. Same thing with finding your friends: stop looking for them and you'll find them. I always had this theory that if you stand in one place long enough, you'll get a ticket. I remember being on tour and I didn't have tickets for any of the shows, but I knew people, and I knew that somebody would know somebody with an extra. That's the first way: you tell everyone you know that you're looking for a ticket,

More parking-lot madness, Philadelphia, 1986 (PHOTO BY STEVE EICHNER)

and they tell everyone, and it goes from there. Another good way is to stand by the will-call line, because someone'll get a ticket and they'll have an extra, and if you're right there, you'll get one. But you can't look too sad—you have to be on the ball: "Got an extra? Got an extra?" But never looking too sad. That never works. Or if you look overanxious, that never works either.

You can always scalp and buy if you have the extra money, that way you're gonna get a ticket for sure. Another way is to stand near certain people: a security guy or boyfriend and girlfriend—a couple, because they may get in a fight, she walks away, he doesn't want to go into the show, he's gonna sell his ticket or he's gonna give it away. I would listen to conversations and watch people and keep my eye on them.

I always got into shows—somehow. I was only shut out of a couple. And if you don't get in, you go and hang out in the parking lot with all the people who didn't get in—I hung out with a lot of people! And you have fun. It's never a bummer. It's always worth the trip.

Ken Fine, aka Kew, 36, organic T-shirt salesman, Liberty, ME:

I've had a few fiascos. I once lost my ticket in Oakland and walked back, retraced my steps, went back into the bar we were at, an all-black-folks bar in Oakland, and said, "Has anybody seen a ticket on the floor?" And they looked at me like, "You're back here again? You're really pushin' your luck, pal." And then I walked back to the concert, totally dejected, head down, and there was my ticket in the gutter!

Greg Martens, 31, entrepreneur, Portland, ME:

I remember one year I had an extra ticket. I was young and I didn't have any money, so I was looking to scalp it. I walked up to the door, I was going to sell it to the first person that asked me. This guy looked me in the eyes and he was so dosed I realized right then and there that I could never sell a ticket for more than face value. I asked him how much money he had, which was about five bucks. I'd paid eighteen for it, but I just gave it to him for what he had. "Take it!"

Ricky Begneaud, 37, Cajun chef/caterer, Mill Valley, CA:

In 1980, the Grateful Dead came to New Orleans. It was the second time they'd played Louisiana in about fifteen years, and this was only my second show, so this was a special time. It was a two-day acoustic run. By this time, I was more involved with the music. I'd been listening to it a lot and I understood it better since my first show. It was a big deal for me. I was *so* into these shows. A bunch of my friends and I bought as many tickets as we possibly could. We rented a big white limousine, and we were sitting on top of each other because there were over a dozen of us.

We got to the show, opened the limo doors, and piled out. I whipped the tickets out of my pocket to disperse 'em to my friends, and of course hundreds of other people came over because they wanted to get in. People I didn't even know were trying to grab the tickets from me, but I finally handed them all out to my friends. I gave the last ticket to my friend, and suddenly I realized . . . I didn't have a ticket! I said, "Wait a minute! None of you guys would even be here if it wasn't for me! I don't have a ticket, so I guess I'll hang out in the limo." I couldn't believe I did this. I had everything so planned, but I'd left myself out! I was dealing with so many people, trying to negotiate everybody's well-being. Turns out, I'd given my friend Mike Kenney a ticket early on in the evening because he wanted to sit in a "special" seat—seat no. 13 or something. He realized he had two, so he gave me one back and we went in.

Annie Harlow, 36, green grocer, New England:

In 1978, our family life was falling apart. I was a teenager, my dad left home, my mom was depressed. Christmastime comes around, and my mom asks me what I want for Christmas. "The only thing I want for Christmas is to see the Grateful Dead the last night at the Winterland." We lived in Boston. She'd say, "Oh, Annie, I can't do that for you dear. Love, I can't. What would you like for Christmas?" "The only thing I want for Christmas . . ."! I brainwashed my mother! I kept repeating it. It was a mantra I was reciting. It was funny because my mother realized the only thing that would make two of her four children that were Deadheads happy would be to have tickets to the Winterland show.

So, my mother called Bill Graham and spoke with Bill. My mother was amazing! She knew how to deal with him in his way, on his level, without sounding like a fry-head or a psycho who would kill him if she didn't go to the show. Bill Graham sent my mother four tickets to see the shows at the Winterland. My mother bought me a round-trip ticket with a week's stay in San Francisco. Everything was unbelievably secretive until TWA called to confirm and I answered the phone and found out all about it. But my mom came really close to totally surprising me with these tickets under the Christmas tree. I freaked out: "I can't believe it! You're the best mom in the world!"

Anyway, I flew out to San Francisco and met up with a friend out there who was taking my second ticket. I went to Bill Graham's office to pick up the tickets, and that was the first time I had any sense of the whole Grateful Dead thing as a business. I walked in and there was rock-and-roll stuff all over the place. I brought flowers for Bill's secretary because she was so helpful and nice, and she really liked my mother. Bill and his secretary said that my mom was the nicest person that they had dealt with in securing Winterland tickets. I was ecstatic.

Stuart Wax, 37, music manager, Los Angeles:

The greatest gift is when you have a few extra tickets and somebody says, "How much! How much!" And you say, "Just a smile or a hug. That's it." And they can't believe it. It's exciting when the person gets their miracle, their ticket. Then, part of my getting off on it is just walking away from them—not trying to connect with them or anything. Just letting them have it in their hands and really believing that they were blessed with this good time.

Jerry and Stuart Wax

3

Getting In

Cree McCree, 47, writer, New York:

G iants Stadium, 1991: We were blessed by the gods that night, who not only canceled their scheduled thunderstorm, but lured us to the perfect parking spot, then waived the standard Dead-show rules of Waiting and Standing. We cruised straight up to Will-Call, where our ticket packet miraculously contained an extra pair—instantly donated to our friend Jono Manson, who appeared, serendipitously, at precisely the right moment. Then it was into the vast, ominously stark shell of Giants Stadium, where Little Feat had long since come and gone and the anticipatory buzz from the rainbow bedecked-and-bedazzled crowd began to swell.

Jeff Brown, 36, landscape architect, San Francisco:

I t wasn't that tough to get into shows back when I moved to San Francisco in 1978. I was nineteen. It was so easy and so much fun, kind of like, "How many burritos are we gonna get?"
I've seen a couple hundred Dead shows. I followed them around a bit on the East Coast when I was first getting started, back when

they were playing colleges in the 1970s. The most I've done in a run was when they did the Warfield in San Francisco. I think they did twelve nights, and I made it to nine shows. It was great. All you had to do was hop on the bus, go down Mission Street, and you were there. Things were different.

Gina, 31, Blues Traveler's personal assistant, New York:

The last time I saw the Dead was in 1994, the run they did at Madison Square Garden. I became friends with Justin Kreutzmann (Billy's son). He took care of me, I got into all the shows.

Back in the old days, Greg (Martens) was this guy who would always get me into shows. He was a T-shirt vendor and he ushered, and I'd always say hi to him and kinda flirt with him because I thought he was cute. He was always cool to me. He'd always ask me if I needed a ticket: "Sell some T-shirts, I'll get you a ticket." Greg doesn't sell T-shirts anymore, but now he's hooked with the band because he knows Vince Welnick.

Richard Yaker, 26, futurist engineer/visionary, Los Angeles:

A few months after Brent (Mydland) died, I'd bought two tickets to see Jerry at the Warfield in case I could find somebody to go with me. But nobody in my circle of friends was yet into the Dead or Jerry. I only knew people from work, and I didn't even know that many people there because I was trying to get a handle on *work!* So, I went up to the show by myself, and even though I'd been living there a few months, I was forty-five minutes away from San Francisco and I'd only been there a few times. I didn't really know my way around. I parked near the Warfield, which was kind of creepy because it's a pretty bad neighborhood.

Unfortunately, I didn't know that then. Being from New York, I thought, "Okay, this is a city, and I'm from the city—no big deal." But I didn't know my way around at all. In New York, I can walk around not being a tourist and be wherever because I know where I'm *going!* Here, it's not that scary, but I didn't know where I was going, so being in an unknown situation was kind of weird. Also, I had a ticket to get rid of, and I'd *never* had an extra I had to get rid of at a show! I didn't think it would be a problem, but I was by myself. I got near the Warfield and it was weird because a crowd was outside, and all of a sudden I felt okay because I was amongst people. Without even really talking to anybody, something about the vibe and everything—I felt at home. That had never happened to me before. Usually I think, "Oh, I'm by myself, who am I gonna talk to? What am I doing here!" *Self-conscious!* But I didn't feel that way at all. It was really easy finding somebody to give my ticket to, and going into the show was totally sweet.

I don't even really remember the show exactly! Everything was sweet, I remember that. I've seen Jerry at the Warfield so many times since that night they kind of all blend together. I remember the stuff before and after the shows, but once I'm in, it tends to stream together with every other time.

Ken Fine, aka Kew, 36, organic T-shirt salesman, Liberty, ME:

There have been some momentous shows I've missed, that I tried to make it to but didn't. Sometimes the shows I've missed have become even bigger milestones than the ones I made it to. Like the time I tried to drive all the way across the country to make it to the closing of Winterland. It became this race against time. I ended up making it to Santa Cruz at about 12:30 A.M. and gave up. I didn't go all the way up to San Francisco because I had just driven three thousand miles—struggling against the elements: freezing rain, and all this other adversity. I just said, "Oh, well." I heard the tape and said, "Well, I tried!"

Annie Myles, 24, music manager, New York:

After a couple years of not being in the scene at all, I ended up running smack into the Grateful Dead scene down in Georgia by accident in 1988. I didn't realize they were there, and I ran into some old friends of mine. So I decided to go to the show. It was really weird; I was very pensive, and I felt like I was coming into it from a very alone point of view. My friends had been on tour and they were all caught up in the scene and everything, and I kind of walked into the show by myself. It was really eerie. Really quiet. There was no line at the ticket gate. I walked right up, and everyone was like, "Good evening. Welcome to the show. Thank you very much for your ticket." It was "dead" silent, no preshow screaming or anything. I thought it was so bizarre.

It was a killer show. I had a blast.

Annetta Pearson, 51, artist/homemaker, San Francisco:

After a few shows, I found that I could get around by my-self. My husband and I brought many newcomers to the Grateful Dead, and we have this one couple that we in-troduced to quite a bit of rock-and-roll frivolity. We're known in our crowd for taking care of seating arrangements. Greg knows his way around, so everybody looks to him as being the person in charge. You can always count on him.

Anyway, we were going to a concert at the Polo Field in Golden Gate Park. The Jefferson Airplane were playing. It was one of the first big concerts they had at the Polo Field after a long hiatus of not having any. A friend of ours is a big Jefferson Airplane fan, and we agreed that we were going to meet slightly behind the soundboard on Jerry's side—no matter who plays, we always refer to that side of the stage as Jerry's side. When we got there, we're winding our way through the crowd, and when you know where you're going, you just cut through like a knife through butter. We get there,

Phil Lesh at Madison Square Garden, 1992 (PHOTO BY CHRIS FLUM)

and there's no soundboard! And here's this sea of people. We went right to the spot where the soundboard would have been, and there were our friends, sitting right in place in the middle of this sea of people! I thought that was quite awesome that we could pass that trick on.

Steve Eichner, 30, R&R photographer, New York:

I had this one classic Grateful Dead experience with my friend Steve McGuinness, who was a really crazy, breaking-the-law-all-the-time kind of guy. He and I had driven down to Washington, D.C., to a friend's house. We ran out of money there, so we were stuck. We went out to try and siphon enough gas to get back to New York. But then we heard from these thirteen-year-old kids that they had tickets for the Dead show down in Hampton, Virginia. Steve and I were like, "Holy shit! We'll get these kids to pay for our gas to go to the show, and we'll figure out some way to make money there."

Then McGuinness has a bright idea go to a drugstore, and the next thing I know he's stuffing white T-shirts and dye down our pants. So we basically robbed this drugstore for Rit dyes and T-shirts. We went and made up twenty tie-dye T-shirts, and we got those kids to pay for our ride down to Hampton. It was a miracle. We got out of the car, sold all our T-shirts, hooked up with tickets, doses, a big bag of weed, and enough money to get home. We went into the show, enjoyed it, partied it, and then we gave those kids a ride back to Washington, and we drove all the way back to New York in glory.

I remember another immaculate experience I had in Hampton, Virginia, the year before this one. I didn't have a ticket, and I was standing there looking at a security guard, concentrating really hard on him. He was looking back at me, and I walked up to him and I said, "You're standing between me and my life. Step aside!" And the guy let me right into the show! I willed him away!

I've had my share of getting shut out of shows too. I've definitely sat out in the cold while other people have seen the show. My thing was always to sell stuff on tour. The first day of tour I learned you can make money and support yourself. I mean, you could make a hell of a lot of money, but at that point I didn't care. If I had enough money to see the show and survive, that was enough. I'd wake up

Comin' and goin', Philadelphia, 1986 (PHOTO BY STEVE EICHNER)

in the morning and start cruising the parking lot for a beer, and then I'd get a bagel, and I'd have a pocketful of tabs. I look back on it and it's like, I should've been arrested! I went from car to car and I sold a hundred hits of acid for two or three dollars each. Blatantly! But I was young, and it all worked out.

Hartford, Connecticut, is a really hard place to get in free to Dead shows. Some friends and I were just standing by this back door, and it popped open, we all ran in, and the Dead were into the first set singing, "So glad you made it!" from *Give Me Some Lovin'*. It was a moment of sheer high because of the adrenaline of the door popping open, running in past security guards trying to grab us, and having the Dead singing right to us!

Norbert Verville, 30, chemist, San Francisco:

December 8, 1994, I went to see a Grateful Dead show at the Oakland Coliseum. I drove to the south gate to park in the back lot, and as I was getting my change back from the parking attendant, he said, "Did you know there's a cop behind you? I think you're being pulled over." I look behind me, and sure enough, I'm being pulled over. So I pull over and the police officer comes up and says, "Did you know you've got expired tags and a broken taillight?" And I said, "Yes, I know I've got both of those." He asked for my license and registration, so I gave him my license and registration and told him I had a bunch of outstanding parking citations for about $500. He said, "Okay," went back to his motor-cycle, and started talking to someone on his radio.

By that time, three of his other buddies arrive, get off their bikes, and start circling around my car, looking in as I'm sitting there. There's a big ol' bag of kind bud on the seat next to me under a news-paper. So I'm just sitting there, and the cop eventually comes back, gives me my driver's license, goes to the back of my car, and starts writing on my rear window with a wax pencil. He comes back and says to me, "Sir, we're going to impound your vehicle. Will you please get out of the car?" He's standing right there so I couldn't really make a move for the bag of weed. So I rolled up the window, left the key in the ignition, got out of the car, and tried to explain to him how I was going to do the registration the next day, but he wasn't going to listen to me. He wrote me out a ticket for a broken taillight and new registration, gave me the ticket, and said, "Enjoy the show, sir." That was it. I'm standing there going, "Oh, well!"

I walked up to the parking attendant, who'd been watching the whole thing, and I said, "Do you think I could have my seven dol-lars back?" And he just looked at me and said, "Sure," and gave me my seven bucks. So with a Grateful Dead ticket in one hand and a police ticket in the other, I went in to see the show.

Annie Harlow, 36, green grocer, New England:

One time, I only had tickets for three of four nights of shows. Something got wrenched and I didn't have a ticket. So I went to the concert anyway because I had to be there. I'm outside and I'm walking along this alleyway next to the auditorium, and this police dog jumps out at me and nips me! I start freaking! I didn't do anything, I'm walking, I wasn't stoned, I was straight . . . well, I might have smoked some pot, but, you know, that's kind of straight! Anyway, I was so bummed, and the cop of course blames me. But my bite wasn't really bad, so I went around to the back of the building, kind of freaking out, and met up with a friend of mine.

We were standing there and this guy comes out on the fire escape and yells, "Go through that door or get away from that door!" Well, what would you do? We went through the door, and we were right next to the stage, right up in front! Okay! I can live with this! That's the only time I ever snuck into a show. It was really great. I was ordered to do it!

Trey Allen, 27, R&R caterer, Nashville, TN:

My partner Tom and I were broke. We were stuck in this massive traffic jam getting into the amphitheater to see the Dead, and I got out of our VW bus and started selling shirts in traffic. We ended up selling every shirt we had, and we were sitting on this bundle of cash, which was not for us to go home and put in our bank accounts. It was money that we made to continue our experience. And if the money would take us to Thailand, we'd go. It was that whole Kerouac thing.

So we sold out all our shirts. I had some good friends who claimed to have the inside track about the Dead. There's this whole funny thing in the Dead experience of just silly rumors. They just spin off. We were hanging out after the show, and this friend came up and said he'd heard the Dead were playing Red Rocks, Colorado, as Mother McCree's Uptown Jug Champions, which is the original name of the band. So we hop in the bus, we were about the tenth vehicle to leave the parking lot, and we drove all night to Red Rocks. We get there, and it seems the only person gracing the stage for the next three weeks will be the old man down there sweeping it! There was nothing going on!

The whole VW bus thing . . . you hop in one, and you're like, "Will this thing make it? We can get it, and we can drive it as far as it will go, and if doesn't go anymore, it just doesn't go anymore." They sort of have that going on. You don't really know! We'd pull into gas stations out in the backwoods. I remember seeing these three old men sitting down on a bench watching people come and go. I'm sure it's what they do every day of their life. We pull in with our bus, there's no one around, we pump our gas, pay, and then the bus wouldn't start. I push it out of the lot, and Tom tries to kickstart it, and we hit the street and it just sort of disappears away from the station. From where these old men were sitting, it must've looked like we could still be pushing the bus right now! I remember looking back and seeing these old guys grinning and laughing!

Jerry Miller, 51, Moby Grape/Jerry Miller Band guitarist, San Francisco:

Back in 1980 at Laguna Seca, me and my friend Will, we're in his Porsche, he's got plenty of money, but we're not gonna pay to get into a Dead show. It's a matter of principle. Moby Grape played with the Warlocks. We park the Porsche a long ways away, hike in, make it through a bunch of roadblocks, and we finally get up there. I'm sneakin' in, there's this fence, and I'm gonna go leap over that fence—no problem. So I leap over this fence, and what I don't realize is that on the other side it's not the same height, it's way the hell down! So I'm waiting for the earth to hit me. Man, when it did, I landed right on my side, and I was so bruised. I limped my way in there, so we did finally smuggle ourselves in. It was ridiculous. That was the last time I ever tried any of that shit, relatin' to the old days, sneakin' in somewhere.

4

Getting High

Dan Wilson, 49, Street artist, Sacramento, CA:

Back in the sixties, the Grateful Dead and I were kind of neighbors in the Haight/Ashbury. I remember one time my roommates and I were hanging out at Yerba Buena Park, which was just up the street from where we lived on Frederick, and right around the corner from the Grateful Dead's house. Well, that day I had in me a real good kind of a mescaline derivative in tablet form. And this was the first time that my friends and I ever turned on to anything like that. And we were trying to be real scientific.

We received some excellent instructions from a college professor on how to do this and not get blown away too badly. So we're sitting there in the sand at the park that Sunday afternoon, and the Grateful Dead just happened to be playing down on the Panhandle. Every once in a while, the music would just come floating by on the wavelengths. . .on the wind. I remember I was digging my index finger into the soil to make a little hole in the ground, and then all of a sudden the mescaline hit me. The wind was just howling around in circles around my head, and the trees were all waving back and forth. I was really gone for about eight hours, and the Dead's music was a catalyst for the whole thing. I was digging this little hole in the earth and I remember saying, "My God! I'm injuring this ground!" I got real defensive about destroying the earth. It was an interesting little reaction. I'll never forget that day.

Steve Brown, 50, filmmaker/Dead's aide-de-camp, 1972–77, San Francisco:

I remember one time we actually got our limo driver high. That was a good lesson to ourselves not to share anything with anyone who couldn't handle it. This driver missed the turnoff, and if you missed the exit, it was twenty miles before you could turn around and loop back . . . all this at two or three in the morning after a show! We all sort of looked at each other, going, "What have we done to ourselves by getting this guy high?"

There's always that kind of danger on the road because all of a sudden you've brought in an innocent party to your world of controlled chaos. So, unless they're wired—or rewired—to be the kind of people we were because of "conditioning," then sometimes these outsiders just kind of lost it. We were used to being high on the road and functioning under various states of altered consciousness, which is something neither to be ashamed or proud of. In either case, it was a challenge. It often led to interesting times. In restaurants, there'd be what we used to call mels, short for "melons." The Deadheads were included in our scene, but anyone outside of that was the world of mels. Whenever we stopped to eat along the way, we'd be kind of exposing ourselves to a very surreal world, and we had also probably altered ourselves, which added to it. In those kinds of experiences, you had to open yourself up to being able to step into them, survive them, and step out of them.

Richard Yaker, 26, futurist engineer/visionary, Los Angeles:

I had a "Watchtower" experience at a Dead show in Albany, 1990. I was tripping, and "space and drums"—especially when I'm tripping but even when I'm not—don't really do it for me. I want them to play a song but they just drift off. Drums is kind of cool, but space is sort of melancholy, it's dark. And whether I'm tripping, straight, or anything, I'm just not into dark

Wheels keep turnin', Philadelphia, 1986 (PHOTO BY STEVE EICHNER)

stuff. I'm way more into light stuff. So I'm sitting there, it's dark, my eyes are shut, and they go into this transition. I had no idea what they were gonna go into or whether it was just gonna be a jam. My eyes shut, I started seeing this image—like I was flying. It was kind of this Alice in Wonderland thing, really light blue crayon-color sky with really puffy clouds, and there was a walkway that was contoured like I was coming over a hill, a horizon like you're going around the earth. There was grass on either side of this walkway, and I was speeding rapidly across it. I couldn't see my legs or anything, so I was kind of flying, but it wasn't like I had wings. I was eye level as if I was walking, but the scene was flying by me. Then all of a sudden I started seeing roses on either side of me. It was like in cartoons where a lawn mower comes along with flowers flying up. So the roses are flying up and coming along on either side of me. And then all of a sudden there was a tower in the distance. I realized at that exact second that the band was transitioning into "Watchtower." I was really freaked out because I was tripping, and I thought, "Wow, my subconscious knew what was going on way before I did, and it created these images, and my consciousness didn't get it till now!"

There was a run of shows in New York at Madison Square Garden, I think it was September of 1987. My friends and I didn't have any dope, we went to the show, and for whatever reason I brought along "tools," "apparatus"—lighter, bowl, and all that. We were sitting there, and toward the end of the first set, the people sitting next to us said, "Shoot! We have nothing to smoke our dope with." And I handed them my tools and said, "Well, here it is." During the break, we all got totally baked. I was totally straight for the first set, so I could compare it with the second set where I was totally high. It was really weird. The way I concentrated on the music and how I dealt with things was different. I have recently self-diagnosed myself as having ADD, attention deficit disorder. I have a really short attention span, and I never actually realized it. I have a lot of trouble concentrating. I got through school because I'm extremely smart, but I used to get in tons of trouble because I'd forget homework assignments, or I'd make stupid mistakes because I wasn't paying attention to the directions. Well, getting high kind of emphasizes all that, so when I'm at a show and I'm really high, I get to this point because shows can be so long where I'm self-conscious or I'm thinking about other stuff, checking out other people—my mind is wandering. What I think about and where the music takes me—I'm very tangential because of that. Where the music took me when I was straight and where it took me when I was high were two totally different places. When I was straight, I was thinking about the music and them playing, and then when I was high, I let the music take me, I was into the emotion of it, and it took me totally different places. One experience was more external, and the other was way more internal.

John Popper, 27, Blues Traveler harmonicist, Princeton, NJ:

I remember one time I didn't have a ticket but I went to a Dead show to try and find Bob (bass player for Blues Traveler) at Brendan Byrne Arena. I went home for the weekend and asked my parents if I could borrow their car. They didn't want me to go to Brendan Byrne Arena, so I just said I was gonna get a pack of cigarettes. I got in the car and drove to the show to find Bob, figuring my parents would go to bed soon and think I'd just gone to get cigarettes.

When I got to the gig, I couldn't find Bob, but I'd brought my harps because that always gets you out of a jam. Somebody gave me a tab of acid, which I happily munched down. I ran into some people and started jamming a little bit, but they were all playing Dead songs. I didn't know any Dead songs, but that was okay, I could just play along. Then they started seeming really weird, their faces started melting, and suddenly I realized I might not have been thinking forward when I ate that tab of acid because now I was really getting kind of lost. I was in this very big parking lot. So, I started jamming with a different group of people to take my mind off it, and everybody knew these Dead songs. This was right after the show was over, but as far as I was concerned, the show was going on for eight hours. I was tripping! So this soon grew into a seething crowd of people who were just growing and growing, and they were all singing along. I started to get this closed-in feeling and figured I better get out of there.

It turns out that Bob and Dave (Blues Traveler's manager) walked right by that mob of people surrounding me to their car to go home. So I'm wandering around, the parking lot is thinning out, and I don't know why, so I better just sit in the car until the acid wears off. I turned some music on real loud because, you know, it's psychedelic. But all I could get was this cheesy—not Muzak, but it was just a really bad radio station to be tripping on, so I figured I better just get the hell out of there and drive home. A lot of bottles were in the parking lot, and I said to myself, "Well, I'll just drive across. These are tires, they can take it."

So I'm driving, and I wound up on the other end of this sports complex, it's totally dark, and I can't find *anybody!* Somehow, I got into this weird thing. I'm driving on off-ramps, and the whole time my car's going *boomboomboomboom* . . . I figure that's just me, I'm tripping. But about forty-five minutes later, I figure I better check. One thing you should never do, by the way, is drive under a blinking light when you're tripping, because suddenly there are rabbits everywhere. So I get out of the car, and semi trucks are whizzing by. When they thunder by, it's really freaky. So I check the first tire, it's fine. Second's fine, third is fine; the fourth tire is searing and melting into the ground, steaming, because I'd been riding on the rim for an hour. So I go back in the car, and I don't know how to use a jack even if I could find where the spare tire was. So I'm sitting in the car going, "Shit. Shit. Okay. Sooner or later, a policeman will pull over and see if I'm okay. If I sit here long enough, a policeman will have to come." So I start preparing a statement for the policeman when he shows up: "Officer, I have a flat tire. Could you please send a tow truck. . . . Officer, I have a flat tire. Could you please send a tow truck. . . ." No problem. I can say that.

Eventually a cop shows up, I get out of the car, and I walk up to him. He rolls down his window, and I say, "I got me a big ol' flat tire right over there!" For some reason I just got into trucker talk. The cop looked at me and said. "*Ggrhzghggrhzg-ghrgghz*," and I swear to God, the cop had the head of a bee. And then he just drove away. Eventually a flatbed truck arrives, he puts my car on the truck, we're driving away, and he goes, "That'll be two hundred and ninety-four dollars." Of course, I don't have any money. So, I had to call my mom at six in the morning from Newark and ask her for her credit card number to repair the flat tire I'd gotten after sneaking off with her car. Later the flatbed truck guy was like, "Oh, *here's* your spare tire!" So, I just drove home.

That was me going to a Dead show by myself.

Chris Flum, 28, "cool dude," Orinda, CA:

One time in Los Angeles at the Forum, I spent five bucks on a balloon and was walking across the parking lot, took a big ol' hit off of it—"Wha-wha-wha," and *boom!* I hit the ground. The balloon went shooting out of my hand, people were chasing it. I was on the ground and I got all wet: I'd fallen in a trail of piss. Across the street were some apartment complexes, and they had their sprinklers going right on the side of the road there. I took off my clothes, butt naked, standing there on the side of the main road, all kinds of cars driving by. Nobody seemed to notice me butt naked, scraping myself on the ground! I was so disgusted. I had urine on me. Other people's urine. I decided right then I was never gonna do another balloon. And I never did.

Another thing that never mixes with the Grateful Dead, to the best of my knowledge, is cocaine. They are two totally separate entities. It's more of a psychedelic thing to me. In fact, probably the stupidest thing I ever did at a Grateful Dead show was snort cocaine. You can't relax and enjoy the show anymore. It's stupid. It's like, "Okay. Let's go out to the car. Fuck the show. Who's turn is it to rail 'em up?" I hate that.

The most heroic thing I've done at a Dead show when some guy was too high and fell, cracked his head open, and I carried him to Dead-Med.

I see many shows straight now because I like to drive there, which means I want to drive home too. I always have big fun.

Sheila Rene, 56, music anthropologist, Texas via San Francisco:

As far as drugs and the Grateful Dead, I think people enjoy it more on drugs than when not. Those people say, "I just don't get it!" if you can get a little something in them, even pot, they begin to understand. I don't know why that is. You can do it without drugs. It has been done. But drugs enhance the experience. Jerry always rolled the biggest joints I ever saw! When they first started out, acid was legal, and it was a mind-expanding drug. The best nights I've ever seen the Dead, I was on acid. I realized the tribal community, the oneness of it all.

Annie Harlow, 36, green grocer, New England:

Some of the most fun came from the camaraderie of friendship. One time my friends and I were all really high for four nights of shows. My friend Pete always reminds me, like, "Remember when . . . you lured Johnny Miller's Comet up onto the common? Remember, you just coaxed it up there and he followed you, like he was possessed by your energy? And then when the tailpipe came off!" We drove around for the rest of the night all over this lily-white, suburban, affluent community with this raging tailpipe!

We raged so heavily and did things . . . it would be a book of Grateful Dead blessings. Stories where there's no way it could have happened except you were on drugs and you just came from a Dead show. We never got pulled over, we never got accosted in any way. It was amazing.

Jerry Miller, 51, Moby Grape/Jerry Miller Band guitarist, San Francisco:

Neal Cassady stayed at my house one night. He was quite a character. We were trying to capture sunlight with a whole bunch of mirrors! And we couldn't find enough mirrors. We were breaking mirrors to make more mirrors as fast as we could find them, trying to slow down the sunlight, capture the speed of light. Of course we were pretty well gone that night. We had them all through the house, little bits of mirror—glass all over the floor. And in the morning we got up and made popcorn without a lid! Said, "Fuck it! This is fun!" Then when we came down, we had all this to deal with! Glass all over the floor, popcorn everywhere, oil paints all over the place.

David Gans, 41, radio producer: *Grateful Dead Hour;* author: *Playing in the Band* and *Conversations with the Dead,* San Francisco:

We camped out at the San Jose box office, bought tickets for four shows in August at the Berkeley Community Theater, and went. We drove back and forth every night, from San Jose to Berkeley and back again, tripping our socks off. I was house-sitting for my friend Craig, and we'd come home really stoned at two o'clock in the morning and play with his kittens till morning. One time we went over to this Alpha Beta store at dawn for supplies and encountered an entire family of harelips doing their shopping. It's the kind of thing that sticks in your mind, weirds you out a little bit. I guess that's when they do their shopping.

John Perry Barlow, 47, Dead lyricist/cyberspace pioneer, WY:

During the time that Weir got involved with the Grateful Dead, I actually was off pursuing my own East Coast Orthodox version of the same thing, at the hands of Dr. Timothy Leary. While Weir was taking the acid tests with Kesey and the Dead, I was off in Millbrook sitting in the lotus position and taking the whole thing very seriously in a spiritual sense.

True American Deadheads, Squaw Valley, 1992 (PHOTO BY TREY ALLEN)

I didn't really know what Weir was up to, and then sometime in 1966, a guy we both knew at our school, Fountain Valley, wrote me a letter and said he'd seen Weir in a band called the Grateful Dead someplace down in San Diego, and he thought I might be interested. I spent some time trying to find out who they were and how to get ahold of them, but surprisingly there was a disconnect between the East Coast and the West Coast. There was some intolerance between the two different strains of acid-head religion that had developed in each place—a tendency to view the other one rather harshly. The West Coast was much more about music and bacchanalia. It was just, "Let's all take acid and see what happens," and in its way, each way had its merits. I don't fault either one of them at this point, but at the time I had my religion, and it made it hard to penetrate into Bobby's.

But then the Dead finally came to New York in 1967 and I saw Bobby for the first time in three years. We hung around New York all afternoon. They were staying in this fleabag of a hotel. I didn't know any of the rest of the band, and I spent the next two weeks with them, pretty much continuously. I brought them up to Millbrook to meet Timothy Leary. I drove with Bobby, Phil, and Phil's woman, a girl who was singing with Frank Zappa. God, I wish I knew what has become of her. She was amazing. Her name was Uncle Meat. Uncle Meat was a sly, witty character. Real sexy and real sly. She'd come up with these lines that were just so deadpan. Anyway, she came up to Millbrook with us.

Several things happened that day; one of them was that the Six Day War broke out. And the other one was that *Sgt. Pepper's Lonely Hearts Club Band* was released in New York, or at least that's the first time I'd seen it in a record store. I got a copy and brought it up to Millbrook, so it was the first time that the Dead and Timmy heard it. We got up there and played it in this very Eastern Orthodox setting, with the lights just so, and the incense just so, and the cat piss on the Persian rug smelling like it did, and everybody being pretty reverent! We all sat around and listened to *Sgt. Pepper's Lonely Hearts Club Band*. It blew my mind. Timmy at the end of that record said, "Well, at least my work is over," and it was pretty clear what he meant: that the idea of LSD was now pretty well loose in the culture and transmissible in some coherent fashion. Here was this rock-and-roll band in England—who were surely in a whole different mode—able to know exactly what had happened to us. It had happened to them, obviously. It was like control group in a way. "Yeah, it happens to them too."

Herbie Greene, 52, R&R photographer, San Francisco:

At the closing of Winterland, we were high, and I was with somebody who'd never been to a show or been high before. The way it was set up . . . it was stacks and stacks of seating. There were tiers. The thing was like starting from the top and going down, the colored lights and the people and all that stuff—it was like descending into Dante's inferno. That was the impression I got. The Blues Brothers were playing, and there was all the insanity of the people around the band. They were very insane people. Lots of Hell's Angels types and ruffians and people who were nuts. You think backstage is weird now, you should have seen it then! I mean, intimidating! The whole thing had an edge to it that was brinking on insanity. If you check out the Grateful Dead movie, it has that edge to it. You can tell, the nitrous scene and all that, and the cocaine and all that bad stuff. There's that nasty edge to it.

Now it's different—at least for me. Maybe that's still there, but I don't think it is. It's more of a family thing now. There were always kids there. My oldest daughter grew up backstage. All the little girls loved Bobby, chased him around.

Tom Constanten, 51, pianist/composer, San Francisco:

I think the role of drugs is overstated for both good and ill. I think I can say categorically that drugs really didn't do much ill. People who would sit around and get stoned all day would probably like to sit around all day and do nothing anyway. They don't need drugs for motivation to do that, it just helps them do it a little more enjoyably, perhaps. Or entertainedly. Likewise, I think there's a lot of inflated claims for all the glorious things that came from drugs. All they did was open doors for things that people were involved in anyway.

Drugs were a fun part of the whole scene. I'd hate to see it without drugs, but I don't think they were the crucial genie in the bottle that either the detractors fear or the proponents claim. Much ado about nothing—in both senses. I mean, even a good acid trip can be like a Saturday-night drunk: you open the spigots and flush everything out, so to speak. Which is a great thing to do. I think it's better to have that than not have it, for sure.

To my knowledge, I was the first person to import LSD to Las Vegas in the early sixties.

Parking-lot minstrel on wheels, Philadelphia, 1986 (PHOTO BY STEVE EICHNER)

Jerry Garcia (with guitar), Rick Begneaud (left of Jerry), and friends
sailing on the San Francisco Bay, 1986 (PHOTO BY RICK BEGNEAUD)

They all had these affectionate names: "Blue Lagoon" in a little blue
vial. These brown pills they called Brown Reknown; there was Startling Burgundy and Plum Pretty, a purple liquid. There were the
capsules that looked empty and I called them the Emperor's New
Clothes. I was a dealer to the dealers. Crap dealers, roulette dealers, a lot of good friends in those times.

Of course acid was still legal back then, as was peyote, which you
could virtually mail-order. What a great way to grow up! We'd go
out into the desert. There are some wonderful places out there
where you can't be sure what planet you're on by the time you're
floating. That was the milieu I was used to when I came to San
Francisco. People here were taking acid to hear music. It sure helped
rock music do what it does even better.

I remember one time when I was playing with the Dead, we had
a gig in Boston. Jerry, Phil, Owsley, and I were out dining, Owsley
was pouring tea for Jerry, and he poured it all over the table! It
overflowed the cup, it overflowed the saucer, and it started over-
flowing the floor! Jerry said, "Here's the man who we've been en-
trusting our body chemistry to. Look what he's doing!"

Pigpen was the best person to have with you when you were having a trip. He was a princely, gentle person. Utterly wonderful. If you got dosed accidentally, which happened to me once or twice, he was sensitive, very different from what you might think if you just saw his picture.

Rachel Clein, 13, student, Marin County, CA:

I remember going to a Dead show in 1989 when I was seven with Catie Broomhead, her husband, Bud, and their daughter, Celine. We were sitting on the grass, and there were a bunch of guys next to us who were really stoned. One guy was lying on his back, throwing his hands in the air, no matter what was playing—even if *nothing* was playing. He was dancing on his back to no music! I don't think much of drugs. They're kind of pointless. I've learned never to do drugs.

Dan O'Neill, 53, cartoonist, Nevada City, CA:

A former partner of mine was one of the guys behind the camera—they had about ten cameras going—for the Grateful Dead movie. Well, they'd put acid in some ice cubes, then put beer in this big white tub of ice cubes. So, every time someone popped a beer, they were getting it off the top! Wiped out the whole territory! Later, they were looking at the footage, and all that was on the film was a naked lightbulb hanging for forty-five minutes!

Twenty years after the revolution, we're talking mid-eighties, I refused to cut my hair because when Reagan got elected, I didn't want anyone to think I was responsible. Anyway, lo and behold, the Grateful Dead came up to Grass Valley. About nine thousand people were there, and this beautiful woman comes spinning up to me. She's spinning like a top, all jangles and beads, swirling around. She had her three nieces with her, another generation spinning around. They're all spinning around me, and they put their fingers in my mouth, and I thought, "I know what this is!"

So pretty soon I'm flying like the rest of the crowd. The cops got really nervous. The day went on and on, and the Dead kept playing. They'd start a song and just keep noodling around on it for hours. On it went! The cops were really freaked out because it was the quietest and happiest crowd they'd ever had. They thought there must be really big trouble if there's no trouble. They didn't want the Grateful Dead ever to come back again because they'd never seen an audience flying so high.

PHOTO BY JANICE BELSON

5

Getting Busted

Steve Brown, 50, filmmaker/Dead's aide-de-camp, 1972–77, San Francisco:

In 1974, I went on tour with the Dead to do merchandising promotion at the concerts, handing out free stuff and signing people up for our mailing list so we could sell to a bunch of fans through a direct line of communication. We had a gig in Missoula, Montana, where there's this large gorge known as the Gates of Hell, and when you're on the road with the Grateful Dead, a place with a name like that deserves a visit. So, in the afternoon, Bobby Weir and I checked it out, then went to see a movie. I think it was *Blazing Saddles*—something to do with the Wild West, outlaws and all that. I mention this because it seems appropriate to the following story, what with the Dead being these kind of cowboy, outlaw, hot-rod boys from California.

The day after the Missoula gig, we had to fly to Vancouver, so we had to make sure we didn't go across the border "beholding." Before we left the hotel, we made sure everybody was cool. We got in the car and were asked yet again if everyone had in fact taken care of not having any "things" with them that they shouldn't. Everyone said yes.

Jerry and I had been talking on the plane, and when we landed in Vancouver, we came out together and stood there while the customs officer inspected our luggage. They were checking everybody's bags, especially this troupe of Grateful Dead members who were kind of conspicuous in their appearance. Even in Vancouver in 1974, we really stood out. Not that we were dressed outlandishly, but we were a group of guys that looked like we might be from San Francisco—and we *were!*

So anyway, there I was standing next to Jerry as the customs officer proceeded to open his suitcase and pull out T-shirts, Levi's, and there, to everyone's astonishment, was this giant, oversized baggy with a donkey-dick-sized Maui bud-and-a-half sitting in it! Bright green! That wonderful Maui green. And I got one of those feelings they call a "grand clong"—a giant rush of shit to the heart. Jerry just sort of nervously stood there as the guy held it up to him and said, "What is this?" to which Jerry replied. "I believe it's tea. A fan gave it to me." And the guy opened it up, smelled it, and then looked over to the exit door to this young, long-haired hippie who looked like he could've been with us. The customs officer signaled for this "hippie" and asked him, "What is this?" holding up the baggy. The guy looked down at it, looked over at Jerry, looked back at the baggy, then looked back at Jerry again, recognizing who the fuck it was he was looking at, and he told the officer he didn't know what the stuff was. I had this momentary flash that we'd been given this blessing, some kind of miracle, that we might be getting away with it!

But, it wasn't to be because they proceeded to take the baggy *and* Jerry to a little back room somewhere and hold him for a while. We immediately called our lawyer, and he told us to get the most expensive and powerful lawyer in Toronto . . . *fast!* We got the best we could, and within fifteen hours, Jerry was out.

Steve Eichner, 30, R&R photographer, New York:

One time me, my roommate Tom, and our friends Karen and Lance were all at some Hampton shows with no tickets, but Tom had a counterfeit ticket he'd doctored. We used to do that a lot, take color Xeroxes of tickets and perforate them—there were so many ways to scam in. So . . . Tom had a counterfeit ticket, and we watched him go in. We thought it was cool, he must have gotten in because he disappeared. But then we saw Tom coming out in a pair of handcuffs. He looked right over to me, stares me in the eyes as they're putting him into a van, and he mouths the words, *"Help me!"*

The cops took him downtown and booked him. They wanted $150 to bail him out, and between the three of us, we had maybe $20. Karen went crazy. She took Lance's hat and went through the parking lot at the show, person to person, saying, "Our friend got busted! We need bail money!" Three hours later, when the show was over, we got everybody coming out of the show, and she collected something like $120. It was one of the most amazing things I'd ever seen. People were totally sympathetic to it. Then we went back to the police station with all this money, and they let him out.

Waylon Jennings, 55, rhythm-and-blues country musician, TX:

We played at Kezar Stadium. They had this brilliant idea of me and the Rolling Stones . . . uh, me and the Grateful Dead together—which was wrong! It didn't work. But, I went in there and I told everybody that worked for me and all the band before we went down there, "Get all the water you want. Anything you want to drink, do it now. I don't care if you open the bottle, don't drink nothing while you're down there." They said, "Ah, whadya mean?" I said, "Them guys do some serious shit!" And they really do! I said, "Just don't take no chances 'cause they'll play a little trick or two on ya too."

Sure enough, there was this kid named Larry. Larry would take a button and stay up for three days, if you told him it was dope. Here he come, and they give him some. He said, "I have found God! And I know exactly where's he's at. Matter of fact, he's probably in one of the Grateful Dead's pockets!" It took us three days to get him straightened up. Well, on the third day . . . I mean, it just kept goin' on. We did that, and we wound up in El Paso without him. Me and Richie decided we was gonna go over to ol' Mexico, the Juarez. Well, we were in a car that half the Hell's Angels and probably half of the damn Grateful Dead's guys had been in when we went across that border. Now I can just see 'em sayin', "Hey, you dropped that." "Ah, I'll get it." "Naw, I don't need it. We got more." Sure enough, we come back across that border, and I had emptied my pockets, but there ain't no way to get everything out of that car;

Fans of all ages, Cal Expo, 1985 (PHOTO BY DAN WILSON)

there's about two roaches, all kinds of stuff. We were dead as we
came around the corner . . . they had dogs and everything in the
car findin' all this stuff. We get outta the car, and here comes this
Mexican guy, one of the guys that's searchin' us, sayin', "Waylon!
Waylon! Waylon! I didn't recognize you on your driver's license."
It said Jennings, Waylon. He said, "Where you playin' at?" and I
said, "Where do you *want* me to play!" 'Bout that time I looked
around and he said, "Oh. Where did those roaches go?" And Richie
had swallowed 'em.

Jeff Brown, 36, landscape architect, San Francisco:

I've known Chris (Martensen) since he was about six or seven
years old. The woman I fell in love with in San Francisco, Patricia Rose, is his aunt. He lived out in Grand Junction, and
we would visit from time to time. He was kind of a rowdy kid, he
did the usual juvenile-delinquent kind of things—but nothing serious. He wasn't doing armed robbery or stealing cars or anything.

Last time I saw him he was about nine years old. Eventually he managed to put together a Volvo station wagon and was essentially touring with the band. Just a real sweet kid, beautiful young man, having a good time touring. He would drop in on us in SF from time to time and visit, we'd go to shows together. He was getting by, dealing a little bit of acid at shows, but also selling sandwiches! He'd sell peanut butter sandwiches for a dollar apiece. I mean, the kid was not a big-time dealer. He just wanted to get to the next show. He was just taking a little bit—no big thing. He was at that age in life when, you know, he must of been in love with I don't know how many different women, and they were all in love with him, and he was just enjoying it.

Then somebody he knew on the East Coast got busted and gave his name to the agents, and the agents set him up at a Dead show. He got busted in the Haight for dealing a couple hundred hits or something—it might not even have been that much. But some small quantity of acid, and he got busted for the weight of the paper the acid was on. It was a real drag because they wanted to slap this mandatory minimum of ten years on him. While he was waiting sentencing, he was in a halfway house and got a job with Bill Graham Presents, ushering at Dead shows! It was such an irony. I remember driving him home after the shows to the halfway house because he had to check in at a certain time for curfew. I don't know how he got around the tests they must of given him.

He became something of a cause célèbre because here's a young kid with a ten-year minimum. The local papers picked up on it. There's some guy, a prison inmate himself, who writes articles for the San Francisco Chronicle from time to time, who did a piece on Chris. So Chris was awaiting sentencing, and sure enough the local judge said no way would he give him ten years, and he gave him five years instead, and then the feds retried him, trying to get their ten-year sentence back on him. He's become the public figure/scapegoat for the mandatory minimum. He's in federal prison now, and they keep bouncing him around because he gets a lot of attention.

It's rough when you think a young guy like that could lose ten years of his life. It's sad, but I think it's funny and ironic that he worked for BGP. They're using his case to change the laws, so there is kind of a silver lining to the story, it's not a complete bummer. And I think, I'm not entirely sure, but I think he's learning to play bass guitar while he's in prison.

6

Getting Off

Ricky Begneaud, 37, Cajun chef/caterer, Mill Valley, CA:

There was a show the Dead did in Louisiana in 1980 that was magical for me. I came out of there, and I could tell you every song, every note—*everything* that happened. First, I *didn't* get thrown out like I had the night before! Second, I didn't have to deal with taking care of a huge group of people or holding everybody's hand at one time. It was just my friend Chuck and I. I could just be with the show, focus on the show, and this was my third show, so I was hearing all these songs for the first time live, which was amazing to me. I always knew them on the records and tapes, but to actually be there, thirty feet in front of the stage, listening to this music, was amazing! I didn't do any drugs that night, I just had a couple beers. I was high as could be just being there with the music.

After a little tour in the early eighties, my friends and I were on our way back home to Louisiana. I pulled the Jeep to the side of the road, stopped, and said, "You know what, guys? We haven't heard 'Scarlet Begonias' yet. I don't know if they're gonna play it, but let's go to Atlanta." We didn't have tickets or anything, and my friend Rick said, "Ah, I don't know." I said, "Look. We're here. Let's just go. I'll drive." We drove all night, got to Atlanta, and we got these incredible 14-row center seats! I'd never seen the Dead that close. It was great. It was a whole different thing because you begin to see their personalities, and you get to see interactions between them and stuff like that. And I was still hearing a lot of these songs for the first time live. It was really special.

In those days, I watched Garcia a lot. Then I started focusing on Phil sometimes, and I'd think, "Wow. I never knew he was doing all that kind of stuff!" On Bobby, it was like, "God! That's what that sound is! Oh, yeah!" And then I'd watch the drummers and I was like, "Whoa! There's other members in this band!" It was really a transformation when finally I'd sit back and listen to the whole band together. It was a really special time.

Dan Wilson, 49, Sacramento, CA:

One of the most memorable times I ever had was over at the Fillmore. It was a New Year's Eve bash—the Grateful Dead, Jefferson Airplane, Big Brother—the "big three." Ushering in 1967. Paul Butterfield also showed up to do a little jamming on his harp. We literally danced till dawn. We were in there until at least four in the morning. And the bands were just great. Everybody seemed to love it. They never sold booze or anything in that place. It was cool to be able to go that long and come out fresh as a daisy.

Caryn Shalita, mid-20s, actress, Los Angeles:

Probably the most overwhelming emotional experience I've ever had at a musical event was at the Bill Graham Memorial in Golden Gate Park. All these bands were playing, and I don't think it had actually been confirmed that the Dead were gonna play, but how could they not? I mean it was Bill Graham . . . they'd *have* to. They'd *want* to. I never knew Bill, but I had been in the same place with him once or twice, and I really wish I had talked to him because, having read his autobiography, I think he was an amazing man. I would've really loved to have talked to him. I do know his son David from college, Columbia. He was a class-

Trey Allen (right) and friends, Squaw Valley, 1992 (PHOTO BY LEIGHANNE
CHANDLER)

mate of mine. The fact that somebody my age lost his father really
freaked me out. Besides who Bill was in the music industry, he was
somebody's dad and that got to me.

The people who'd worked with him for years and years must have
been totally floored and upset too, so I knew it was gonna be an
emotional show. But I don't think anything I could've done to pre-
pare myself for that day really would've worked because there was
something eerily magical to it. I don't even know how to explain
it. It was not of this world. There was a completely unique sense of
energy floating around Golden Gate Park that day. It was a *beautiful* day. There were about one hundred thousand people, and everyone was there for the same reason. There was such positivity and
such sadness happening at the same time, but it was all kind of okay.

I remember the Dead opened up with "Hell in a Bucket"—and I
thought it was a very strange choice. I thought, "Well, that's interesting. I wonder what they're trying to say with this." Maybe I was
reading into it, but I felt like everything they were saying was some
kind of message to Bill. Maybe it was like Bill is "going to hell in
a bucket," which may very well be true, and I hope he did "enjoy
his ride." Anyway, they did that, and then they segued into "I Know
You Rider," which also says "I'm gonna miss you when you're gone."
Okay, I can see that. While this is all happening, there's this noise

Catching some Zs in the parking lot, Eugene, Oregon, 1990 (PHOTO BY TREY ALLEN)

coming from above. Now I have to mention here that I have definitely been in my share of altered states at Dead shows, but I was sober for this. I had *nothing*. No drugs, nothing.

So, as I was saying . . . there was this noise coming from above, and I thought, "What is happening here?" Planes were flying above the park while the Dead were playing, "I know you rider, gonna miss you when you're gone." And then a plane would go, "*Whooooshhh!*" It was as if they were doing it on the beat. It was really strange. I don't think they could've planned that. It just kind of happened that way. So, I'm looking up, and there's all these black dots in the sky. It was really weird. Meanwhile, the song is continuing, the planes are flying, and as the band got a little bit more into the song, the black dots had come close enough so you could see that they were actually pink carnations raining from the sky! Flowers all over the entire field! I thought, "If I were tripping right now, I would be in a serious state of *wow!*" I wasn't, but I could still appreciate it. I knew there had to be someone there right at that moment who was completely flipping out!

Only the Dead could have thought of something like that and carried it off. No other band could do that. The emotion . . . I felt like their music carried to the sky that day. I really felt it. Sometimes people accuse them of not trying hard enough, or that they don't have it anymore. Yeah, okay, they're normal guys, they get tired, they don't do such a good job at work sometimes, but when they're on, they're *on!* You can't be on a hundred percent of the time every day. But on this day it was clear that it mattered to them, and I really felt something from them that I don't think I could've ever felt before. I don't think it was a question of age or how hard they were trying, I think it was just how much they'd invested in what they were doing. I was crying because the emotional aspect was so overwhelming. I was sad, but at the same time it was so beautiful. I knew I was seeing something that was really special and something that would never again happen. I'm really glad I was there. It was sad that he died, but what a tribute! If I were Bill, I'd be looking at it and thinking I had some good friends. That day gave me the shivers.

And that feeling stayed with me for a while. It was a very peaceful day and people were so kind to each other. I don't remember seeing anything negative. The sun was out and everybody's hearts were out, and everybody's hearts were linked and in the same place. It rose to this level above where we normally exist. Not many bands could ever do that, and I don't know that I've ever even seen the Dead do that. It was superhuman. My life didn't change because of it, but. . .every day I try to find something that's gonna give some kind of a spiritual connection to something, and that day gave me my dose for a while! Bands usually put together big productions with lots of lights, big stages, and have all the special effects, but this day the Dead just had themselves, some grass, some flowers, and they managed to create something so amazing from something so simple. And, they were in the place where it all started. Maybe this gave them a sense of closure and gave them their chance to say goodbye to Bill. That message had to go far because he's not here anymore. He's somewhere else and they needed to reach him.

And I think they did.

Annie Myles, 24, music manager, New York:

I hadn't been to a show in two years, and I didn't really know that I wanted to go. I'd heard a lot of bad things about the Dead tour. I just wasn't into it anymore.

I had the best time of my life! I snuck my way down onto the floor—by just *walking!* I had no hassles from anybody! It ended up that the security guards wouldn't let anyone dance in the aisles—except me! I was dancing with six police officers and security guards. I had them all doing the line dance, and the tango, up and down the aisles! Right in front of Jerry. I swear to God the band was laughing, like, "Oh my god, what is this chick doing!" If anyone tried to step out into the aisles, the guards would say, "Get back! You're not allowed to dance in the aisles!" And yet, the seven of us were sashaying up and down the aisles, the police officers were hooking arms and doing do-si-dos around each other. I was dying!

It was the purest example of people uniting under music, because there is *no way* that I would ever associate with a police officer or jovially get down with them at a show. The music just sliced through every single boundary I could ever have had with them. It was a really cool way to come back to shows. The pure soul of the music was still there. It was still uniting people who dared to unite!

The last shows I saw were in 1993 at Madison Square Garden. Again, I had a great time. I went by myself. I was in the front row. It was killer.

Getting Hooked

Chris Flum, 28, "cool dude," Orinda, CA:

I 've seen well over a hundred shows. Probably under two hundred, though. The first time I went back East to see the Dead was in 1988. I just happened to be visiting some friends, and the Dead were coming to town. I said, "Yahoo!" My friends had passes. East Coast people with passes . . . "Yahoo!"

So there I am, 1988, backstage at another Dead show, Madison Square Garden, having big fun. Then Ramrod hooked me up with passes, and I went to nine shows in twelve days, and then to Philadelphia and a couple other places. I went to a ton of places catching Dead shows. "Yahoo!"

Ricky Begneaud, 37, Cajun chef/caterer, Mill Valley, CA:

A fter a show in 1980 in New Orleans, my friends and I went to another friend's house, and I remember standing in the kitchen by myself for about two hours! I was rerunning

Jerry, Bobby, and Billy jamming in Golden Gate Park, fall, 1975 (PHOTO BY JANICE BELSON)

the entire show in my head. I remembered *everything* about that show. I couldn't go to sleep. It's hard to describe really because it's one of those things about really wanting to be in that place as much as you could think about being anyplace on the planet. I thought I was hooked on the Dead before that, but that show really made sense to me.

There was nobody down in Louisiana for me to go listen to the Grateful Dead with. There was nowhere to play tapes and hang out. I was going to college and selling real estate. Because I was still living at my parents' house, I'd tell them I was going somewhere for the weekend, then I'd hop on a plane and go somewhere to see the Dead. Sometimes I'd tell my mom, but my dad would have freaked out if he knew! They used to say, "Don't you have anything better to do with your life than following some rock group around?"

My mom finally understood. She once told one of her friends, "Well, you know, he travels around going to see the Grateful Dead, but the funny thing is, he gets to see them all over the country! He travels and sees all these places that we never get to see!" That was true. That was part of the fun thing about touring, you got to go around and see other parts of the country. You would never dream of going to Oklahoma City. Why would you need to go there? Well . . . to see the Dead!

I've never done an entire tour. The first little tour I ever went on was when they did three cities in Florida and then ended up at the Fox Theater in Atlanta. I went down with a couple of my buddies, Mike Kenney and Rick Welch, and cooked Thanksgiving dinner for my uncle, Robert Rauschenberg. Then we went up to Lakeland, Florida, then to Gainesville, Florida, then to Gator Alley or whatever that place was called, which was a spectacular show. Then we went to the Fox in Atlanta, then home to Louisiana. That was a great tour. I really got into the Dead then.

Gina, 31, Blues Traveler's personal assistant, New York:

The longest I went on the road with the Dead was about three weeks. In 1985, I moved to New York, and I continued to tour heavily all through that period. Every time I got a job, I told them that when summer rolled around, I had to go to Wisconsin for a week for the Dead shows. I finally found a job babysitting for these people who'd been Deadheads in the sixties and were now professionals. In fact, that's the reason they hired me! I said, "I'm a really good baby-sitter, but . . . I *have* to see the Dead every year, and I have to go to Wisconsin every summer." They understood!

I went for ten years straight to Alpine Valley. That was my favorite place. I lost a lot of jobs in the process, but I'd always get one back, and I'd make good money on the road, selling stuff. I was real low profile on tours. I did a lot of drugs and just kind of kept to myself and made money. I wasn't really into socializing, I was more into making money and seeing the show.

On the Dead tour, I never felt afraid that some guy was gonna try and take advantage of me. A couple times I'd be in a hotel room, and a guy would say something like, "Can I give you a back rub?" And I'd just say nicely, "No thanks!" And when I'd say that, then I felt comfortable. And I always stayed with a big group of people.

Annie Harlow, 36, green grocer, New England:

The Dead "took a year off" in 1975. I was freaking out, like, "I'm born too late!" At sixteen, you're a total loser anyway, and you think that life should revolve around you, but then you find out you came too late. I thought I was only going to see one Grateful Dead show my whole life. It was juvenile travesty! Nineteen seventy-six comes along, I'm now seventeen, and the Grateful Dead are going to play four nights in Boston at the Music Hall, which is a small theater. Of course, I have to go. And gosh, does it coincide with my eighteenth birthday, the graduation of high school? Oh my god! So my second show was actually my third, fourth, and fifth show. That was superimmersion at that point. I turned eighteen with the Grateful Dead in the Music Hall. I didn't go home for a week! It was June 9, 1976, and that was the same week I graduated, so it was a major party! Major launch. There was so much power now between this group of friends I had from growing up together. The Music Hall was so small, it was so hot, it was so intense . . . it was just energized! I remember them playing "Dancing in the Street," and afterwards, my image of it was everybody *was* dancing in the street.

Richard Yaker, 26, futurist engineer/visionary, Los Angeles:

Some people go, "Wow, this person is God." I don't know where that comes from. That's not for me. I've traveled to shows here and there, but they were all weekend getaways.

Ken Fine, aka Kew, 36, organic T-shirt salesman, Liberty, ME:

From college in Maine, I transferred to Santa Cruz for environmental studies, and I lived in Santa Cruz for five years. Living on the East Coast and going to school on the West Coast, I made some cross-country trips just for the New Year's Dead shows. I'd go home for Christmas and then just make sure to hightail it back for New Year's. Some trips were successful, some were . . . unsuccessful!

Annie Myles, 24, music manager, New York:

I've been to about seventy-five to eighty shows. I'll always consider myself a Deadhead!

Trey Allen, 27, R&R caterer, Nashville, TN:

I've sold beer, food, but the best thing I ever did was sell T-shirts.
Total bootlegs. Sometimes you don't do the whole tour just because you might be hanging out at somebody's house having a
good time, and you wake up and think, "Do we want to drive all day
or just hang out?" To me, as I got into it, the music was more important, but I'd have to say just the scene was always what I was into. I
was totally into collecting tapes and all of that. I've got closets full of
them, about three hundred tapes. It's more or less a big eyesore now!
But it's funny that you'd have really bad-quality tapes that sounded
horrible, but they were so important to you. Sort of like a sound track
to your evolution.

My favorite time was the tour in the summer of 1990. This really good friend of mine and her boyfriend, who I never really knew,
we decided we were all going to do this tour together. I got shirts
printed up, they were really great shirts, probably the best thing I've
ever sold before on a tour like that. People went crazy. It was an
Aztec design with the five stages of life on the back and a sundial
on the front. I painted them, which took about two hours. It was
amazing the reactions I got. When people came out of shows, they
just got sucked right into this design, they were oohing and aahing
at it. But for me, all of this pulled me out of the bullshit life that
I was programmed into. The summer of '90 was definitely the
biggest, craziest summer that I've ever had.

Steve Eichner, 30, R&R photographer, New York:

For three years, I got really into it. I'd go on tour, and I made
a lot of friends. I survived by selling tickets or loose doses.
I was a real ninja—I prided myself on being able to get into
shows for free. In the early eighties, before In The Dark came out

and they got real popular again, it was real easy to get into shows for free and scam. I'd go from show to show, selling T-shirts or stickers. I knew people who had stickers, so I'd get a guy to front me one hundred stickers for a dollar apiece, and I'd sell them for a dollar fifty each, and then I'd have fifty bucks and that would be my ticket and my doses and my bag of weed for the night. I was really into it. I'd go from city to city that way, catch a ride with someone.

When you're on tour, you keep seeing the same people over and over, you keep interacting with them, and you're in foreign cities together, so you have this bond going and you help each other out. The longest run I went on, we drove out to San Francisco from New York, me, my friend Adam, and two girls, for the shows at the Berkeley Greek Theater, and then we followed the tour all the way back East. I would hitchhike to shows and figure out some way to get in—or not, and just hang out with the people. It didn't even matter that much if I couldn't see the Dead. It was more the whole experience of that community.

8

Getting Onstage

John Popper, 27, Blues Traveler harmonicist, Princeton, NJ:

lues Traveler has had a long relationship to the Dead because of our association with the Grahams—David and
Bill. I met David playing at a Barnard gig back East. He
saw us, liked us a lot, and figured he could manage us because he
was getting out of school. So he told his dad about it, and Bill ap-
proached us. He had us opening for the Neville Brothers less than
a week later. He flew us out to open for Lynyrd Skynyrd. At one
point, they were making the Doors' movie in San Francisco, Bill
was producing it, they needed some musicians to be in it, so we got
in the movie, in the park scene. The day we filmed, we also opened
for Garcia that night. It was a really San Francisco-y gig. To be
filmed in Golden Gate Park for the Doors movie and then go to
the Warfield to open for Jerry Garcia—we were all freaking out! It
was really cool. When we got to the Warfield, I think it was Jerry's
personal manager, Steve Parish, who said, "Okay, boys. Now no
metal tonight!"

We went and had a good set. We were very nervous, the guitar
didn't work when we started, so we had to start over again. But that
was okay. Looking back, that was kind of entertaining. We just had
a ball. I remember watching Garcia playing. This music was just sort

of oozing out of him. He just kind of telegraphs music right into you. It was a great thing to see.

The next time I played with Jerry was when Bill died in the fall of 1991. Bill had always been trying to get the Dead and Blues Traveler together, but it never seemed to happen. I just wanted to go to Bill's memorial and be a part of it any way I could. And David wanted me to be there, so I flew out for that. Garcia didn't seem too keen on it, but he would do it for David. So David wanted me to meet Garcia. I'm at the festival and David said, "I talked to Jerry, and you're gonna sit in with the Dead." I was torn because it was a sad day, but it was a cool thing that I was going to sit in with the Dead. I met other members of the Dead, Phil and Bobby, and they were all very nice.

David wanted Jerry and me to have some sort of dialogue, so he took me into Jerry's tent backstage. When I got in, Jerry's eating a hamburger and I'm just standing there staring at the floor. All I could think of to say was, "I'm a flurry of emotion." And Jerry said, "Me too," with a long sigh. That was about it. I think he started to get a little annoyed with me and he said, "This song will be in D." I said, "Okay," and I just started fidgeting with this little telescope I had, I think he got amused by that. But I just really had nothing to say to this man, and here I was left in his tent! David left, and it was me and Jerry hanging out. And the only thing said was, "I'm a flurry of emotion." Eventually, Dave came back and got me.

I remember hearing a tape of Carlos Santana once, trying to sit in with the Dead, and Carlos gave up all his chops early and the Dead just kind of made him run out of things to say musically. So, when I got up to play, the one thing that kept running through my mind was, "Don't try and blow your wad. If you play impressively, you're gonna look stupid." So I really held back, and David said afterwards, "You should have gone nuts." But I knew if I'd gone nuts, they would've gone after me. So I held back and they really had fun.

Within the next week we were opening for Garcia at Madison Square Garden. Apparently he told someone afterwards that we blew him away. It just seemed to me, without having ever really talked to the guy since, that after I demonstrated a little self-control, he decided that we—Blues Traveler—were okay. I've always got the feeling that they thought we were too . . . metal is the word they use. But I think we're just younger. I think when they were younger, they hit a lot more spots when they were playing, especially on Lesh's part. Phil Lesh used to go crazy.

John Perry Barlow (left) and Timothy Leary (right) with the author, New
York, 1992 (PHOTO BY STEVE EICHNER)

Bob Rupe, 38, Cracker bassist, Richmond, VA:

I think the capacity at the show Cracker played in Oregon was
35,000 or 40,000. Over the three days we did about 115,000.
That's certainly the most people I've ever played for . . . or
played in front of! I tell you, the Dead audience is tough. The deal
is, with the Dead audience, they want to see the Dead. They don't
really care about anybody else, and anybody else up there before the
Dead is just in the way. But we sort of moved our set around a bit.
We didn't play all the heavy Cracker stuff, we ended up pulling out
some folk tunes, and we had Morgan, the girl who used to be in
Camper Van Beethoven, come up and play fiddle.

We got some stompers going a little bit, and they seemed to warm
up to us. Then, on the third day, we actually got an encore and the
crew let us go out and do it, which apparently is pretty unheard of.
It was really cool getting an encore and getting the okay from the
Dead crew—who are all really great people. I probably had one of
the best Grateful Dead experiences, I guess, of just about anybody
out there! I had a really great time.

Their whole production is very well organized. I mean, the Dead have been doing this for about thirty years, and they know exactly what they're doing. They know who needs to be there, who doesn't, how to set things up to get 'em to move smoothly. As far as shows go, I've never seen a more professional production and security setup. Not "pro" like gestapo, I mean pro like the right attitude, how to handle everybody and not come off like Nazis. It was very well done. I was impressed.

Tom Constanten, 51, pianist/composer, San Francisco:

Playing with the Grateful Dead, when it worked, it was wonderful—like music in general: when it works, it's wonderful; when it doesn't, it can be very sucky. I was a newcomer, yet I wasn't. I'd known Jerry and Phil since before they knew some of the other guys in the band. And it was only because of my being in the clutches of the air force that I hadn't been with them before.

The technology of the time wouldn't allow sufficient amplification of a keyboard to give me anything resembling a dynamic range so I could be at all expressive. I felt I was shouting, musically speaking, to be heard at all. You can't be very expressive when you're at the top of your lungs all the time. Also, I had no instrument at home to practice on. The only time I played was at the shows or the rehearsals, so I had to do a lot of thinking on my feet. The military doesn't pay a lot, and there were at least two places that didn't like the band's credit rating well enough to let me buy a piano from them. The instrument consideration was one of the suckiest things.

Of course, in the studio, that wasn't a problem. All multitracking. At that time in the studio, the Dead were learning what they were doing also. Everybody was making it up as we went along.

Every "Dark Star" we did at the Fillmore East was like there were angels or something who made things work for us. I think part of that had to do with the fact that when you played for the New York audience then, you knew they were critical. But when they're approving, it gives you this incredible lift.

Jerry Miller, 51, Moby Grape/Jerry Miller Band guitarist, San Francisco:

Moby Grape used to play a lot of double bills with the Dead. We'd sit up there in the little upstairs room at the Fillmore, with say, the Dead, Big Brother, Moby Grape, and the Airplane. We'd all sit up there and chew the fat, laugh. They'd rotate, each band got to play twice at most venues. So, whoever played first also got to play fourth, which was a perfect place to play. The idea of top bill and all that, the only way you could tell probably was to look at a poster, and then they shared that pretty evenly too. It was pretty cool. There were short breaks between bands; Bill Graham ran the show, so it wasn't long breaks!

I've always said, "If it wasn't for the Dead . . ." The Dead was the strongest draw here. They were the epitome, the beginning of the psychedelic scene. They actually got it started, we just winged in with them. The Dead and the Airplane always helped us out, got us into the Fillmore and the Avalon. Then they'd come to the Ark, which was an after-hours place over in Sausalito. On weekends, they'd do the Fillmore and after hours, if they still wanted more action, they'd come over to Sausalito and play on this old ferryboat called the Ark. We'd jam till six in the morning, Janis Joplin and everybody. We kept going, and then at six in the morning they'd serve eggs and bacon to all the hippies. A Bloody Mary if you wanted it.

That was such extreme fun. We always had the Ark to go to. The Sons of Champlin would come over, we'd have these big jams. Four in the morning wasn't nothing. Everybody was still having fun, jumping around. The police weren't extra heavy, once in a while they could be, but overall it was pretty loose. You never had to worry about getting stopped for having a binky (translation: a joint). You never got in much trouble for that. We used that in a song.

David Gans, 41, radio producer: Grateful Dead Hour, author: Playing in the Band and Conversations with the Dead, San Francisco:

In October 1978, Weir got me up onstage to watch at Winterland one night. Along about 1982, I had fairly regular access to the stage. To me, it was really cool to be able to watch the musicians interact that closely. Being a musician myself and playing in bands, I'm used to the weird perspective of being on-

Deadhead with his favorite head, Alpine, 1987 (PHOTO BY STEVE EICHNER)

stage. Instead of hearing it through the PA the way it's supposed to sound, you're hearing it from this incredibly distorted place of being right near one set of speakers. You learn how to hear what's going on from that perspective. It was a tremendous privilege to be able to watch the musicians from that close up.

Sometimes it was a weird thing because there are people on that stage who thought I was an intruder and that I'd sort of barged in and pushed my way in there, and they weren't particularly welcoming. After a while, I figured out that being onstage wasn't important enough to endure all of that weirdness. I didn't want to be the bearer of weirdness, and I didn't want to be the recipient of weirdness. Having had the experience enough times, being up there and seeing it, I was able to just go back out to being among the audience where I was much more comfortable. I realized that I was happier among my friends in the audience, that it's okay to be a Deadhead, a spectator, a fan, and go out there and listen to it from the seats where you're supposed to be to hear the music.

Timothy Leary, 74, chaos engineer, Los Angeles:

The first time I ever got onstage with the Dead was the first Human Be-In in Golden Gate Park, January 4, 1967. It's a powerful memory. It was miraculous. That was the first time there was that kind of show in numbers. There was no advertising, only underground radio and word of mouth, and *wow!* They jammed, and suddenly forty or fifty thousand people showed up. It was awesome. It was a small little stage, and with Hell's Angels around, there wasn't room for anybody else!

We thought, "Shit! Good Lord! Look at all these people!" We got a sense of the demographic power the music had. Of course Owsley was there, but the Dead! They were the only band I remember from that day. I went to a lot of their shows in the Panhandle.

Bill Cutler, 47, musician/producer, San Francisco:

Pat Campbell played bass in a band with Jerry, and he played in my band, the Heroes. He was at some sessions once with me and Jerry, at my house and at Hyde Street Studios. When my band was forming, we opened for Jerry's acoustic band, Good Ol' Boys, at Margarita's in Santa Cruz. Pat played stand-up bass for them and electric bass for Heroes. We had a lot of fun down there at Margarita's. Jerry was in a great headspace. He's a great musician, probably a better musician today, but in some ways his enthusiasm for music was so great then, his energy was so unstoppable. I remember being backstage . . . we weren't supposed to open the show, but somebody canceled and we went on at the last minute. I was just stoned out of my mind. I said, "Jerry, I'm too stoned to play!" Jerry goes, "Hey, man! You're never too stoned to play! That's the first rule in rock and roll: You're never too stoned to play!" I said, "No! Don't make me go out there." But he did, and I played the set. I heard it later, and it sounded great. I couldn't believe how good it sounded. But at the time, I was just flying and I was nervous! I went out there in front of Jerry's crowd not knowing how they would accept us. They just roared! They loved us! They gave us an encore and everything. Jerry made us feel so at home. He made it clear to the audience that he was behind us as a band. It was a great moment. It was that kind of stuff. Jerry really gave me a chance to move in among a new music community.

Waylon Jennings, 55, rhythm-and-blues country musician, TX:

One time we played somewhere on a One Hundred and somethin' Street in New York, with the Dead and the New Riders of the Purple Sage. See my problem was . . . I realized, "Hey, this is a no-win situation for me 'cause here I am,

I'm a loner, and I look like to them little kids that come to see the New Riders, I look like that son of a bitch that just left that told 'em theys gonna kill 'em." Yeah. So that was a no-win situation. I got outta there!

Ramblin' Jack Elliott, 62, folk musician, San Francisco via Brooklyn:

In 1971 or 1972, I played in New York with the Grateful Dead and the New Riders of the Purple Sage. We were there about a week, playin' different gigs. The first one was at Madison Square Garden. The second one was somewhere in Long Island, and the third one was in New Jersey. Bobby loaned me a guitar for those gigs. It was the only time I ever actually played with them. I was on first, then the New Riders, and then the Dead. Well, I didn't like the audience. They just got off the subway and they were still walking to their seats.

Then there was the time I had a gig to play where I was opening for Jerry at the Santa Cruz Community Center. They had a bad sound system there and people couldn't hear me, so they weren't listening 'cause they couldn't hear. It was a rainy day. I was very pissed about the crowd reaction. It was bad. I went home and went for a ride on this horse named Brinkham late at night. I got lost up on top of a mountain and couldn't find a trail to get back home. I figured I was gonna spend the night sittin' cross-legged underneath my horse's belly. I was sittin' under there hangin' on to his front legs with my hat on, just touchin' the bottom of him with his saddle on. I finally did find my way home, but I caught a bad cold.

I had to play another gig the next day opening for Jerry after getting stuck all night in the rain, so I could barely sing. When I got up there, they called the gig because it was outdoors in the mud in the football field at Sonoma State college in Cotati. So they put it off till the following week. They gave us a rain date. I went up to do the rain date and I was over my cold and I sang okay.

Another time I played my favorite gig in Denver and there was a Grateful Dead concert the same night. After my show, I went and hung out with the Dead. I remember hanging out backstage before the show, and I was amazed that Jerry would be so congenial as to visit with me, right on the stage when the curtain was closed, right before the show. I thought, "You shouldn't do this to a performer, hang out and talk to 'em like this." He didn't mind. He was just happy to talk. But I remember him warning me, he said, "Don't get in the way of a gorilla." I said, "What?" He said, "Don't get in the way of a gorilla. You'll never be invited back." That was very good advice and I've never gotten in the way of a gorilla. I'm always very careful about them backstage because if you trip one of those guys when they're carrying those hundred-pound speakers around . . .

Ramrod and I are the best of friends, so I'm not too worried about him. He's always my best friend when I go to see a Dead concert. He's the one who welcomes me in.

Jerry Garcia, Greek Theater, Berkeley, California, 1966
(PHOTO BY DAVID SEABURY)

9

Getting Backstage

Chris Flum, 28, "cool dude," Orinda, CA:

It was never my goal to get backstage and meet the Dead. A lot of people would kill to be in my shoes. I've been to well over a hundred backstage shows.

The best thing about backstage shows is there's a bathroom, and it's easy to enter and exit, you don't have to deal with the crowds. For back-East shows, the best thing about backstage is that there's not that many people and they also cater. So you can get your ice cream, you can get your hot pretzel. And at Oakland shows, you have beer!

Everybody's really nice back there. It's like family, and I've been there so long, I recognize and know a lot of the people, so it's like going and seeing my old friends. If I have to buy a ticket, that means I don't get to see my friends who have become friends particularly through backstage passes. I'm not one of the lucky few who gets a BGP (Bill Graham Presents) or GDP (Grateful Dead Productions) laminate, but when I really want to go to a show, I will get a laminate or a stick-on. I'm always prepared to buy a ticket, but 90 percent of the time I know if I show up and somebody I know sees me, they're gonna get me a stick-on.

I know people who have taken advantage of the system, gone out and sold their tickets, stuck on their stick-on, brought back bad people, snuck people through, taken laminates, and that's all bullshit. Milking the meal tickets. There are so many people who do that, and to me that's so wrong—taking full advantage of the privilege of being backstage. I don't like people who take advantage of the system. The system isn't there to take advantage of. That's why they've changed the system a lot over the last couple years, because people took way too much advantage of it.

One time when I went back East on a tour, I got two laminates and four tickets, so that was for every night of every show. One of the guys I was with was the biggest jerk in the world. He'd take the extra stick-ons and the extra tickets and sell them to people and keep walking people through the backstage exit using these stick-ons. He got cut off, cold cut-off. I told on him, other people told on him. Now he doesn't get passes anymore. He doesn't admit that's why he doesn't go to shows anymore. Yeah, right! If you didn't milk the system, then you'd still be there, buddy.

The only thing you see backstage that's out of the ordinary is that a couple narcs walk by, and it's obvious that they're narcs and not Deadheads! You just look at them and think, "Why are you trying to weasel in here? What has anybody here ever done wrong to you? So people may dose a little bit, party a little bit, but are we hurting anybody? Have you ever seen a Deadhead hurt somebody?" You certainly don't see fights at Dead shows. I mean, go to a heavy-metal show where they chug tons of whiskey and get in fights. That just doesn't happen at Dead shows.

Bob Rupe, 38, Cracker bassist, Richmond, VA:

When we opened for the Dead in Oregon (1994), it was cool back in the dressing room. We could bring people back there and hang out and party and do whatever we wanted and not get hassled by anyone. It was great.

I met this photographer backstage. An older guy. He's a musicologist who's been hanging out with the Dead forever and was taking pictures and stuff. Anyway, we were talking about old music, and he's one of these guys that just loves to pontificate about old music because he knows everything. I don't fault him for that, I mean, I think it's great that there's people that collect this information.

Lounging before the show, Alpine, 1987 (PHOTO BY STEVE EICHNER)

I asked him, "What did Dylan listen to?" He said, "Oh, Dylan listened to this guy and that guy, these old Irish folksingers from the twenties." And I said, "Well, I'd be interested in finding some of that if you have it in your libraries." And, as it happened, he had a big case of cassette tapes with him! He said, "Well . . . ," and he looked through and he pulled one out and said, "Well, it's the only one I have with me." I said, "Well, I'll just give you a call and maybe you can mail it to me." And he said, "Naw. Go ahead. You can take it." I thought that was very cool.

Lauren Astra Esley, 20, writer, San Francisco:

At the 1991 New Year's show, my friend and I were in the parking lot at the Oakland Coliseum and we met a relative of mine—a Hell's Angel—and went backstage with him. The Dead were already playing, so we walked to the stage. Security was tight, we were shuffled around, I couldn't find a place to stand, so we decided to go back outside to the lot. We went to a drum circle, and all of a sudden, people started to do a countdown to the New Year. The drums got louder and louder, and when the count got to "*One!*" some guy standing on top of a school bus sprayed a huge bottle of champagne on the crowd. It was fun, but the really funny thing was that this was the sixth countdown I'd witnessed that night.

Deadheads are rarely on time.

Caryn Shalita, mid-20s, actress, Los Angeles:

There's something different about the Dead than any other band: their scene backstage. Having been around the music scene in Los Angeles and San Francisco, I've hung out backstage with various music people and I really don't like the atmosphere at a lot of places. It's very stuck-up and very self-important, and really not user-friendly at all. Last year, my husband and I were backstage for the Dead's Chinese New Year's show in Oakland, and I have to say that it was the best backstage experience I've ever had. I've never been somewhere where, first of all, you could have as much fun backstage as you could outside because there was so much going on. They had set up this whole video arcade, a Ping-Pong table, and all these fun things to do, and sofas and whatever.

But the thing that struck me the most was that there were all these people wandering around backstage, like really normal people that you'd think you'd meet going out to get your mail or something, hanging out with these little kids running around everywhere. And it just struck me: what a family-oriented thing. There's no age that's exempt. At most rock concerts, people fall within a certain age range, but that's not true about the Dead; you can have anybody from age three to age sixty and they belong there. For me, that's something that makes them different—besides their music— just *how* they are. It sets them apart from other bands. It gives you a sense of this huge family reunion because everyone's there with their kids, everyone's eating and drinking and listening to music, and . . . *getting along!* There's no attitude stuff happening. The people who are there are all very friendly towards each other and even to people they don't know because there's a security about it, I guess.

I love little kids, so I check them out because they're always really interesting. That's something I always wonder about too: I try and put myself in the mind of that little kid and think . . . because my parents never would've taken me to a Dead show, ever! My mom listened to Frank Sinatra when she was fifteen, the straightest people, musically, you can imagine. Now my mom actually likes the Dead. She has certain songs she likes and recognizes. But I never ever would've been taken to a concert as a kid, so I always think from the kid's perspective: "Wow, what's this kid taking in right now!" There's so much going on, and the kids are so receptive to that high energy. I try to feel what they're feeling. It was so strange because you could lose yourself back there. I mean there was really that much to do. They had one of those little basketball hoop games. You could play the games. That was a whole section in and of itself, and then the other section was a living-room-type setup, and it's like you forget where you are. At one point we were like, "Oh, God, the second half of the show probably started! We should go!"

Getting backstage was not something I tried to do. Our friend just happened to give us passes. We didn't even know. I think she just gave them to us for the hell of it. I mean, it was fun, but I don't think there's any big deal about it.

Ken Fine, aka Kew, 36, organic T-shirt salesman, Liberty, ME:

I remember one time some of my wild college buddies were doing this "try to sneak backstage" thing. They were getting into a lot of shows that year and coming back with wild stories about smoking a joint with Jimmy Cliff, and all these people. Up until then, I was really captivated by this magical thing about the Dead, that they were these gods up there, and the magic they were pulling off with the crowd and everything was just so fascinating. I'd been reading books about some of the weird coincidences that had happened in the Grateful Dead's lives—it seemed like such a charmed thing. At the time, I didn't know Brenda, my future wife, too well. We had just met on kind of a coincidence through some mutual friends, and she recognized me because I looked like my brother. I thought she was neat, and I had a pair of tickets to see the Rhythm Devils on Friday, February 13, 1981, at the Marin Veteran's Memorial Theater. I think it was the only time they ever really played shows as the Rhythm Devils. This was during the time Mickey, Billy, and Phil recorded the sound track for *Apocalypse Now*. They did one weekend performance with the guys they'd worked with: Airto Moriera, Flora Purim, Mike Hinton, and a few other people. It was mostly percussion. They did these special shows celebrating the percussion work they'd all done together on this

Let's go for a ride, Philadelphia, 1986 (PHOTO BY STEVE EICHNER)

soundtrack. So I had these two tickets and I said to this wonderful woman Brenda—who is over on the other side of the house right now—"You wanna go?"

Well, our ride fell through, so we decided to meet on Route 1 and hitchhike up from Santa Cruz. With these huge backpacks on, we started hitchhiking at three in the afternoon. It didn't go very well. It was getting late by the time we got our first ride from some student from Saudi Arabia who had all the money in the world and a great big car. He dropped us off at the last line of BART, which took us into downtown San Francisco. As we transferred to a bus, we popped some mushrooms. We were feeling pretty high as the bus crossed the Golden Gate Bridge! We're cruising Marin County and finally the bus driver stops at the end of this long driveway and says, "This is it!" So we get off the bus with our big backpacks, and we hike down this driveway, through the parking lot with all these cars, and as we get close to the building, the door flies open . . . the show had just ended! These two people came storming out like they just had a fight. "That show sucked!" And the next kid comes out and says, "That was great!" Brenda and I are looking at each other: "Wow, now what are we gonna do?" I look to the left and see a side door pop open. I said, "Come on, let's go this way!" We walked to this side door. It was the backstage door, and Merle Saunders came out. He held the door open, smiled, and said, "Hi!" And we just walked in!

There we are standing backstage with our backpacks on, in the wings with the ropes and the curtains and all the switches that work the lights. The show had just ended, so everybody was just kind of bustling around. A couple of big Harleys were parked back there, some big roadies were milling around, and there was a table with some snacks and coffee. Brenda and I are standing there, higher than kites, and I said, "Well, we'll just be cool, and if someone asks us to leave, we'll leave. But if we just act comfortable, then we'll just hang out." So, we're hanging out, and finally somebody comes over and says, "Want a cup of coffee? The rum balls are really good too! Have one of those chocolate things." So we took our backpacks off and we're hanging out drinking coffee, eatin' snacks, and people are chatting with us a little bit. I decided to roll a joint in case we met somebody and they wanted to smoke. I get the joint rolled and Brenda says, "You know, everybody seems to be going around that corner." So we put our backpacks back on and we go around this corner and we see some stairs. We go up these stairs, we get to the top of the stairs, and there's this long curving corridor, and as we curved around, we suddenly realize we're in the room with the band! Mickey Hart was right there having a heated conversation with Joan Baez, so we walk past him—with our huge backpacks on!—and next to him was Phil having a conversation with Mountain Girl. They were having some kind of major thing too, and I just stood right next to Phil and said, "Hey, do you wanna smoke a joint?" He looks up at me, and I'll never forget his hands—they were huge and all callused, beat-up, with tape wrapped around them, tears all over them, and they were just trembling. He reaches for the joint and says, "Oh, don't mind if I do!" He draws hard off this joint and hands it back to me. I put it in my mouth, and I'd rolled the damn thing too tight! It wouldn't smoke at all! So I'm going, "Oh, God," standing there, and Phil's still in this conversation with Mountain Girl. I quickly busted the joint all up, put it in my pipe, got it lit, handed it back to him, and he goes, "Oh, no thanks, I don't smoke."

So there we were, still hanging out like a couple of fools with our backpacks on, but I guess we were lovable fools because nobody seemed to mind. Phil got up and kind of walked off, and Mountain Girl said, "Well, I'll smoke it!" So we smoked it with her, and Phil was making all these joking comments, like, "Oh, you would, you hussy!" So it was a joking-around scene and we were just hanging out. Then Phil comes back over and Brenda says to him, "You know, we hitchhiked all the way up here, and we were too late. We didn't even see your show." And it was so funny because Phil goes something like, "Now, young lady, when you buy a ticket, it's your responsibility. You have to be here to make it to the show. Now there's nothing I can do to help you with this. I can't get you a ticket for tomorrow or anything." We said something like, "No, no, no, it's cool. That's not what we want."

Then we started rapping with Phil about us being from Santa Cruz, and he said, "Oh, I always wanted to play there on the campus!" I remembered in *The Book of the Dead* it talked about how one time Phil was traipsing through the woods and heard music in the distance, and it was Moby Grape playing a concert at what they called The Quarry, which was a natural amphitheater in the middle of the Santa Cruz campus. So he was all excited about playing there someday. I said, "Oh, yeah! I can put together a gig for you and it'll be great!" So we hatched this plot where everything would have to be clandestine and no one would know that the Grateful Dead were coming. We would set up the PA system and say it was some other band or something. So Phil was pretty psyched up about this, and he was saying, "Now, it's vitally important that no one must know!" I was right into it with him, like, "Yeah, we gotta do this and that . . ." I really felt like I was relating with him because that's how my friends had always planned things: "Now we gotta do this . . ." Anyway, we raved about that for a while, and I told him I could definitely put it together and I wouldn't tell a soul, and I'd let him know what was happening. We were both semiserious about it. But . . . one thing led to another and he slipped away to go do something. Brenda and I kept hanging out, and as I said, I figured if I just keep smoking and it smells really good and anybody wants some, I'll share, and if nobody minds, we'll just hang out, and if they ask us to leave, we will. And no one did, so we stayed.

People were coming and going. Billy came in with his drumsticks in his back pocket and said, "Anybody seen my kids?" He looked around the room. "No kids?" and he walked back out. It was a pretty casual scene there backstage, which made me realize that these people were just regular guys. I think Mickey, Jerilyn, and some other people were hanging out on the other side of the room. Then Phil and Airto came in and they "assembled" in the corner for this meet-

Dead dog-day afternoon, Philadelphia, 1986 (PHOTO BY STEVE EICHNER)

ing. Brenda and I just sat there quietly, and I was able to kind of eavesdrop on what they were talking about. I got the gist that they actually rehearsed things, that they actually work at putting together these shows, they don't just get up there and play rock and roll and it's real easy and they have a good time. They're really busting their butts.

I was fascinated because they were all talking like: "Yeah, and tomorrow night on that part, we're really gonna go after that. We're gonna hit that part hard! We're gonna blow 'em away!" And I realized that these guys are working hard to put on these shows. This music doesn't just fall together like nothing. I'd seen Phil's hands ripped up, and listening to them talk about how they were really gonna push for a certain arrangement of the song—these guys are human beings who are wonderfully talented and have great technical backup, but they're just musicians who are working their butts off to put something good together for their audience. It really changed the way I looked at the whole thing.

Then I became fascinated with the technical aspect of everything. "Oh my god, look at these cables! Look at this stuff these

Smilin' at Cal Expo, 1985 (PHOTO BY DAN WILSON)

guys are using!" I really respected them as musicians, just regular guys who go out on the road for a long time. It's hard work! I've since played guitar in a few bands, so I know what it's like to put on a show. And then to see the Grateful Dead. I mean, you're doing these interviews with these people who've been to all these concerts. Well, Garcia's played *every* concert! Those guys are hardworking guys. Luckily, it can be a hell of a lot of fun. That night listening to their meeting was a real turning point for me. I saw that they're just regular guys.

So ... they had their meeting, and things started winding down. This one musician had come over and talked to us a little bit—his name was Freddie Fleck. He made some of the talking drums they were using at the time. And I think it was Jerilyn who finally told us, "It's time to go." She was wearing a black spider-web dress. She had long blond hair; she was Mickey's old lady at the time. She said, "We're all gonna go home now, so you gotta gather up your stuff. We gotta leave the building." So, we gathered up our stuff, and then they started offering us money for a hotel room. My wife says we took the money, but I don't remember. I don't think we did. We had our tents and our backpacks—*huge* backpacks! I still can't believe that when I handed Phil a joint, I was wearing a huge green backpack! Pretty goofy. I'll be curious if Phil remembers that night because it was certainly memorable to me. The impression I get of those guys is that they have a great sense of humor, and they've probably seen some freaked-out Deadheads, but I'm sure they've also met some really neat Deadheads that are fun to talk to. As I said, this night was a real turning point for me where I no longer consider these guys as some kind of strange godheads.

I've met Phil since, shook his hand backstage, said hi, but I never had the opportunity to say, "Do you remember that night, blah, blah, blah . . . ?"

Ricky Begneaud, 37, Cajun chef/caterer, Mill Valley, CA:

In 1981, my friend Lou Tambakos got me some tickets for the Greek Theater shows. I brought him a bottle of champagne, hung out. Then I went to the show, and somehow I got put on the guest list, I got backstage passes. I guess Lou put me on some sort of special list. I went up to will-call and I literally skipped back to show my friends Rick Welch and Cliff Broussard these special backstage passes I got. It was special because the Greek is so special and it was my very first backstage show, plus we got to sit in special seating. It's so easy to see the band from there.

That was the first time I really connected with how this was home turf for the Dead. They were actually *home*, so there was different feeling for me at that show. And, we got to go backstage! We didn't really meet anybody, but we were totally excited. Absolutely.

Rachel Clein, 13, student, Marin County, CA:

I've never really liked being backstage. Last time I was in the kids' room, what I remember most about it was two girls bragging about their ponies and their big closets and how they just redecorated their room. I'd rather be out front listening to the music. I usually go with my dad, and we watch the show from the audience.

Greg Martens, 31, entrepreneur, Portland, ME:

I go backstage, but I never force myself on that scene. When I stopped vending, I was just standing in the parking lot because I didn't know what to do anymore, and my friend came up to me and said, "Well, it's time you meet the band," because he'd been hanging with the band a lot. The next thing I know I was in talking with the band. It just happened. That evolution of going to shows for ten years and not pushing it, taking care, and all the good things I did in the parking lot—not ripping people off. That good karma just came back to me. It was at the Oakland Coliseum, and the next thing I know, I was in Vince's dressing room and asking him if he could play "Lucy in the Sky With Diamonds" for me. He said he didn't have the sheet music, but he'd go buy it and that it would take a while for Jerry to learn it. Then about a year later, they played it. That's one of my most famous Grateful Dead tales you could ever print. I brought some friends of mine back to meet Vince, and I'd keep on him about, "Have you practiced 'Lucy' yet?" My friends were like, "Ease up on him!" I kept going on, "Damn! I want to hear 'Lucy in the Sky With Diamonds.' It's my favorite." They'd been playing a lot of Beatles' songs to that point, and I thought that would be a neat song for them to play.

Jerry Miller, 51, Moby Grape/Jerry Miller Band guitarist, San Francisco:

Backstage I was usually doing my own thing. Nothing really that crazy, just chatting and hanging out. I smoked many joints with Jerry, but that's what you did then. All you had to do was breathe up near that dressing room at the Fillmore or the Avalon!

I remember Jerry needed a string one night, his roadie come tearing in there with this stuff for him, and this big old redneck is standing there like he'd never been there before with this crew cut kind of deal, and the guy stepped on his toe a little bit, and the guy starts chasing him, running past me, runs right up to the dressing room, and the guy knows he's behind him, chasing him, and getting ugly. He gives Jerry his strings, takes off his shirt, and he goes out there, and the guy is still standing there, and this roadie has got muscles like Arnold Schwarzenegger, but you couldn't tell because he had a loose shirt on. So he comes out there and says to the guy, "Did you have something you wanted to say to me?" And the guy was speechless! I didn't like the guy. He didn't fit. Besides, if your toes get stepped on in those situations, they're gonna get stepped on. Don't get rednecked and ugly about it. The roadie was getting strings to Jerry, so that was more important than worrying about this guy right then, but after he had free time, he could go back and say, "Okay. What were you saying?"

John Perry Barlow, 47, Dead lyricist/cyberspace pioneer, WY:

I don't know when this was, maybe '76, maybe '77—yeah, coming into '77. The Dead were playing New Year's Eve at Winterland, so it must've been at least that early. This was the last New Year's Eve at Winterland. I had come out on a whim just at the last possible moment. I'd just gotten together with my wife. Well, we'd been together awhile, but this was still a strange zone to her a little bit.

In any case, we'd been up onstage, and I had taken a powerfully large dose of LSD, and so had she, I think. We were up onstage and Weir had this girlfriend at the time, Janice, she was just like . . . mist. She was cute. Cute, but *real* light. Real diaphanous. She just kind of drifted off at a certain point, and there was this zoo going on backstage that was I think the worst I've ever seen it. Maybe it was just because I was really high on acid, but it was like the night circus. It was Fellini on bad acid. It was like the ninth circle of hell. Everybody's face was melting off, even if you weren't on acid! Oh, man, twisted, contorted people dressed in all these extravagantly startling bad clothes. Yuk! It was the seventies. The seventies was not a pretty decade. It was ugly. And I'd been on the ranch for quite a while at that point, and I wasn't used to it. I was doing my own things, and I'd pretty well adapted to that other environment.

Anyway, Weir's girlfriend had taken off, and because it was the last New Year's at Winterland, Graham was truly gonna kick out the jams. I mean, it was gonna be Circus Maximus at midnight, and he was gonna descend from the clouds as Uncle Sam, some sort of psychedelic Uncle Sam. It was really gonna be special. Well, right before midnight, Weir says, "You gotta go find Janice. She's backstage someplace. I can't leave her out there for New Year's. I want her onstage. Can you go get her? I gotta stay here." So I said, "All right. I'll go look." And I went back into this crawling mass of horror. I looked high and low. I couldn't find her anywhere. I couldn't find anybody I'd ever seen before in my life, in fact! There was no solace to be had. So, it's about five minutes to midnight, and I come back to the stage entrance, and I presented myself to go back onstage, and there was this huge black guy. He was like a linebacker for the Raiders guarding the stage. He said, "You can't go up there." I said, "Yeah, I can. I'm John Barlow." He said, "*Nobody* can go up there." I said, "Listen, I wrote the song that they're playing right now. My wife is onstage." He said, "I don't care. If you were Presi-

dent Carter, you couldn't get on right now." And I was feeling kind
of panicked about this. Right at that moment, a couple of what appeared to me to be obvious groupies flounced on past, and neither
one of them was President Carter. I thought, "Well, fuck this! If
they can go, I can go! Screw it!" So I went past, and this guy
grabbed me and threw me up against the wall, and it just unhinged
me, and I had the strength of a thousand men that you've got on
LSD sometimes, and I came back at him and hit him so hard that
I dislocated his jaw. Which I didn't know at the time, but I knocked
him down sideways. Hit him really hard, but I bounced away from
that shot the wrong direction—not towards the stage, but away.
Back into the hellhole!

So then I just sort of faded back. I thought, "I'm gonna let this
ride for a little bit. I'm just gonna bide my time." So I went backstage and I suffered through the turning of the New Year and whatever explosive activity was taking place out on the other side. And
I was in hell! So after about twenty minutes of people hugging and
grimacing and kissing, it's finally time for me to re-present myself
. . . I think it will have blown over by then. Besides, in my view,
much time has passed! We're not even in the same geological period anymore. This is not the view of the guard for whom this whole
incident is still fresh as the moment it happened! The paramedics
have come, the cops have come, I come back, and the next thing
I know, whang! I'm in handcuffs and charged with assault! I'm being
led out onto the street and I'm thinking, "Uh-oh! This is serious!
Here I am without any ID whatsoever, high on LSD, charged with
assault, holding drugs, and there's no good end to this. They're just
gonna take me away, and Lord knows if anybody will ever see me
again." Truly a paranoid moment.

Turns out, Alan Trist—he ran Ice Nine many years, good friend
of mine, originally came onto the scene as a close friend of Robert
Hunter's—way back, before there was a Grateful Dead. He's English. Lives in Oregon now. He was too fine-tuned a unit to be in
that society as long as he was— Anyway . . . I didn't know he'd
seen me. All I knew was that I was in irons, and that I was being
hauled off into the belly of the beast. I'd been an antiwar protester
so I'd been handcuffed before. But this was different. Never for
doing something that could conceivably be a crime as far as I was
concerned. Then I went into this thing thinking, "Maybe I really
hurt this guy," which I had, actually. But I also . . . I got outside and

Bill Graham working on Golden Gate Park concert featuring the Grateful Dead and Jefferson Starship, fall, 1975 (PHOTO BY JANICE BELSON)

I had this sort of patriotic moment where I thought, "Now wait a second. This is America. This is not Bolivia. What I have to do now is to get really clear and focused and explain to this cop precisely what happened without any bullshit whatsoever. To the best of my ability to even speak!" And I was having some difficulty doing that!

"I just have to make human contact with this guy. He's my fellow American! He's not a pig." Right? So I start in on him, and I'd pretty well gotten this accomplished. In fact, he's taking off the handcuffs when we are descended upon! Turned out that Alan Trist had seen this go down and had immediately assembled all the troops he could think of, including Hal Kant, our lawyer, who is a true piece of work, John McIntyre, who was then managing the band and can be a truly operatic fussbudget, *and* Bill Graham, who was still dressed as a psychedelic Uncle Sam with plastic confetti hanging off him! They all jump this cop and demand my immediate release. The cop puts the handcuffs back on, and now it's like I'm booty! I'm being held hostage because this group of people is putting a lot of pressure on the cop, and not going about it right at all! I'm trying to explain, "No! No. Listen, just leave it. I think we got it covered here." I almost got hauled off after that because these guys were so insistent on having me released.

So, I was rescued. Sorta. By Uncle Sam! It turned out that Janice, Weir's girlfriend, had gone down into the garage underneath Winterland and curled up in the car and gone to sleep, so there would've been no way I could find her.

And so it was that I entered that year. . . .

Now *that's* problems with security! This guy was too willing to turn himself into a machine. The problem with him was that he had his orders. It turned out that the women that went past were Graham employees. One of them was Bill's personal secretary, which I didn't know. So there was a good reason why they went by me.

Bill Cutler, 47, musician/producer, San Francisco:

I went backstage at all the shows at Winterland. I really enjoyed that because there was such an extended family there. So many fascinating people were into all kinds of things besides the things that everyone talks about, like LSD and the Grateful Dead. There were American Indians, environmentalists, filmmakers, animals, children . . . it was amazing! I went quite often to Winterland and also to the Carousel and the Fillmore. I recall going to see the New Riders quite often too. I became friends with John Dawson from the New Riders, and I pitched him some songs, which eventually didn't get recorded by them, but my girlfriend, Judy, and I used to get together a lot with John and his girlfriend, Elanna. But what I remember best about those backstage shows was really a feeling that you just don't have in rock events now. That sense of "anything could happen." Bringing people up onstage at the last minute that you didn't expect to see—the nonnavigational kind of thing that just took place.

It was very complex backstage, some of which had to do with the Graham and the Fillmore people, some of which had to do with the Dead. But it was exciting because it was unpredictable. I recall the night that Winterland closed. I went to that show, backstage, and I had a wonderful talk with Jerry. Winterland used to have a backstage that was like a catacomb, and then way down in the back was the final room, this big chair way in the back. I remember the sun coming up, and Jerry and I were smoking some joints or something at about five in the morning when the whole thing was over. We were both talking about how it was the end of Winterland and how sad that was going to be. I could walk to Winterland from my apartment! But the Blues Brothers played that night and they were hysterical! Those two guys sitting around talking with the Dead. I can't even remember the jokes, but it was the feeling of the wit of Dan Aykroyd and John Belushi at their prime sitting around riffing, stoned out of their brains with the Dead and all the other people on the bill. It was incredible. It was just amazing. It was the end of something, and it was the beginning of the Blues Brothers' big acceptance as a serious act. Everybody knew we were moving on, but nobody really knew what was going to be next. Even today, I almost cry when I go by Winterland. It's been torn down, and there's those ugly apartment buildings there, and I think, "How could you take a piece of history like Winterland out of San Francisco, a town this hip? How could they let that happen?" Thank God the Fillmore has been restored.

I don't remember a specific conversation that Jerry and I had that morning after. It's more the feeling of the two us walking out at the end with about five or six other people and realizing that we would never walk out of Winterland again. I remember Jerry telling me, "Man. It's really heavy. This is the end of an era." I said, "Yes, it is."

Winterland is where I always went! I'd walk down there, I knew all the guards, I could go backstage. It was an incredible experience for me as an artist because I got to interact with people. I heard my song "Home to Dixie " played by Kingfish at Winterland as the encore, with everybody lighting matches in the audience. It was so exciting. I was standing there onstage thinking, "God. Matthew and I wrote this song in a haze one day and here it is, and five thousand people are digging it!" That kind of thing happened a lot at Winterland.

10

Getting Silly

Jeff Brown, 36, landscape architect, San Francisco:

One time when I didn't get into a show, I ended up setting up the postshow festivities in the hotel room we had for the night. I got this little plastic bowling set at Kmart and set it up in the hallway after the show. And since it was New Year's Eve, we were able to get away with it. The hotel was just crawling with tie-dyes. And even the people who weren't Deadheads were there to party, so it was a fun scene.

We did some hall bowling late into the night. The security guard eventually came up and told us we had to quiet down, but we were able to get him to roll a few balls with us before tearing down the lanes.

Paul Perme, aka Trinket Guy, 31, Gila Monsters harmonicist, KY:

What I do is fill a little purple velvet Crown Royal bag and I fill it with knickknacks. I mean, I put in everything. Lately, through the last couple of years, I'll put a Gila Monsters tape in there so someone'll know about our band. And I put buttons and all the little things I've collected through the years: little coins from other countries, little bits of my own personal things. I cruise around at the shows and try and trade it with people. It's kind of in the same tradition as the old, old medieval days—Renaissance. Trading. You can't really go to too many places nowadays and do that.

It's like the Renaissance fair. It's so cool. Every time the Dead come through, it reminds me of that, because I do a lot of fun, whimsical things—I juggle, I play congas, and all these things I can do, I can let loose there. But my trinket bags, each one of them I make per night when I go to the shows, and I walk around and I try and trade them for things. There are always those people who say, "No way, I need money" or "I need tickets" or "I gotta get to the next show." But there's always somebody at every single show who has traded me, even if it's the last moment and I'm getting into my car, and I'll walk by and there'll be somebody in the parking lot with something to trade me.

I made a list of some of the things I've traded for over the years, so if anybody reads about this they can say, "Hey, I remember that, I got that guy's stuff!" I've gotten about three different T-shirts, and those are tough ones because those are the vendor guys. You gotta really work. You gotta really get them into the mystery of it, like there's something in that trinket bag they really need—not want. They feel the bag: "Oooh, what's in here?" And all the people around are like, "What's in the bag!" And no one can see what's in the bag until after the trade. Then usually they dump it out and give it all away!

I've gotten a voodoo doll some lady was walking around with. It had a little mask on it and she said, "Don't take off the mask! If you do, you shine it in someone's face and you give them the big curse." So she gave me that and I was like, "Oooh, cool! Here, you wanna trade for what's in here?" And there was this little mystery going on. We did it. She didn't even look in it. She just walked off. That was a cool one.

Then one time I saw this guy walkin' around with this pineapple on his head, and I traded him. That was no problem—a pineapple. It was like, "Here, man, take it."

I've gotten a couple of hats. Those were okay. I've gotten numerous stickers, but usually it's not just one sticker, you go to a sticker guy and pick three stickers, because what's in my trinket bag? Sometimes there's three stickers in there.

I got a geo puzzle one time, which is this cubic thing that you can bend and twist in all kinds of weird positions. That was a pretty cool trade.

Emergence of a happy camper, Philadelphia, 1986 (PHOTO BY STEVE EICHNER)

I've gotten food. I got a falafel. And a burrito. And last year was a cool one because it was one of the last things at the Vegas shows as I was leaving. This guy had a liquid timer, and he said it was ex-actly fifteen minutes—like an egg timer—and it was this purple gross ooze stuff, you turn it upside down like an hourglass. He *loved* it, and his girlfriend asks me, "What's in the bag?" and I said to myself, "Here we go!" I was just walkin' by holding the bag, and she says, "What's in there?" And I said, "I'll trade ya." She says, "What's *in* there?" I said, "I'm not gonna tell you." The guy was saying to the girl, "No way! You're not trading my timer!" She says, "Yeah! Come on! Let's find out what's in the bag!" Actually, that was a cool trade for them because I had a Jerry Garcia CD in there.

I always walk away with at least one thing, and they walk away with many. I travel around a lot, especially over the last few years. I've kinda settled down now with the band and stuff, but I've done Worcester, Massachusetts; New York; up through Maine; Florida, Kentucky, Colorado . . . so I pick up stuff all over the place and fill my bag up.

Chris Flum, 28, "cool dude," Orinda, CA:

I am the nuttiest person. Chinese New Year a few years ago, I went to a show at the Oakland Auditorium totally straight. I have a video camera, and I do this thing: I hold the camera up to myself and I face dance. You can't really move your body because then you're shaking the camera. So I'd always face dance.

I'm right out in front of the stage, and Jerry is just staring at me, laughing at me. This has happened at multiple shows. While he's playing, he's looking down at me, and he can't help but laugh when my face is going in all these weird contorted positions. I look like a *freak!* Plain and simple, I am a freak. And I'm totally straight. I'm a little twisted in my own self. People say I'm weird, but I don't think I'm really weird. Everybody else is weird and I'm the only normal one.

Anyway, there I am face dancing and everybody's turned around watching the dragon go by in the Chinese New Year parade behind us. There's just a little light guitar music going on, Jerry's playing, and I turn around and he's staring *right* at me. I tap my buddy on the shoulder, and he looks around, and Jerry's still staring right at me with this huge grin on his face. We slowly tap our whole group, there's about ten of us. Everybody's saying, "Jerry's staring at Flum! Jerry's staring at Flum!" and here I am doing this major weird face dance into my camera. I was perfectly straight, but I'm just mental. My friend got a great picture of Jerry looking over his glasses right at me.

Dead-inspired art, Alpine, 1987

(PHOTO BY STEVE EICHNER)

In 1992, I went to a show with my buddy Eric at the Oakland Coliseum. He'd listened to the Dead, but it was his first show ever. So I take him and he's trying a little herb, and it happened to be *epic* herb! Next thing I know, Erick turned a pale white and his body got really cold. So I got him to Dead-Med.

Later, backstage, my friend Paul—who was roommates with Eric for four years in college—comes up to me and says, "Hey, Chris, how ya doin'?" I'm like, "Great," and I keep telling him I have to go over and see a friend of mine over in Dead-Med. So I keep running to check on Eric, and by this time Paul's kind of concerned, like, "Hey, is your friend okay?" And through the whole show I never correlated the two things, that these two guys were roommates for four years, and that they were best friends, and that Eric came all the way down from Lake Tahoe to go to his first Dead show!

So I'm in there hanging out with Eric, he comes through, he's okay, we leave the show and get to my house. I said something about hanging with this guy Paul all night. Eric was like, "What? Paul was with you!" That was one of my more confused, stupid times at a Dead show. It was really funny to me afterwards that I never tied the two things together. Whenever we're all together and we talk about it, we laugh.

Buck Henry came up to me at a Dead show at Shoreline once. He was doing little interviews and he interviewed me. He asked me, "What are spinners?" I turned around to show him, but I realized you can't spin at Shoreline because it's on a hill! So I said, "Well, I'd like to show you, but there's nobody spinning. If you start spinning here, you're going to the bottom! Walk up to the top and you'll see the girls spinning around with their beautiful dresses flung out. That's a spinner. Once in a while you'll see a couple guys doing it, but they're not as beautiful."

My friend Quentan Park is a true Deadhead. True to the end. He always wears straw hats to shows. He wears these hats until they get holes in them. At the end of the show, we just shred them. He always takes the bandana off the top and goes out and buys another straw hat. For every run of shows, at the end of it, we tear up his hat. A tradition.

Stanley Mouse, 55, poster artist extraordinaire, Sonoma, CA:

At one time Garcia and I resembled each other. We looked a lot alike before he got gray. Once, at a Dead show, during a break, I was out in the audience and this guy came up to me, handed me a hundred dollar bill, and said that he was a real fan, and said, "Will you sign this?" I said, "Sure," and signed it. He was real happy and said thanks and he took off. Later, he came back to me and said, "This isn't your name!" He thought I was Garcia and had signed another name to his bill. I said, "I'm not Garcia! That's Garcia on stage."

Annetta Pearson, 50, artist/homemaker, San Francisco:

At the Philadelphia shows in October 1994, we were supposed to meet a few people there, and we were looking for this one particular person. Now there you have assigned seating, so she knew exactly where we were going to be, and in fact her tickets were right next to ours. We had sent them to her so we knew eventually she'd make it, but she was late. It was right before the show was about to begin, and I'm looking for her in the hallways, and I thought as long as I was there, I might as well go to the bathroom.

So I walk towards the bathroom, and here is this huge line. This arena looks very much like the Oakland Coliseum: big and round, and the bathrooms are downstairs, down two flights of stairs. So I went down the stairs and I got in this line just expecting to wait forever, and the line is moving, and the line is moving, and the line is moving. People are walking down the stairs, all in a single-file line, all the way down the stairs, and I'm thinking, "Wow, this is fast." At the bottom of the stairs, right there at the opening of the bathroom, is this little short woman, she must have been four feet

Sky's the limit, Telluride, Colorado, 1987 (PHOTO BY RICK BEGNEAUD)

ten, five feet max, maybe late fifties, dyed-blond hair, with a megaphone, saying, "Two to the left, six to the right, eight to the right, seven to the left . . ."

I get up to where she is. There's two sides of bathroom stalls, eight bathrooms both sides, and they all have big numbers on them. And she is literally barking out orders as to which bathrooms to go into. "Two to the left, two to the right . . . That's it!" Every once in a while she'd holler, "Six to the right? What's taking you so long? Hurry up. There's people out here! One to the right, three to the left . . ." I was like, "Yes ma'am!" And I ran into the bathroom, went as fast as I could go, and dropped a piece of toilet paper on the floor—oh! Better not do that! Cleaned up, went back out, started to go back upstairs, but thought, "Oh, no. Better wash my hands!" I could just picture her yelling at me if I didn't! This was a spotless bathroom. I couldn't believe this woman was doing this. She had real fast comebacks to people's remarks. She didn't engage anybody. She had this heavy New York accent, barking out these orders as to what to do and where to go. I only wish that I had recorded some of her repertoire while I was sitting there on the toilet, peeing fast of course. She'd break out into song, or you'd hear her yelling at someone. I couldn't believe it. There must have been thirty people in line, and we were in the bathroom in less that five minutes. I'd never ever seen anything like it.

So every break during the show, I'd go down there and talk to her. Her name is Rita. She was part of the security team, and she's been doing this for eighteen years, and as far as she knows, she's the only one in the country that does that. She said, "Oh, you know how girls are. We piddle around and it takes us a long time in the bathroom. My goal is to make sure they're able to see the show." I asked if she did this for all the shows, and she said, "Oh, yeah. Every one. For eighteen years. It was my idea. I invented it. I said, 'Paint numbers on the doors and I'll take care of it.'" She said the hockey fans love her, that they actually wanted to take her on tour. This was her second job, she had a regular job working for an alcoholic rehab for twenty-five years.

I was fortunate enough that night to have a backstage pass from one of our California friends. Backstage there was only one bathroom, so you had to wait and wait for your turn. I told the women in line, "Listen. You've got to go down to the bathroom, door number X. It's Rita's bathroom. You gotta go up there. You'll be able to walk up there and go to the bathroom faster than it'll take you to wait here."

It's one of the sight-seeing things: if you go to the Philly shows and you're a woman, you've got to go to Rita's bathroom. It's a hoot! Later on that night I was down there again because I kept doing little interviews with Rita, and I saw this woman I'd talked to backstage and she said, "My God! You were right. You were going on and on about this bathroom and about this woman. I had no idea. You were right, it is a sight-seeing tour! I'm gonna bring my friends." I love to turn people on to this. Don't go to any other bathrooms but Rita's. This was the best bathroom experience ever.

I learned to stilt-walk at Wavy Gravy's summer camp, and I've become quite an avid stilt-walker. I stilt with Women Walking Tall, which is a huge group of about two hundred. Every once in a while they do different performances. Wavy knows I'm a member, so he considers me one of his students that's gone on to bigger and better things! It's fun. One day our artistic director got a call saying that people at Grateful Dead Productions Office had heard about Women Walking Tall and were interested in having them join the Mardi Gras parade. Since I was Deadhead, and only one of two out of those two hundred women, she asked if I'd take care of it. I said, "Sure. Gladly!" I arranged for passes and all that, put together who wanted to go. They wanted twenty stilt-walkers, but a number of people couldn't go out that late. I got a call from one girl who said her girlfriend Tamar wanted to join. She just wanted to be wherever her girlfriend was, so I arranged for her to do it. Tamar was from Israel, she'd been here for a couple years, and she didn't know anything about the Grateful Dead. So, we're waiting for the parade to start, and you have to wait about an hour. You're outside, waiting for the giant door to open. The coliseum has a huge door at the end of one hall where they open it like a great garage door; it rolls up to take in circus elephants and anything else. So, we were waiting, there's all this anticipation. You're among a whole group of crazy floats and people doing all sorts of weird things. But it's a relatively small crowd compared to the sixteen thousand screaming fans that are on the other side of that door. So Tamar joined us, got her stilts on, and we went and stood in line. Later on I found out that the whole time she was waiting, she thought the Grateful Dead was some sort of a religious rite. She thought it was some church putting on a ritual. She was thinking it was maybe two hundred or three hundred people in a church. She didn't know as the doors opened that she was gonna go into a room with sixteen thousand screaming people. One of the people that fell that night said that that alone would be enough to catch you off-balance! Talk about a Dead virgin!

Having all those people looking at you was wonderful, but it's treacherous! Walking on little tiny sticks on slippery cement floors with Mardi Gras beads all over the place. Of sixteen people, six of us went down. And I almost went down twice. You get right back up again, but you don't want to fall on cement in a crowd. One girl practically did the splits!

John Perry Barlow, 47, Dead lyricist/cyberspace pioneer, WY:

Several times Weir has gone out into the crowd in disguise, to experience that whole scene. One of them was at the Oakland Coliseum in 1976 when they were playing with the

Who, and Weir wanted to hear the Who from the audience. He put on this crazy, incongruous outfit: a panama hat, dark wraparound sunglasses, and a wild Hawaiian shirt. He was like a Hunter Thompson character. Out we went and cruised around. He couldn't get comfortable out there. He just constantly felt uneasy, obviously. We kept trying to sort ourselves into a condition that would work. Then another time, I kept telling him about what a cool place I thought the village of the Deadheads was, which he'd never seen before. This was in 1988. There's an invisible guard-all shield between the band and the scene. You don't realize how completely impermeable it is. But if you think about it, how could the band go into the audience? For one thing, if the scene is out there, then the band is working someplace.

So, this was down at Laguna Seca. I was talking to Weir how cool it would be if he could come out and see the scene and how it was. Calico, a Hog Farm lady, a great ol' gal, was listening to this conversation, and she said, "Well, you know, I've got a skeleton suit that would fit you." So we put Bobby in this skeleton suit. He went out, and a number of people knew about it, and they all had to be a part of it, they all had to see this go down. He was definitely a skeleton with an entourage. Talk about a Dead fucking giveaway! Everybody knew! "Hey, Weir's walking around the village in a skeleton suit, everybody. Come see!" They were respectful in the way of Deadheads. Deadheads don't go into a feeding frenzy over this stuff. They're smart enough to recognize that it ain't Weir, it ain't Garcia, it's not even the Grateful Dead—it's the funny thing that arises in the space between them and the Deadheads. There's no point in getting too pumped up about it. Bobby liked it. He was surprised by it. He definitely wasn't prepared for it. That was at the height of the parking-lot scene's formation.

Bill Cutler, 47, musician/producer, San Francisco:

I recall meeting Bill Graham for the first time. I was up at the Sweetwater in Mill Valley. Bobby Weir—this is a digression, but it fits in—Bobby opened one of the very first studios at his house. Nowadays, everyone has a studio at their house, but in those days, like in 1975 or 1976, it was very rare to have a studio—espe-

Dead car art, Philadelphia, 1986

(PHOTO BY STEVE EICHNER)

cially a twenty-four track. It might have been a sixteen at first that he converted to twenty-four, but anyways ... He lived in Mill Valley, and over his garage he built this studio. It had a tree going through it. He's still living there. I don't know what the studio's doing now. But at the time, Steven Barncard, my old buddy, and Robbie Taylor, who is now the production manager for the Dead, but was a jeweler in those days, he wired the studio up. They hired Robbie because he had these great hands, all these thousands of wires. And those guys lived in the studio as they built it. When it got done, Bobby wanted to give it a test run, so he invited Heroes up there to cut their first stuff there. We cut four or five things up there at that studio that became a demo that we shopped. Jerry didn't play on that stuff, but all kinds of people helped me with it: Dan Healy, Robbie Taylor, Steven Barncard—all those guys.

During the time that we were cutting stuff up there, Bobby took a bunch of us out to the Sweetwater. In popped Bill Graham, and he promptly sat down next to me. I've long forgotten who we went to see, but what I do remember is that Graham was there. It was maybe ten or eleven at night, and everyone was kind of buzzed. Bobby introduced Bill and I—I'd seen him a lot backstage but we never really talked. Graham said to me, "What kind of food do you like?" You know, Bill Graham started as a waiter in the Catskills. Anyway, he said to me, "What's your favorite food?" I said, "Bagels and lox," and he said, "Ah! I love bagels and lox. I want some right now! I'm gonna call Lindy's in New York and I'm gonna have some bagels and lox flown out here overnight, and we're gonna stay up all night and eat them tomorrow!"

My girlfriend Judy and I were still living in a basement at the time. A ham sandwich was a big event; we were collecting coupons and stealing steaks from the supermarket to have dinner. The idea that some guy was going to get a private plane and fly bagels and lox out—we'd all debated and decided you couldn't get good bagels and lox on the West Coast. Bill went for the telephone, and I grabbed him and said, "You can't do this!" I was horrified! Everybody just cracked up, and eventually we talked him out of getting the bagels and lox.

Then I didn't see Bill for a while. The next time I saw him was at the Fillmore at the Carousel after the New Riders. They always had weird bills there, like I think the New Riders played with Miles Davis. I was backstage, and Bill Graham had this way of being real nice or just snapping at you, depending on what happened. There was this incredible spread of food back there, really nice finger foods, and everybody was nibbling on it. Bill looked at his assistant and said, "Get me a Hershey bar." I said to him jokingly, "You've got all this food back here and you're gonna eat a Hershey bar!" and he said, "What are you? The picture of health?"

Tom Constanten, 51, pianist/composer, San Francisco:

One time on tour, we were at the airport and Weir was reading the paper. In all honesty I should've done this myself, but I egged Pigpen on to do it: he set fire to Weir's paper while he was reading it. I was the instigator. It was like, "Oh! Oh! Bad, bad, bad boy." They got mad, but it blew over in about a half hour.

Another time we were on a plane, coming in for a landing at La Guardia, and Garcia said something like, "I think the pilot's got us too far over. We're not gonna make it." And Weir would get that voice of his and scream, *"We're all gonna die! Aahhh!"* The flight crew knew pretty well to brace themselves when we marched on the plane.

When *Yellow Submarine* first came out, Phil, Jerry, Owsley, and I all saw it together. We were on the road in Detroit. We found this movie theater, and we drove what seemed a long way to go to it, and we sat in the front row. We were giggling and laughing the whole time. It represented an incredible validation for what the band was doing. I remember we all walked out after the movie was over and all we could say was, "Wow."

Ricky Begneaud, 37, Cajun chef/caterer, Mill Valley, CA:

One time I went on a little tour with my friends Mike and Rick in my yellow Jeep, and we listened to the great musician Ernest Tubb the whole way from Lafayette to Lakeland, Florida. It's a great album with guest artists like Willie Nelson, Charlie Daniels, and all these different people. There was this one song with Loretta Lynn called "Thanks Alot." We knew every word of every song on this record!

So, we make it to the Dead show, and during the break, we went to get a slice of pizza. My friend Rick's in the bathroom taking a pee, and Mike and I are in this huge line waiting for pizza. We're almost to the front of the line after about fifteen minutes, and all of a sudden I hear something out on the house PA. I ran out there and couldn't believe what they were playing. I ran into the bathroom, grabbed Rick out of the stall, and said, "Come on!" He says, "What're you doing?" I said, "Just come on!" I went to Mike, who's next in line for pizza, and I said, "Come on!" He said, "You're nuts." I said, "Just come on!" So we go into the house and they're playing "Thanks Alot" on the PA! We all just looked at each other and went, "Hmmmm . . ."! This is the last thing you'd think they'd be playing: Ernest Tubb. That was really wild.

The next night, Mike, Rick, and I were all on our own little trip. Rick had my hunting vest on, and he'd turned it inside out, so it was deer-hunter, fluorescent orange! And he had this paper Uncle Sam hat on. It was a fun, crazy show. The music was great. We had the best time.

In 1980, at a Los Angeles show, my friend Rusty and I had great seats, and I called to invite this guy Lou Tambakos, who'd been sending me really cool tapes for a while. I'd only met him on the phone, so I told him what seats Rusty and I would be in that night. When the show started, all these empty seats were in front of us, so Rusty and I gravitated to the better seats.

Now I didn't even really know what Lou looked like. Later on in the show, I turned around and I saw this guy down the way. We kind of looked at each other, but that was it. The next day, I called Lou and I said, "Why didn't you come over to introduce yourself and talk to me?" He said, "I did. I went to your seat number, and I said, 'Hi, Rick,' and the guy said, 'Hi,' so we had a conversation for a few minutes." It turns out he was talkin' to a guy named Rick but it wasn't me in my seat! So that was Lou's first nonexperience with me!

Another show that really rings a bell was in 1988. The Dead were playing at Laguna Seca in Monterey. We had a barbecue pit on-stage, and we just barbecued and drank beer all afternoon. It was so great! I *love* to barbecue. It's one of my favorite things to do. I *love* to listen to the Grateful Dead. And here I am, on the stage, barbecuin', drinkin' beer, hanging out with all my friends, listening to the Dead—all afternoon. It was killer.

During the show, Weir came up to me and said, "Go call Shannon and have her go to my house." So, here I go, I walked into the production office, I called Shannon—my wife—who's still up in Mill Valley; I had a list of things she had to get for Weir and bring to the show. "Go up to his house, go into his bedroom closet, and in the cabinet you have to get a mustache, a wig, some glue, a baseball cap . . ." The people in the production office were looking at me like, "Huh?"

Laguna Seca had a big parking lot scene. It was like being in a village. You could come and go, but you could also camp out and do what you wanted there. Weir had never been in the parking lot, or at least it had been a long, long time since he was able to. How could they go out there? If Garcia walked into the parking lot, he'd be mobbed five feet in and he wouldn't get to see anything. So we got Weir rigged: he's got this straight, shoulder-length wig, a little mustache, a little Grateful Dead cap, and a tie-dye T-shirt. Here we go! Weir is like a kid in the candy store. It's like he's at his first Grateful Dead show. He's wanderin' around, realizing there's this whole world out there, talkin' to people, and he was fascinated by the Deadhead buses. He'd just pop into someone's bus, not even knock, just walk in. He'd stand there and . . . he looked good. You couldn't tell it was him. I mean, you'd have to know who he was, and even then it was hard to recognize him.

My friend Michael Nash and I tried to keep tabs on Bobby because he would just wander off. We kept saying, "We gotta watch this guy!" Then, Weir pops into this one bus, and Michael and I follow him in. He scopes it out, looks at all the shit hanging on the walls. He was amazed. This one guy on the bus came up and introduced himself. We're sitting there talking for a few minutes, and all of a sudden I thought, "Oh, no. This is the time we've waited for. He's gonna recognize Bobby." The guy pointed at Weir and said, "Hey, man! I know you!" We thought, "Oh, shit! We're way in the depths of the parking lot. We'll never get Bobby out of here once everybody knows it's him." The guy said, "Hey, man! I know you. Weren't you at Alpine last week?" Bobby said, "Yeah . . . ," and the guy asked, "I met you at Alpine, didn't I?" We're thinking, well, yeah, Bobby was at Alpine last week—playing! It was so weird, because Weir was shaking his head "Yeah." Then Weir said something to cover himself, and we all slipped out of the bus.

Michael Nash went back in to tell the guy, to make his life. He said, "Do you know who that really was?" and the guy said, "No." Michael said, "That was Bob Weir." The guy said, "No way." Michael said, "Go out and look at him again. Think about it. This is the only way Weir can see the scene. That's Weir. He was on your bus." We totally must have made this guy's life: Bob Weir was on his bus! Like anybody would ever really believe it!

Bobby was totally jazzed. He totally dug it. You gotta realize, when the Dead do a show, as soon as the encore is over, they're in the van, and they leave the show immediately. They never get to hang out. They never get to know what really goes on in the whole scene out in the parking lot. That's what the scene really is!

Herbie Greene, 52, R&R photographer, San Francisco:

I met Neal Cassady. He scared me to death! Because he was a maniac! You were either scared of him or you were enthralled by him. He was a terrifying guy. You were definitely dealing with an insane person. I mean, the guy was a loon! He was brilliant, he did all this stuff, and he talked . . . but that was terrifying to me. Ask Bob about it. We were breaking a lot of rules, but there was stuff that was way over the top, and he was one of them. The stories are true: he drove, he never looked where he was going. It was like he could see around corners! Bobby said, "Herbie, *never* get in a car with him. You'll never make it. You won't make it." Cassady was just another dimension. He was what he was. Born to be.

Ramblin' Jack Elliott, 62, folk musician, San Francisco via Brooklyn:

I don't know which birthday it was, but John Barlow, Bobby Weir, and I ended up later going into San Francisco in somebody's car, probably John's. So we went to this nightclub, had a few drinks, then we left there and Bob lay down on the sidewalk, perhaps the better to view sighting up the hollow tall spire of the TransAmerica building that was pointing up at the sky, for he needed guidance about which way was up. I don't know! That reminded me of something, and I said, "Okay!" I suddenly had an inspiration. I knew where we had to go, so I became the tour guide at that point. I said, "Okay, everybody in the car!"

We all got in the car, I gave directions, and we ended up down at the *Balclutha*. I'm a permanent member of the crew, having worked on the rigging back when they first bought her. She was built in 1886. She's one of the oldest steel ships ever built in the world. She's one of the first ships ever made of steel. Up until that point, they'd been making sailing ships and steamers out of iron. Iron still is a very good material for ships, but they thought steel was better 'cause it's stronger, and you can use thinner steel than you could iron, and it's lighter. Thing is, it'll rust through quicker.

Anyway, we went down to the *Balclutha*, we arrived at the dock, and I said, "Aboard the *Balclutha*!" You don't just walk on there. The night watchman came down and said, "Who goes there?" I said, "It's Ramblin' Jack and some friends." And he said, "Oh, Jack! Come on board! How are ya, man?" So we were welcomed on board, and this is about two o'clock in the morning. I wasn't aware that they were getting ready to have an eclipse of the moon in a few minutes. He says, "Welcome aboard. Show your friends around," and he just stood back and left us alone. I said, "Well, the first thing we should do is get a bird's-eye view of the ship. So, if you'll just follow me, gentlemen . . ." I took them up aloft into the rigging, and we climbed up to the third yardarm up there, it's called the four upper topsail yard. Drunk out of our minds, but still we could hang on. Nobody slipped. Nobody fell. We went up to the yard there, and it had the sail, it was only half a sail really be-cause full sail would be maybe too expensive, or maybe it might put too much pressure on the rigging in the event of a storm . . . I think it was probably due to expense. Because the sail was only like the starboard half of what would be the upper topsail, and it was printed with all this beautiful old-fashioned lettering, and it said, "Last, Cape Horner. Open to the Public."

So we climbed up there and we were standing on the footropes with our bellies lying over the yard and our elbows resting com-fortably on the yard, and it was there that we saw the eclipse of the

Eyes of the world, Cal Expo, 1985 (PHOTO BY DAN WILSON)

moon, and I said, "Happy birthday, Bob! Welcome, John. This is where I like to hang out when I come to San Francisco." That was the first time I ever met Barlow. I'm sure everybody concerned enjoyed themselves to the utmost. It was like an acid trip. We were not on acid by the way. It's always important to mention this in a Grateful Dead story, that we were *not* high on acid on this particular day.

One time Barlow invited me to come up to his ranch in Wyoming. So I went up with him in the Cadillac. That was great. I've been there when Bobby's been there. A couple or three times. And I've also been present when Barlow was having long phone calls with Weir at two o'clock in the morning, one of which was back when Barlow used to drink heavily. There was a skunk that had been hanging and living under the floor of the milk room, which was off the kitchen. It's a beautiful, big, log ranch house with a nice dining room and a kitchen and a living room and an office room, kind of a parlor and some bedrooms upstairs, and there's a piano. This skunk . . . John was on the phone talkin' to

Bobby and he heard the skunk in the milk room and said, "Take the phone, Jack. Talk to Bob. I gotta go see about that skunk." So I said, "Oh, okay. John just heard a skunk in the milk room, Bob, and so he's gonna go off and visit with the skunk for a while, and so here I am. Well, how you been anyhow?" Then, all of a sudden, I heard a rifle go off. Barlow had taken a .22 rifle with him. So he comes back holding his head in grief. "Oh. I only winged him. He's gonna die a horrible death." Not only that, not only is the poor skunk gonna die a horrible death, but it's gonna stink under the kitchen milk room!

Rachel Clein, 13, student, Marin County, CA:

A t Jerry's daughter's birthday party in 1992, I remember Jerry lighting her birthday cake, and then later playing music with a few friends—David Grisman and some other people. Jerry is very quiet.

Another time I was at their house, and his daughter really liked to play hide-and-seek. We were playing upstairs and she liked to hide in Jerry's room a lot, so I was looking in there for her. It's pretty big. There's a bedroom, a bathroom, and an adjacent closet/dressing room. It was the first time I had been in there. I didn't know which door to take to get out of the room, so I got lost up there in Jerry's room. Eventually I found my way out.

Dan O'Neill, 53, cartoonist, Nevada City, CA:

B ack in the sixties, Sam Andrews was my roommate, and he later became part of Big Brother and the Holding Company, so I wound up backstage with all them clowns, mostly Big Brother and the Airplane when it was all going down at the Fillmore and the Avalon. We often wound up at the same places as the Dead and everyone else.

There were at least two hundred people in every house all the time! There were hordes of people. I remember one time I went under the sewing machine where nobody could step on me! "This is where I'm gonna crash!" I got tired of getting stepped on.

This was my early training in hippie land.

11

Getting Out

Tom Constanten, 51, pianist/composer, San Francisco:

This was pre-limo time, 1969. Jerry, Pigpen, and I had to take a cab back to the hotel after our show at the Fillmore East. So we find a cab, which was evidently waiting for us, get in the back, get two blocks, and the cabdriver hands a lit joint to the backseat. He tells us his name is Patrick and he's our greatest fan.

We're going through lights and he's describing what it's like to be out all night on acid. Somebody would come in and yell out the address, and he'd say, "Easy! I'm rushin'. Just tell me right, left, or straight ahead." He told us all about shooting the rapids of Times Square at night, all the lights, the New York thing. Whoa! Best of all was that he spoke English!

Quite an amazing night.

Ricky Begneaud, 37, Cajun chef/caterer, Mill Valley, CA:

We had a few casualties one night at a show in New Orleans in 1980. We started out with nearly fifteen people, and only four made it through the whole show. This one girl who came with us kept going down to the front of the stage, and security kept sending her back. She did this about five or six times. Finally, they were gonna throw her out, so I went down to help her. There I am trying to be the good guy, and the guard grabs *my* shirt and yanks me out too!

I was totally shocked.

Jeff Brown, 36, landscape architect, San Francisco:

I remember one time we all came out of a show and we were in the parking lot, and we always try to use the parking lot for transition. There's always people hanging out, there's always music, playing ball, nitrous . . . whatever. So we all kinda wandered over to the rent-a-car, and my friend Annie Harlow has the keys and all the beer is in the trunk, and the chips, and everything's in the trunk, and people's coats are in the trunk, and Annie is messing around with the lock. We're standing around chatting and a few minutes go by, and she can't get the trunk open, so somebody else says, "Here, let me try it." And we're all standing around watching this, and then we realize it's the *wrong car!* We weren't that far off. We were just a few cars or maybe an aisle over.

Richard Yaker, 26, futurist engineer/visionary, Los Angeles:

I had a problem one night *after* a show at the Warfield. I forgot where my car was! I had that kind of panic where I was saying to myself, "Okay, I'm in a city I know nothing about, I've only been here a couple of times, I will know this city eventually, but right now I don't, it's late and dark, and I'm not sure where my car is." Luckily, I'm good at remembering landmarks, so it didn't take that long to find it.

Trey Allen, 27, R&R caterer, Nashville, TN:

Eugene, Oregon, summer of 1990. It was Little Feat and the Dead, and this was the start of a West Coast tour. these were the peaking shows of my Dead experience. The whole idea of going to Eugene and seeing how beautiful that place is. I

Hold on to your head, Philadelphia, 1986 (PHOTO BY STEVE EICHNER)

went strictly as a fan, no work, no nothing, which was just great. It was a very sunny day, and very high! I flew in from Nashville with my buddy Michael Nichol. He is just out of control. He's an unbelievable guy. You have those people you run across in life who are on their own shelf of life. We're both dosed out of our minds, full on Eugene, full on beautiful. So we go into the show, and I lose him immediately, before the show even starts. I run into some people, hang out, see the show, and then afterwards, I run into Michael as I'm walking out.

We walk out together, walking all over the stadium, checking things out. As we walk into the parking lot, I look down and Michael doesn't have any shoes on! I'm like, "Oh, dude! Did you come in with any shoes?" He said yes, so we turned around to go back into the stadium. Michael's talking to the security guard at the gate, who won't let him in because he doesn't have his shoes on! At this point, Michael is still trying to grasp the thought of coming out with his shoes off, and not being able to get back in because he doesn't have his shoes. When you're buzzed like that, you can't even fathom it. Especially after that show. It was unbelievable. So, I went in to find Michael's shoes, without even starting to find where he was sitting or anything . . . I mean, this was a full-on stadium. I knew he was on the floor, so I wandered around. You can just imagine—people leave and lose all kinds of stuff. There are people all around "ground-scoring," and I just kept looking all over the ground and found Michael's shoes! I walked back out and gave 'em to him. He was really psyched because we were fixing to embark upon a gravel parking lot.

Jeff Brown, 36, landscape architect, San Francisco:

We always made it home. And a lot of times we didn't have a ride. You've got to be close to the people you're with. There's never a problem getting home. It's often been a really enjoyable experience—hitchhiking. Our rule of thumb is: "Stay in the tripping lane."

Ken Fine, aka Kew, 36, organic T-shirt salesman, Liberty, ME:

My date and I had had a terrible hitchhiking day, we missed the show, but we ended up talking with Phil Lesh backstage and having a very memorable experience. Then, everybody was leaving, and we went to the bottom of the stairs, said good night to people, opened the door, and it was pouring rain! So there we were with our backpacks, looking out this open door at this rainstorm, and this guy Freddie Fleck came down the stairs and said, "Where you guys going? You want me to give you a lift somewhere? It's pouring." So we said, "Okay. We're gonna go to a motel."

We get in his truck and he says, "Why don't you guys just stay at my place?" So he carted us up to his place in the Oakland foothills and we slept in his little one-room apartment. He showed us the new drums he was working on for Billy. He was in the band with them, one of the backup percussionists. We helped him feed his horses the next day, and he gave us a ride back to the Marin Veteran's and he said, "I can't get you tickets, but come in with me for the sound check and get on line and I'm sure you'll get a ticket." So we waited on line, got our tickets, and we saw one hell of a show. It was just fabulous. They did a special thing for the basketball player Bill Walton that night: they set his foot up on the stage and they all did this little drumstick thing around his foot when he was having all his foot problems. It was a great show, and then we had another ordeal logistically getting home! We ended up hiking a long way with our backpacks and setting up our sleeping bags within sight of San Quentin Prison. Eventually we got home the next day. It was quite a first date. Since we were able to do that together, we've pretty much been able to do everything together since then!

PHOTO BY JANICE BELSON

12

Getting Disillusioned

Dan Wilson, 49, street artist, Sacramento, CA:

There was a turning point in my association with the Dead. It was on Haight Street. My buddy and I went down there one night, and it seemed like some of the audience was really starting to get detached and so far out on their trips that they would probably never come back. It was distracting for me to be listening to the band and having some of the audience members "nerving" or "unnerving." Freaking out, you know? So I didn't see the Dead again for a long time.

Mostly I stopped seeing them because I'd moved. I got out of college and into the war thing. I refused the draft after five different physicals during and after college. Finally, it came to the point where I had no other choice and that was it—I refused to go. They told me at the physical I better hang around because "you're going to be indicted by the FBI. Don't try and go anywhere without telling us." And these guys in their Ford Fairlanes would be out in front of my house, parked, reading their newspapers, just making sure I wasn't going anywhere. That really kind of changed my whole outlook on life. I got pretty bitter. I never did follow through on my communications major, and it definitely ended the baseball career I was hoping for. I just tried to maintain an income and work, down in East

Oakland mostly. I did everything, from working in a cannery to painting houses. All labor jobs. I've had thirty-four jobs since high school. That's the way it went for a long time.

Kim Weiskopf, 48, TV writer/producer: *Married . . . With Children*, **Los Angeles:**

I remember when Dan (see above) was on the lam from the draft board. That was a real paradoxical time. Frankly, a lot of us, including myself, were staying in school at that time just to stay out of the army. You know the movies like *Forrest Gump* or the Oliver Stone films where you see what Vietnam may or may not have been like? Well, a friend of mine who was the art director on *Forrest Gump* has been after me for years to write the *other* movie, which is: What was going on *here* during that era? I tell him it makes me so damn uncomfortable to recall it. Every day was . . . well, obviously it wasn't as bad as being in Vietnam and being afraid some sniper's got you in his sights all the time, but there was this real weight, a sense of the pending doom.

This was a feeling that I had and a lot of us had at the time. The Grateful Dead were the most unstructured of the bands, consequently they were the first album you reached for when your head was in a certain place. You didn't particularly want any kind of soothing music. It was about upheaval. That's what was going on at the time—*upheaval*. I'm getting worked up thinking about it now.

Steve Brown, 50, filmmaker/Dead's aid-de-camp 1972–77, San Francisco:

When I stopped working with the Dead in 1977, the negative parts of that culture were bringing everybody down. What had been magic years ago was turning pretty ugly, and I was just too close to the personalities involved to appreciate the whole thing anymore. Also, once you've been on the road for five years, it gets to be pretty old. I have to say the Grateful Dead are great long-distance runners with the road thing. I admire their tenacity in being able to put up with it all these years.

Cal Expo, 1985 (PHOTO BY DAN WILSON)

Gina, 31, Blues Traveler's personal assistant, New York:

I was so glad I had Blues Traveler to fall back on, because the Dead thing changed so much. It was kind of sad. I couldn't make a living anymore, I couldn't even hardly get a ticket, and the whole mail-order deal was so out of hand. I'd get rejected and it was like, "Fuck, I've been seeing these guys for ten years. Whadya mean I can't get a ticket!"

Annie Myles, 24, music manager, New York:

After a few years of seeing the Dead, I stopped going. I was searching for different levels of consciousness. I was into mind enhancement. All that way of thought came about from the people I'd met at Grateful Dead shows, but I decided to try to carry out the "silver" route because I was finding a lot of peo-

Billy lookin' on, Cal Expo, 1985

(PHOTO BY DAN WILSON)

ple at Dead shows more interested in getting fucked up than
grooving and having a good
time—growing. So, I took off
for a while and I didn't go to
shows for two years.

I drove around by myself. I
wasn't doing drugs, and I
didn't want to be around the
scene at all. I knew there was
so much more than the Grateful Dead. I was driving around
the country just kind of thinking things out. I was selling
T-shirts, going from town to
town, college to college, meeting lots of locals. I was hobo-
ing around in an old schoolbus.
Right after I bought it, I met
Timmy Vega (artist—singer Suzanne's Vega's brother) at Wetlands
in New York, and we concocted this huge plan about my traveling with him and some other people because I was getting a little worried about traveling by myself in such a big vehicle. He said
that he worked for a band who I'd never heard of, Blues Traveler,
and that they were heading west, which was the direction that I
wanted to go.

We arranged for some of their friends to come on the bus with
me, and I drove their friends out to Colorado. We hooked up with
Blues Traveler, and I started cooking for them while we were traveling around. I was like, "Yeah! I travel with you guys for a little
bit, check out your music. I've never heard you. I might take off.
I'm here. Whatever!" So I went to a bunch of their shows and
they blew my mind! They absolutely blew my mind. To see a
bunch of young people my age who were of pure heart and pure
mind making music that rocked my soul was amazing to me. When
I met them, I was like, "Finally! I've been traveling around this
goddamn country for about four years now looking for some new
buddies. I'm so fuckin' glad I found you! And on top of that, your
music rocks!"

Greg Martens, 31, entrepreneur, Portland, ME:

The day I decided to stop vending was the day I started working for Blues Traveler. It was the Dead's New Year's show in Oakland, 1990. I was getting down on the vending thing. We used to make a lot of money and it used to be a lot of fun, and then it became no money but it was still fun, and then it became no money and no fun. I was sitting out in the hallway during intermission, and all of a sudden, Dan Healy played Blues Traveler's CD over the house system. I thought, "Whoa! What karma!" I was just sitting there by myself, I got up, I knew working for Traveler was meant to be, I knew this was my road.

Jerry Miller, 54, Moby Grape guitarist, San Francisco:

I'm still playing the same guitar I was playing back in the sixties, same amplifier too. I've got a Fender bassman, 1959, that I bought new. They say if you remember it, you weren't there! I was there but I don't remember all of it. It was happening too fast. It was most dazzling, everything that was going on. Sometimes we'd have limousines, and then sometimes we had Volkswagens. We were supposed to do that *Look* magazine thing, when they had the Airplane, Janis, and the Dead—first big national exposure. We were supposed to be in on that. Here we come, right after *Look* had just left, because we got the times wrong, which was a real stupid career move. But we made many stupid career moves. We got our butts chewed out. Jerry said, "You're irresponsible, guys. You just don't know how to take care of business at all." Bill Graham was booking us into his places. He was always a good ally, but he wasn't managing us or anything.

My advice to any young musicians out there is be careful what you sign, and get a good staff, support system, that you trust to help you. In those days, most people didn't know that, a lot of people made the big mistakes on contracts. Also you have a responsibility to set somewhat of a decent example to people who are admiring you, so you don't want to go screwing up—getting busted with too many drugs or acting weird. Just be humble. Keep your friends. You have to set up a good support system for yourself. You've got to sweat like a borrowed mule. Be ready for a lot of rejection. It's a hell of a life.

John Perry Barlow, 47, Dead lyricist/cyberspace pioneer, WY:

I see a lot of the disappointment and the sense of dissatisfaction that the trailing edge of my generation left behind. If you go and do as we did, you will really be holding the bag. You've got to play a very straight game. You've got to not get into any of that insanity. You've got to keep to yourself. Don't go around trusting people indiscriminately as we did, because look what it did for us. But people in their late twenties and early thirties have got it worse certainly than we do. We go on in about the same condition of hopeless optimism. And we are now feeling joined by our children on the other side of those in their late twenties and early thirties.

The leading edge of kids we actually raised are now in their early twenties, and they're a culture that's much more like us than it is like those in their late twenties and early thirties. I'm around a lot of people in their early thirties, women as often as not, who are suddenly realizing that the subtle rules that they played by, that very risk-adverse, cautious, fear-based set of rules is not necessarily prudent, not necessarily practical. And they're gearing up to make some kind of a move. It's a very conservative way to play it. It's a fear-based method, and it get scarier, as all fear-based methods do. It gets much scarier than something else that is more collateral. Otherwise you end up isolated and alone. You end up not trusting anybody.

Herbie Greene, 52, R&R photographer, San Francisco:

I didn't go to many Dead shows for a long time. I wasn't really that close to it. They were doing other things, I was doing other things. I didn't really like the music that much. I mean, I've been to a lot of *bad* shows, embarrassingly bad. I didn't understand it like I do now, either. So in all humility, there was a six-year period where I didn't give a flying fuck about them. I liked everybody around them a lot, but as far as they were concerned, I didn't care. I couldn't understand why my ex-wife, Marushka, would drive all the way to Los Angeles to go to a show. I just couldn't understand it!

PHOTO BY JANICE BELSON

13

Getting Perspective

Dan Wilson, 49, Sacramento, CA:

I could never imagine following the Dead around like some of these people do. I can't do anything that much! My dad always says, "Variety is the spice of life," and he just turned ninety. I think he's right. He's got that Grateful Dead type of staying power, and he's never even heard 'em! But that doesn't matter, because I certainly have. I love 'em!

Caryn Shalita, mid-20s, actress, Los Angeles:

I consider myself . . . I jokingly say I'm a responsible Deadhead, a Deadhead with a life! I've never really followed them around. I think that's a little silly. Like I said, they're just guys, they're musicians, they're wonderful with their music, and they have some things to say through their music, but I don't think that they want people to be following them as much as they do. "Go do something productive and helpful in the world rather than follow us around." And I think people sometimes use touring as a way to escape responsibility. I know plenty of people who have gone on tour. My friend Pete took a semester off and went on tour, but he knew he was going back to school. He was taking a break, and he figured it would be a fun way to spend a couple months, and indeed it was.

There's something about seeing a band that just likes to play—the Dead, the Allman Brothers, Blues Traveler—any of them: they jam and they play music for music's sake. I think that's why live taping is so popular, because every show has its own identity. And people know them. It amazes me when people say "Oh, you have 9/11/91—Port Chester! Oh, yeah, *that* show. Started with 'Scarlet,'" blah, blah, blah. People memorize what's on these tapes! They know them by dates and venues! They're walking Deadbases. I'm not one. I'm not that fanatic.

I can't imagine being overly devoted to a band. That, to me, is giving them more power over your life than musicians should have. You're not developing your own identity. I can understand it, though, because a lot of people are insecure for whatever reason in their life. And like I said, the Dead really do have a sense of security and family about them. And I think a lot of people that follow them are looking for and missing that in their lives and they find it there. Acceptance. A lot of people follow them for a while and then come to the realization that it's time to move on, and they do. I guess that's why there so many eighteen- or nineteen-year-old Deadheads; they're sort of lost and figuring stuff out. I think most of them eventually turn out to be all right. My cousin is an interesting case. He got into the Dead around 1977, when he was in high school. He's a classical oboist so he was always listening to Bach, Beethoven, Brahms . . . and the Dead! And he now plays with the Mexico City Symphony Orchestra.

Stuart Wax, 37, music manager, Los Angeles:

I've seen the Dead a lot, but I never did the eleven-cities-in-a-van thing. I've seen them all over: Denver, Florida, New York, Connecticut, Deer Creek, Indiana, every year—but always because it just worked out that way. Like that bumper sticker that says, "Who are the Grateful Dead and why do they keep on following me?" I always find that I can do work at the same time.

When I was living in Israel for seven years, 1980 to 1986, I'd make my trips to New York around when the Dead were doing their spring tour. I ran Grateful Dead parties in Israel, I had a company called Sugar Magnolia Enterprises. I was working in time-sharing, and I was walking the street, and I saw a T-shirt that said, "I'm from Boston, but I love New York." I went home and printed a shirt that said, "I love New York, but Israel is home." We sold it out from the street. We were all Deadheads. We were in the T-shirt business so we decided we might as well do our own shirts, so we made Hebrew Grateful Dead T-shirts just for ourselves. Everywhere we went, people would go, "Wow! Where'd you get that! How can I get one?" So we started selling them. Then we took them to the Israeli stores, and they said, "Oh, no, Israelis won't want Hebrew." And I said, "Forget Israelis. This'll be the greatest tourist gift." And the most fun we had was when mothers would come into our store and say, "You know, I've been looking all over for a present for my kids. They're gonna go crazy with this!"

Sheila Rene, 56, music anthropologist, Texas via San Francisco:

Obviously, when I got into the music business, there were times I couldn't go when I had conflicts of too many shows going on. I ended up at the hardest shows. I'd pick Kiss if they were in town, because the Grateful Dead were always here and Kiss might not come back for two years. I'd always depend on a couple of Dead shows a year running three or four days, so I could always go back in, rejuvenate, catch up.

David Gans, 41, radio producer: *Grateful Dead Hour*; author: *Playing in the Band* and *Conversations with the Dead*; San Francisco:

The whole band knows who I am, for better or for worse. I've had unpleasant encounters with various people on that scene over the years. There's a lot of mistrust. There's a lot of presuming that somebody is just sucking up for one thing or another. I think that given the tremendous amount of positive regard that is visited upon the Grateful Dead, it's sometimes hard for them to tell when something might be a little deeper than just fandom or appreciation or desire to party with them and suck up to them or whatever. There's a little bit of the starfucker in everybody, like me, who wants to get to know somebody whose work means a lot

State of mind, Cal Expo, 1985

(PHOTO BY DAN WILSON)

to him, but I also took myself seriously enough that I wasn't willing to give up my self-esteem in order to hang out with them. But that didn't mean that other people around the scene appreciated the difference. One of the road crew once . . . I showed up onstage at Red Rocks in 1984, and one of the road crew said, "Why don't you just give Phil your stash and get the fuck out of here." He couldn't imagine that I had any other relationship with Phil than a pharmaceutical one.

I started doing radio in 1985, and I developed a business relationship with the Grateful Dead, and because of the way the Grateful Dead organism behaves, my business relationship with them did not buy me much slack from some people in the scene. Dan Healy, the sound guy, was seriously into radio, and I think he was kind of not thrilled with the fact that I had gotten the license to do radio with the Grateful Dead without making friends with him. He was a tough nut to crack for several years. Plus, being one guy's friend makes you automatically suspicious to some other people. There's a lot of that kind of weird stuff. So I was Lesh's buddy, I had permission to do this radio show, but I had a really hard time getting tapes and getting cooperation and getting any kind of support from various people that I would like to have had a better relationship with.

In 1990, somehow, I was involved in the New Year's broadcast. The experience I had then was absolutely great and fun. It demonstrated a truism about dealing with the Grateful Dead; that is, the people that I've worked with are the people that I have good relationships with; the people that I don't have good relationships with are people that I've not spent enough time with for them to know who I am. Healy was suspicious of me for a long time, and then we got to work with each other and became colleagues and had a good relationship from then on out. There was a team of people: Barry

Scott from KPFA, Jack Ellis, one of Healy's oldest friends, who's been in radio for thirty years, and various support people working on the team. We had a production meeting at my house one afternoon, and we were talking about the kind of stuff we could do in the program, things we might want to do. When you're doing a live broadcast, you need to have some preproduced segments that you can go to when you want to cover for changes, when you need to fill time. You need to have a collection of modules that you can use in various things, and you also have a bunch of information you want to get across, interviews you want to do . . . there's a lot of creative stuff that has to be done working up to the broadcast. We were looking at some ideas about comedy bits we could use to cover, and I had just gotten a CD from Rhino Records of Ken Nordine, *The Best of Word Jazz*, and I held it up and said, "You know, we could use some of this. This would be really fun," and Healy snatched it out of my hand and says, "Ken Nordine! God, I just love this guy." Then I said, "You know what? I betcha if he's got this thing coming out, we could get him to do some things just for us." So we called somebody I knew at Rhino Records, and they got in touch with Ken Nordine. We called Ken from my house, and Healy got on the phone and said, "This is Dan Healy with the Grateful Dead, and we want . . ." And at first Ken goes, "Huh? What?" And then he said he was flattered that all these Grateful Dead guys were so into him, and that he was coming out here to hang out with Tom Waits for that New Year's period. He said he might stop by and meet us all and record something for us for the New Year's broadcast.

The day after Christmas, we went to the Oakland Coliseum and started building the studio on the site. I'm seriously talking "building" a studio: they built double walls with glass in them, they turned a locker room into a broadcasting studio. There was a shower room that became a digital editing studio. We had two guys bring their digital editing systems in to cut material for us. In the middle of all this insanity, Ken Nordine walks in. Healy had arranged for a driver to pick him up and bring him to the Coliseum. So we're doing all this preproduction stuff, there are four shows in five days, and we're gonna go live on the last night. There's marketing going on, we're designing a T-shirt by committee, there's technical wire being strung and equipment being checked out, and every once in a while someone's being schlepped in for an interview. It was just this wild, insanely wonderful experience of dealing. For me it was a legitimacy thing—I'm actually officially doing a Grateful Dead project after being the guy who's getting away with it for five years, and working with Healy, who has an intense style and is a brilliant and very difficult guy. So there's all this stuff of people handling each other, and tiptoeing around each other, and standing up to each other—everybody trying to get committed to the best possible broadcast and getting what they want in the deal. There's this huge amount of stuff going on, and in walks Ken Nordine. Everybody just fell in love with him. Garcia found out Nordine was there, he drops what he's doing, he comes charging into the booth to meet him, shakes his hand, and says, "I was a total word jazz fan in 1962!" Blah, blah, blah.

We invited Ken to be one of our on-the-air people for the New Year's broadcast, and he decides to stay. He flies his son Ken junior out from Chicago to join in on the production team, and all of a sudden we've got this whole new thing happening. I whipped out the record, but it was Healy who leaped out of his chair and picked up his phone and made it happen. I picked it up and showed it to him, Healy picked it up and ran with it, had the juice to get through to Ken, and Ken was interested enough in the idea to make it happen. At one point during preproduction, every afternoon we were testing things. Healy loves to hack together these things: we figured out a way to use digital broadcast technology on the television microwave line, so instead of using telephone lines, which are limited in their fidelity, we used the television link from the coliseum to wherever—a microwave link—and sent a digital signal through that, which involved having a decoder at the other end. It was really, really sophisticated and really, really fun, so that we could have the best possible digital signal going up to the satellite.

In the middle of all this stuff going on, there's a recording session going on: Jerry, Mickey, Hamza Eldin—who opened the Dead shows in Egypt in 1978—and Nordine. We've got Jerry playing an electric guitar through this little dinky amp. Jerry, Mickey, and Hamza do these improvised grooves, while Ken does some of his legendary raps. Just unspeakably wonderful stuff. Ken does this thing with layered voices where he's talking to himself, his internal dialogue. He has a little megaphone to talk into the mike. We're doing this multitrack stuff where we're recording Ken on one track on a DAT, playing it back while he records the second part onto another DAT. He's got this all worked out in his brain, and we're just struggling to get it all on tape so we can have these cool pieces to broadcast during the show. It was fantastically glorious.

One thing you learn with the Grateful Dead is not to expect big shoes of appreciation. Strokes are not coin of the realm in the Grateful Dead world. You're lucky if you don't get reamed for something you had nothing to do with by somebody who has no business yelling at you. It's a very strange social, professional circumstance with the Grateful Dead. It's always made me a little bit uncomfortable but it has its moments of real glory, like the New Year's Eve broadcast. It was a kick in the pants! We broadcast the opening act. We had Branford Marsalis and the Dirty Dozen Brass Band, and we interviewed these guys between sets. I had interviewed Bruce Hornsby in Denver before, so we edited in a bit of that. Dennis McNally interviewed Candace, the lighting lady; we edited in that interview. We had all these different pieces, and it was really a gas. Big fun. We were doing this coast-to-coast broadcast that a lot of stations had signed on to, we had produced this T-shirt that the public stations could use as a fund-raiser around the program. It was a very creative experience that paid off in a really great concert. The band played their butts off that year. We did it again in 1991, and it was equally thrilling and equally insane and equally profitable creatively.

At one point, we put on a long segment, and all charged out to the soundboard to do the live description of the New Year's thing. So there's Ken, Barry, myself, and Jack Ellis talking into microphones with headsets on. The closer it gets to midnight, the louder the crowd gets, the more completely berserk the whole vibe is. Finally the lights go down, the place goes completely ape-shit, and we can't hear ourselves! We have no idea what anybody is saying! We're just watching each other, we can barely even see each other. We're trying not to all talk at once, and we hadn't really figured out who was gonna say what about which thing, so it really just became this improvision. It was unspeakably fun.

What that experience means to me is this: I'd always heard the Grateful Dead encouraged excellence, and I had talked to various people who had worked for them and had described this amazing esprit that happens there. John Cutler told me once, "I'm not only allowed to use the best, I'm required to use the best stuff, and encouraged to do my best work." For me, the New Year's broadcasts were a perfect example of that: to get completely immersed in a project with people who are just insanely dedicated to it and have the time of your life, and get paid for it too. We didn't get a huge amount of money, but I wouldn't trade those experiences for any amount of money. Everybody there got to do his best possible work, and the whole point of it was to show thousands of people across the country a really good time.

I really have not scheduled my life around the Grateful Dead to any kind of meaningful extent. I find that culture a little bit disturbing in a way. It's fine that it exists, it's just unfortunate that the parasites came and started hanging out there. The original scene was a self-sustaining and fairly creative one, and over the years, opportunists came along and started exploiting it in ways that had nothing to do with primary culture. What happened in the Haight is what happened on tour with the Grateful Dead too. Also, just in general, the levels of appreciation of Grateful Dead music and culture have expanded. People who became adherent to the Grateful Dead culture without having really ever been exposed to the source of it. To me, it was the music first. It was the music that brought me to it, and the music that kept me coming back. Over the years, this other stuff came along with it. Like my friend Steve Silberman says, "I went to a show, and then I went to another show, and another show. Fifteen years later, I find that I'm still going to shows." You don't set out to become a fully identified member of a cult. No-

Jerry and Mickey—fun times at Cal Expo, 1989 (PHOTO BY STEVE EICHNER)

body recruited us into this thing. We just kept coming because it was interesting, fascinating, and it was rewarding on any number of levels. Then one day you wake up and you realize that the bulk of your life is involved in your connections with those people. I earn my living . . . I'm a professional Deadhead, for better or for worse. It's an amazing thing. I have a tremendous amount of freedom, creativity, and job satisfaction in my life. I'm self-employed. My day job is listening to music that I've always found compelling and worthwhile. I never, ever would've imagined that I'd end up where I am today when I started going to shows twenty-three years ago.

Bob Rupe, 38, Cracker bassist, Richmond, VA:

I'll probably never go to another Dead show. Opening for them was great, and I wouldn't want to ruin that experience by having to be in the crowd and be mashed up against the front of the stage.

I was really fascinated by the economy that follows them around everywhere. I had no idea what was goin' on. In fact, at one point, I went backstage after walking around and I said to my friend, "You know, it must be a bunch of Jesus freaks out there or somethin', man, because everybody's pointing up to the sky asking for a miracle." I had no idea what they were talking about! I guess they were looking for a free ticket.

I didn't expect the event to be Eden by any stretch of the imagination. I just wanted to get an idea of what was goin' on and had a look around and saw what was happening, and quite honestly, I was just amazed at how authentic the whole thing was. It's like a tribe within a time warp. And seeing them in Eugene, Oregon, too, which is apparently one of the mecca places to go, was great because I don't really get over to the Pacific Northwest too much. It's beautiful. It was June and it was absolutely beautiful outside.

Chris Flum, 28, "cool dude," Orinda, CA:

The Dead are ordinary people. They're just like you and me, or anybody else, except they made music that took generations by storm. And they're still there and people are still listening to them. The thing is, you can't put them on a pedestal, saying, "Oh, they're so great. They're this and they're that." They're just ordinary people.

One in a while there's gonna be rowdy people at a show. Last time I was at the Oakland Coliseum, I walked out from the special seating section to get my favorite thing, a drumstick, because it's got the chocolate at the bottom and it's cool. Anyway, I walk up there and there's some Deadheads kicking the window because they apparently wanted to smoke cigarettes. There's no smoking in the Coliseum anymore. You have to go outside, so they were kicking the window as hard as they could until it shattered. If I'd been ten feet closer to the guy, he would've gone out the window to meet the security guards out there. Instead, he ran away like the little jerk he was. He caused a bunch of damage.

Stuff like that gives Deadheads a bad name. But 99 percent of the time, Deadheads are great people. There are those times that people have bad trips, but then there's Dead-Med, who take care of anyone bumming out.

Tom Constanten, 51, pianist/composer, San Francisco:

From a very generic and general sense, the Grateful Dead helped cultivate trust among people. But to get down to specifics more, I think they represent a bubble, a time capsule, of that era when the vision of all those possibilities was open to us. That is the promise and it's also the hazard, because you go out in the parking lot with your starry eyes and you run into a narc or something.

That's what happened to the Haight finally. I watched it go downhill from 1965 to 1970. Nineteen sixty-six was probably the nicest year. It was like living on a block where all the kids were like you. It was very, very open. Our favorite mode of transportation was hitchhiking. You walked to the corner, put up your hand, somebody picked you up and more than likely dropped you at the door where you were going.

The Dead's house in the Haight was like the nouveau Renaissance, it was like the beachhead of the new world. There was 710, and there was also 710A—San Francisco houses with their multilevels. Seven ten A was the basement apartment, and that was where a lot of stuff was happening as well. Seven ten was like the band's office, and after a while, office means office in any language. I remember one time we had a meeting because we had five managers and we didn't know what their duties were! What does John McIntyre do? Rock Skully?

Seven ten was cool, but a lot of houses in San Francisco were eminently cool. The significance of the Dead house was that as soon as the dance consciousness started happening, there were all these different scenes which were very paranoid because you get busted with a joint and you're in deep trouble. We became aware of each other, and gradually a sense of community arose. I think that was the major outlasting contribution of the concert scene in San Francisco: breaking the bubbles, breaking the inner circles' tension of what had been dozens of little individual scenes.

It's an object lesson of what you can get if there is trust, I think. When it's really open. When it started to come apart was when people came and took advantage of that, and naturally the doors started to come down.

Rachel Clein, 13, student, Marin County, CA:

I think people who follow them around are a little too obsessed with it. People who are devoted to that and almost nothing else, or really nothing else, one day wake up and find themselves hitchhiking on the highway and realize that their life is going absolutely nowhere.

Bill Cutler, 47, musician/producer, San Francisco:

These days, I only see them once or twice a year because I'm involved in my own world, I'm producing other acts, doing everything from hip-hop to alternative music. But in everything I do, I try to bring something from that time. What I did in hip-hop, I covered Bob Dylan's "Like a Rolling Stone" and I got the first Dylan sample in history. I don't think I would have thought of something as groundbreaking as putting Dylan into hip-hop if it hadn't been for the fearless way the Grateful Dead mixed and merged genres. I think I learned to break the rules from these guys. And I also learned the rules from these guys! The rules of how to play well with other people. I had taken acid and all before I came out to California, so it wasn't acid specifically. I mean, I certainly did some of that around the Grateful Dead, but I had done that back on the East Coast, so that wasn't it. It was the musical fearlessness that they have.

I always felt in my personal relationships with various people in that group that we were treated as equals. We always exchanged ideas and felt good about that. It's complicated because my brother works so closely with them that I'm always checking in. I see it from a lot of perspectives. My feeling is that the whole thing is so cumbersome and huge today that I hope they can just tune the world out and write us another batch of great Grateful Dead tunes. Nobody writes a lyric like Robert Hunter; I really appreciate Barlow's lyrics, but there's something about Robert Hunter's lyrics. They're so philosophical and they're just great poetry. They're up there with any great poet you can possibly think of. A lot of the alternative bands that I work with don't realize how important the lyrics become as time goes on. You don't want to write something you're embarrassed about. If you go back and hear those Grateful Dead lyrics from the late sixties and early seventies, they make sense in the context of today's world, and you can't say that about a lot of musicians. Phil's tune "Box of Rain." It's just a beautiful, beautiful, philosophical tune. He did it recently at the Shoreline and I thought, "This is just an incredible piece of work."

14

Getting Older

Dan Wilson, 49, street artist, Sacramento, CA:

I didn't see the Dead for a long time after I got my ear blasted at Altamont in 1969.

One day I heard Mick Jagger talking on the radio—KSAN. That was pretty exciting. I gathered up my girlfriend and my buddy and his big black Labrador dog, Dylan—named after Bob Dylan of course. We went out in my old 1950 Chevy pickup and had a great morning riding down to the show. Stopped and got a bottle of wine and all that. We got about twenty miles outside of Hayward when all of a sudden the Hell's Angels came roarin' up in force and passed us. So we knew they were gonna be there. Of course, I was used to the Hell's Angels bein' around. They were on the Haight all the time, and all the concerts, so they didn't bother me.

Anyway . . . we got to Altamont and the place was jam-packed. Everybody had to get in on the same road. It was a section of un-opened freeway, brand-new, and they used that to get everyone in there. It was so crowded! It got nice after a while, but it was pretty damn tough at first, it was so close and grimy. We went way up on top of a hill for the Rolling Stones part of the show. It was nice. We ate sandwiches, drank a little wine.

Then, on our way out, my buddy got tired of holding Dylan. I said, "Let me run him for you. He's a little hyper." So the dog and I took off on his leash. I didn't run too far—150 yards probably. My girlfriend and Pete were walking behind me. I decided I wasn't gonna run anymore, so I stopped, and that's the last thing I remember. I was patting Dylan on the head, taking a breather on the right side of this roadway, and the next thing I remember was waking up in Merrit Hospital. Turns out some guy in a car had been drinking and hit me and the dog. Apparently Dylan

Deadlocks, Cal Expo, 1985 (PHOTO BY DAN WILSON)

took off, ran over the hill, and we never saw him again.

When I woke up in the hospital, I was complaining about my ear. I couldn't hear out of my right ear. They told me a little blood was coming out of it, but there was a chance my hearing would come back with time. I spent six months recuperating. I was real dizzy, I had a bad concussion where I hit my head on the road, and my left side was pretty well banged up. I dislocated my sacroiliac and had some knee problems. That was my main concern—I dragged that leg around for six months trying to get better.

When I was sitting there in the hospital, I said, "Hey, shit, I'm deaf. And if the other one goes, I'm all deaf. I gotta go see a lawyer because this ain't right. I gotta get the guy that hit me." I went and got a lawyer, and you know how lawyers are, they wanna sue everybody. They got the guy that hit me, his insurance agency, the promoters, the owners of the racetrack, the Rolling Stones—just about everybody. The total settlement was about $18,000, and the lawyers took about 45 percent of it. My hearing never did come back. It was gone. That shot my stereo enjoyment of music. I've got one amp that's blown!

So, the next time I saw the Dead was way later. I'd moved up to Oroville, and I went to see them play in Grass Valley, which was my old hometown—a little town made up of about five thousand people. I just had to go and see my old band, the Grateful Dead, and it was well worth it! I noticed now that I'm older, that my generation is now the parents, and the people in the audience looked just like I remember the Dead looking back in '65 and '66. It was like it never did change.

They're still around! They always struck me as a band that really had the kind of staying power to pull this off, play music as long as they wanted to, and people would be there to appreciate it. It's worked out exactly right, and even better. And now another generation is coming into it. It's really cool that it's happened that way.

Stanley Mouse, 55, poster artist extraordinaire, Sonoma, CA:

In the sixties, there was a great spirit in the air. The feelings were thick. I don't know that it will ever happen again. I think maybe it was like the Second Coming, but nobody really noticed. Whatever it was that was going on, it was really heavy.

I don't miss those days, because they were intense because of the war, free-speech demonstrations, drugs, cops, free love, and revolution in the air. I guess it was all relative. What I mean, the war was scary, but the scene was great fun, so it all balanced out somehow. The slaughter of our generation and the great joy of the spirit—I wouldn't trade those days for now. Just like I wouldn't trade being young again and being there again . . . well . . . it'd be nice to be young again! I miss that. But it's replaced with a mellowness that's really nice. It seems like the recklessness of youth is replaced with a universal overview of life. There was so much going on back then. Just to have long hair was a strong statement. There was a lot of partying. I mean, they didn't say, "Just say no!" The thing to do was anything you could get your hands on. Not a good thing to do.

Kim Weiskopf, 48, TV writer/producer: *Married . . . With Children*, Los Angeles:

Actually, I never saw the Dead play much since the sixties—live anyway. I did actually run into them at the Burbank Airport one time. I knew it was them because

I've never seen so much luggage in my life come off that was all instruments.

I did see them play about three years ago, in 1991. I'm straight now, and have been for about ten years, so that was considerably different. What was similar about it was the crowd. I mean, in a way, they're frozen in time! I don't know how that happened. But the fact that the Grateful Dead are still here makes me feel good. My parents were into swing music, which was completely alien to me when I was young. But kids today can see the Dead because the Dead are still around, and people of *all* ages are going to see them.

I don't think I have changed that terribly much. In fact, I just had a pretty violent political conversation today, it being election day here in California, and I got into a nice shouting match in the editing bay here at work, which was kind of interesting.

I feel privileged to have been there. I really do. Even now, I'm sitting here writing for *Married . . . With Children*. I mean, I've got a pretty straight job, honestly. I spend a lot of time in a room with other people and I've adopted a particular persona—and gladly so. I still have long hair and it's a little grayer than it used to be, but I still embody this persona. So if I say something that's particularly off the wall, somebody will say, "Acid flashback!" And I can go with that!

Ken Fine, aka Kew, 36, organic T-shirt salesman, Liberty, ME:

The most recent show I saw was October 2, 1994. It was great. I don't do acid anymore, but I still get excited. I went with my friend Ian, and one of his good friends is Cameron Sears, the manager of the Dead. That's been a good connection, having a friend who brings me backstage. The reason he's invited to come back anytime is that he's very protective. He doesn't let me or any of his other friends get out of control or do anything stupid. He's spent time with all the guys in the band. He's got no pretense about being buddies with Jerry, and his thing is, "I don't have anything to say to Jerry." And that's exactly why he's so welcome back there. He's not making a scene, and he's very honest and sincere, he's there to see Cameron. Cameron is his friend, and they get together and they enjoy each other's company, and the rest of the guys are just doing their thing.

God, there's a million stories! It's been fun. It's nice to relive the big picture. It's been an important part of my life, and my relationship with my wife and kids (daughter, Adrienne, five, and son Jason, two). They've never gotten to a show yet, but I'm sure they will.

Steve Eichner, 30, R&R photographer, New York:

I've changed. I've graduated. But I still love to go to Dead shows. The last great Dead experience was in Las Vegas when Blues Traveler played at Bally's and the Dead played three days. I was all hooked up with backstage passes, and the great experience was still there for me. What I learned from the whole thing is that you don't need to have money to have fun. That was my whole angle when I was younger because I was rebellious against my parents. They were very money-oriented. My experience being crazy with the Dead got a lot of the angry-young-man out of me. It gave me an outlet for that. It showed me that if you ain't got nothin', you got nothing to lose. You don't need anything

Bobby and Phil, Cal Expo, 1985 (PHOTO BY DAN WILSON)

to really have a good time. If I was in some city and I was down and out and I didn't know how I was gonna get to the next town, and I was hungry, womanless, I could just sit back and listen to the music and that was enough to warm me and get me through the next day. It was never that bad.

If I had to send a message to the Dead, it would be, "Keep goin', man! Keep doing it!" It's amazing that they can get up every day and still jam.

Jerry Miller, 51, Moby Grape/Jerry Miller Band guitarist, San Francisco:

This last Gibson centennial concert they had at the Fillmore was real nice. Everybody was a bit older, they got the kids and the grandkids now, but there still is that magic around. That brought me back a bit, about twenty-five years, seeing a lot of these people. It's always mellow in the midst of great confusion. Everybody realized that everything's not perfect, it's crazy, people look funny, and everybody grooved with it. Do your own thing. Don't get crazy, have fun. Nobody's drunk, and that's nice. Cool space for the kids to hang out.

David Gans, 41, radio producer: Grateful Dead Hour; author: Playing in the Band and Conversations With the Dead; San Francisco:

I created a niche for myself in the Grateful Dead by getting involved inadvertently in the radio thing. I do a good job, I know my stuff, and I learned how to produce a radio show, and I've learned how to distribute the radio show. I had no qualifications when I started. Whether it meant to or not, the Grateful Dead allowed me to become the professional person that I am now. The music lured me. Phil encouraged me, Bobby encouraged me. It is still a really fun job. Doing this music for a living is really enjoyable. There's a drawback to it in the sense of not having enough time to do all the other things that I'd like to do, but as day jobs go, it's just the greatest. I've never lost my enthusiasm for Grateful Dead music. It's been challenging and rewarding every step of the way. The Grateful Dead, one way or another, allowed me to do this thing and thereby enabled me to become an extremely satisfied, fulfilled, middle-class homeowner.

Timothy Leary, 74, chaos engineer, Los Angeles:

The sixties were so amazing because you'd go off and you'd be on the street, suddenly you'd meet someone and they'd say, "Hey, come on over to my place," and we'd take acid. There were several times, you'd bang around San Francisco and you'd meet Cassady or somebody and you'd go over to their place, and somebody would be strumming some chords, jamming. Looking back on it, I think, "Shit, I didn't appreciate how great that was." It was pretty normal: just some guy sitting there playing a guitar!

I was on a bill with the Starship about a month ago in Las Vegas, and we're sitting around backstage for hours. We were saying, "Shit! We were doing this thirty years ago, hanging around backstage."

John Perry Barlow, 47, Dead lyricist/cyberspace pioneer, WY:

Last Dead show I went to was in Denver a few months ago. There was this reporter there from the *Rocky Mountain News* who was doing a profile about me for the business section because I was about to debate John Malone, the head of TCI, a big cable company in Boulder. The reporter'd never been to a Dead show, and he wanted to go to one to get some background for his story. But I told him that the Dead scene is not very characteristic of the current me. But as I explained the metamorphoses of events to him, what had me in cyberspace, and what had intrigued me all along with the Grateful Dead and its scene, I could see a great continuity. Just finding that continuity reexpressed so clearly was sort of memorable to me. The best thing about this whole thing was that he was with me at the concert all evening, scribbling notes, having his life change before his very eyes. He was about thirty-three, never had anything to do with the Dead, never smoked anything—the whole thing. He'd been very suspicious of it and had not had direct contact. And there he is in the very fucking core! It's hot right there, his brain is boiling! It was great watching this guy melt.

Bill Cutler, 47, musician/producer, San Francisco:

The Grateful Dead is such an important part of the cultural history of California, and so many businesses depend on the Grateful Dead: the SEVA Foundation, the Rex Foundation, Wavy Gravy's Rainbow camp for disadvantaged kids. It is such a giant thing. When I knew the Grateful Dead way back when, they were playing places that held five to ten thousand people. Remember, they did play Haight Street for free many times, and they did support the Haight-Ashbury free clinic, and this, that, and the other thing. Now on a regular basis they're playing places that hold sixty thousand people, selling it out.

The pressure is great. So many people are requesting favors that I can't imagine what it must be like to be in that kind of position. Somebody has to be Captain No, somebody has to say no because all the guys in the band are nice. They'll all go, "Yeah, sure. I'd love to play there. When is it? Next Thursday? Sure." They have someone saying, "You can't do that! You're gonna be in Ottawa. You're gonna be in Egypt!" There was a time when the Grateful Dead were one of the only bands that didn't have the kind of management that prevented people from having access to them. So many people were requesting so many favors that after a while, they just had to prioritize things. I think that's really what you see now backstage. They need somebody back there: John McIntyre, Dennis McNally, whoever it might be; somebody directing traffic, just so they can concentrate, get in tune, put a show on, get out of there alive.

Because I do hip-hop, because I do alternative, and I also used to play with Garcia, I'm sort of in the Grateful Dead's chronological generation, and Pearl Jam's musical generation. It's a strange place to be. I find that a lot of the musicians my age that I try to play with aren't interested in playing the kind of music I want to play. I never got off the train. As much as I like the Grateful Dead, I stopped at the next station and picked up on the Sex Pistols, then Chrissie Hynde, then Nirvana. All those things. So, for me, it's not satisfying personally to play, for lack of a better term, psychedelic music of the old style. I enjoy that, and when I get together with those people I do that, but what I feel artistically in the songwriting I do now, I feel I'm part of a music generation of younger people. It's very odd because I find myself playing with guys twenty-eight or twenty-five. In my band, the Mystery Tramps, I'm twenty years older than the guy standing next to me!

15

Getting Close

Dan Wilson, 49, Sacramento, CA:

I remember another day when we were living on Frederick Street, my roommate and good buddy, Bob Landy, came runnin' up the stairs and said: "Hey, Dan! I just saw Mr. Pen!" I thought, "Mr. Pen, who's that?" "Pigpen! I just saw him over at the store!" I said, "What'd you say to him?" "Hi, Mr. Pen!"

So I was out there later and I thought maybe Pigpen would come around. And, by God, he came rolling down the hill from Yerba Buena Park on his motorcycle. It was about four-thirty, on a clear, San Francisco day, and the sunset just hit him right good in the face. You could see all the pockmarks on his face. He looked *so damn tough!* He had his big black shades on and he was ridin' that Harley down the hill and . . . he was our neighbor! That was Mr. Pen.

Steve Brown, 50, filmmaker/Dead's aid-de-camp 1972–77, San Francisco:

The Dead have managed to survive in an alternative mode all these years . . . obviously!

Laughing helped a lot. From the get-go, there was always

more laughing than there was business. When I was working with him, Jerry was a very kind person in the way he cared about people and their lives. Once they started working with the band, Jerry treated them as part of the family, a team thing with a sensitivity to it. There was a personal level to everything. Yeah. We laughed a lot.

One of the most important things I learned working with Jerry is to be honest about what you want, what you will ultimately be satisfied with. The grace of being creative with others gives you something even more than what you singularly brought to it because you conceptualize something that then turns into something finer. The act of creation with a group of people is magic. It's fucking magic. The chemistry of creation is a real high.

It was great to have this experience with the Dead at its points of being fun and high, and appreciating it up close and personal. But after a time, you couldn't really top one more show or one more experience. It's better for me to watch the whole thing now as a member of the audience, but . . . it certainly was fun while it lasted!

Annette Flowers, Dead's Ice Nine Publishing administrator, San Rafael, CA:

Neal Cassady was my link to sitting here in this office today.

I remembered the day I met him back in 1966. He was playing chess, cooking, listening intently to the Beatles' new album *Revolver*, and talking—all at the same time! And he was winning the chess game too. Neal was an amazing soul. He took me to the Acid Test, introduced me to Ginsberg, Ferlinghetti, and a whole bunch of incredible people, and he played matchmaker with me and my first boyfriend, David Nelson, the guitarist for New Riders of the Purple Sage. The Riders used to play and hang with the Dead all the time, and that's how I ended up becoming friends with this circle of people.

A few years after that, I was living in Kentfield, Marin, with David, Cheri—a close mutual friend—and a couple other people. One day I came here to the office with Cheri and hung out while she helped with some house painting. David and Bonnie Parker, who were pretty much running the place at the time, offered her a

Tom Constanten (right) and his
buddy Ron "Pigpen" McKernon at
Tom's wedding, July 26, 1970
(PHOTO BY MICHAEL ARADI)

cleaning job but she didn't want it. There I was, right place, right time, and I got the gig. I really needed the money because I had my one-year-old boy, Che, so I was so glad to get a real job. And I enjoyed it. I liked keeping this place clean. When the sun would shine through that stained-glass window, it felt so good to know I'd played my part.

The band seemed happy with my work because a couple of them had me clean their houses too. Of course, nobody had a vacuum cleaner, so I used to bring my own from home all the time. I remember one time my car wasn't working, so for a few weeks I hitchhiked with that vacuum cleaner. I even rode a motorcycle with it once!

A few months after I started, I was dusting or sweeping or something, and the phone was ringing and ringing—no one was picking it up. Finally, someone yelled from upstairs, "Could someone pick up the phone?" I did, and have been ever since.

My responsibilities have obviously grown over the years, but how it all started was really simple. By Thanksgiving, I'd become an official staff member, and I remember being so thankful for everything. I had a great job that paid well with people I liked, and it all had just sort of fallen into my lap. It was a true blessing.

Being part of this big positive force, helping facilitate the happening of a Grateful Dead show, is the best thing about this job. There aren't many organizations like this. What's going on here is important, and I'm glad to do anything I can to help it along. I love the guys in this band, and I'll help whenever, however I can.

Jeff Brown, 36, landscape architect, San Francisco:

The closest I ever came to meeting the band was my *mom* met Jerry once. I do some sculpture, and I had a commission to do a temporary public sculpture at the Marin Civic Center, out on the lagoon, so we had to pick a location somewhere on the Civic Center grounds. I collaborated with a woman, and we decided to do something in the lake, with a gold-leaf canoe and this fence made out of fennel. While we were installing the sculpture, it just so happened the Dead were rehearsing in the auditorium. The big equipment trucks were parked out there, and I had a friend— Matt Thayer—helping, who really adores Jerry. He's just in awe of Mr. Garcia. And sometime while we were installing this thing, Matt said, "Hey, Jeff, can I take a break and go over there? Maybe I can get inside and listen to the band practicing or something." And my mom, Clara, who was hanging out, says (Jewish accent), "The Grateful Dead? Is that the band you're always going to hear? The Grateful Dead? Matt, is it okay if I go over there with you?"

So Matt and my mom go walking over to the other side of the lake to see what would happen. They come back maybe an hour later, and Matt is just shaking his head and laughing. Apparently they were hanging out, and one of the roadies came over to them and said something about how the band doesn't like people hanging around, that they couldn't get in, and could they please move on. But, you see, to my mother, that's the opportunity, that's her foot in the door: "Ah! Somebody's talking to me! From here, I can get in!"

Matt is a very gentle guy, he was probably ready to go, but my mom starts chatting to this guy, and while she's chatting and talking him up, out comes this guy. He comes walking up the driveway, this gray-haired man. My mom turns to him and she engages him because if he's coming *out* of the building, he must have a way *in* too! And she says, "You know, you should talk to your hairdresser about getting your hair colored. I used to have gray hair like you, but I got it colored. You feel so much better!" And this gray-haired gentleman just gets a good laugh out of that and gets on his motorcycle and drives away. Matt, of course, is just floored. My mom is joking with Jerry Garcia about his hair color. She had no idea who Jerry Garcia was. She *still* doesn't know who Jerry Garcia is!

We joke around about how my mom parties with Jerry, but that's about the closest I ever came to the band.

Then there was the time a friend called me up who was a tree pruner at the time. He needed some help up in Marin. They had a big crew working and they needed some ground crew. It turned out to be Bill Graham's estate. So there I was dragging branches through the poison oak all around these items that Bill came down in from the ceiling in on New Year's Eve—the giant globe, the joint, the bear. These things were all outside, and here I was pruning trees around them. The only other time I'd seen these things was inside some smoky auditorium. I don't think Bill was at the house, but it was fun being around all that stuff.

I've never met the band. I don't know what I'd do! I'd probably be too nervous. Maybe I wouldn't, maybe I could really enjoy it. I don't know. I mean, I go to shows sometimes and I don't even look at the stage the whole show! I'm just busy smiling at my friends and dancing around. It's great that those guys are up there playing, I love 'em so much for doing it! They are such a great catalyst.

I just wanna hug 'em! I enjoy it so much. I just hope that they have rich, full lives. Their hearts should be so full. I'd love to invite them all out sailing, you know? I have a sailboat, a little twenty-two-footer, and I'd love to share with them something I enjoy doing so much: just get in that flow of wind and water.

Stuart Wax, 37, music manager, Los Angeles:

I grew up on Long Island, in a religious-observant Jewish family. I remember writing a letter in tenth or eleventh grade about being in a strict environment, like an all-boys school, a parochial school, how my only escape was when the Dead would come to town. I would go to the shows at Nassau Coliseum or in New York City or in New Jersey . . . and I became part of a whole different world. It was great. It's weird because my whole family is very intertwined with it too. My mother, she's an optician on the Lower East Side, and she used to sell Jerry Garcia his glasses! In 1971, Pigpen walked in with Jerry, and then Bobby came in later, and my mother looked at Bobby and said, "You're with these guys? You look so clean-cut, and so together." And Bobby said something like, "Yeah, I guess I know what you mean." My mother just saw this young-looking, clean-cut guy, and it looked like he had short hair. Then he turned around and he had a ponytail down to his ass!

Another time, my mother went out on a lunch break, and when she came back, one of her coworkers was taking care of Jerry. She asked, "Do you know who this is?" And Jerry said to her, "You know who I am?" This was in the early seventies when nobody really would've known who he was like they would today. And my mom said, "Sure, you're Jerry Garcia of the Grateful Dead. As a matter of fact, my kids are going to see you tonight!"

Jerry once gave me this laminate card that said, "Thrive, Jerry Garcia." I had it for a while, but then once at the Academy of Music in New York, I used it to try to get backstage and this guy took it. I said, "No, you're not supposed to take it, you're supposed to just look at it and then give it back to me." But he kept it. He wasn't a Dead roadie, he was a club guy. He smashed a bottle or something, and I said, "Hey, just keep it." So I lost that card.

We also used to run Grateful Dead nights in Jerusalem. I manage artists/songwriters/producers, and it's always been intertwined with the Dead. I managed Marty Balin for a while; I also did the Jefferson Airplane reunion tour. It was fun when the Grateful Dead office called me and said, "Stacey Kruetzmann [Billy's wife] would like some tickets for the Airplane at the Greek. Do you think you can help?" I said, "Help? It's my pleasure!" That was like the Bridge concert with Neil Young when Jerry and Bobby played, the Dead office didn't get tickets, and I'm close with Neil's manager, so I was able to get some tickets for the office staff. It's a fun thing for me to be able to give back something to the whole thing. Usually in this business, you're either born into it or you're a musician. But I'm neither. It's really a blessing, just like I feel my experiences with the Dead are a blessing.

I have a picture of me with Jerry's arm around me backstage at Laguna Seca in 1987. The greatest thing was that I walked up to Jerry, and I didn't know how to start my conversation. I said, "Jerry, I want you to know that my dad's a rabbi, and while you were in the hospital with a diabetic coma, he prayed for you." And Jerry turned to me and said, "Could you please tell your dad that his prayers worked!" Then we sat down and talked about my mother and lots of other stuff.

Many happy campers, Philadelphia, 1986 (PHOTO BY STEVE EICHNER)

Gina, 31, Blues Traveler's personal assistant, New York:

Blues Traveler opened for the Jerry Garcia Band at Madison Square Garden in 1991. That was cool. Jerry drove up, got out, performed, got back in the van, and drove away. So we didn't even get to say hi or meet him or anything, but the guys were really honored to be able to do something like that—play that big of a room with someone like Jerry. That was their first time doing something like that, ever. Bill Graham set that up. It was right before his accident. Then, when Bill died, they had that memorial in San Francisco, and John (Popper) went out and played with the Grateful Dead on "Wang-Dang Doodle."

Last year, John played at the Rock and Roll Hall of Fame thing at the Waldorf-Astoria when they inducted the Grateful Dead. Afterwards, Bobby Weir came walking by, and John said, "Man, you know, we really love you, and . . . Gina here is a *huge* fan!" John loves to embarrass me, and I embarrass *really* easily. I told him, "Don't you dare introduce him to me, I don't want to be introduced to him." And he said, "No, no. I really want to do this for you. I know how much you love them." I told him if he did that to me, I'd never speak to him again. Of course, he did.

Then Bobby invited us up to his party. Traveler's manager Dave Frye comes in with a wheelchair for John because he still needs one since his motorcycle accident, and John says, "We're goin' up to Bob Weir's to party," and Dave says, "All right. Enough of the jokin', John. Come on, get in your chair, let's go home." And John says, "No, no, Bob Weir just invited us up. He invited Gina and Debbie too." And Dave says, "Okay guys, cut it out," and he looks at me and Debbie, and we've got these stupid grins on our faces, and he says, "You guys are for real, aren't you!" So he says, "Okay. I'll go put the chair back and park the car. What's the room number?"

So we went up there, and it was Billy Kreutzmann, Vince, Mickey Hart, Bruce Hornsby, and Bobby. They were all smoking herb, but they wouldn't let anyone smoke cigarettes in there because Vince had just had surgery on his mouth or something. So Debbie and I went to the hall to smoke, and Chuck Berry came walking up! He asks, "Do we need a ticket to get in here?" And I say, "Yeah, I'm your ticket taker. Slap me five—that's your ticket!" He says, "All right!" slaps me five, and goes in. Debbie couldn't believe I did that to Chuck Berry! That was more exciting to me even than meeting the Dead, because Chuck Berry is such a legend.

What was really cool to me about meeting the Dead was that they were just like us. They were all hanging out together in the hotel room, drinking Heinekens and smoking. And I thought to myself, this is what Blues Traveler are gonna be doing in twenty-five years! It was really cool. It really made me feel good. It was exactly how I pictured the Dead to be, and it's exactly how they are. They weren't eating bonbons and drinking champagne—they were drinking Heineken, my favorite beer! That night was exactly like the getting-a-ticket rule: when I least expected it, it happened.

Annetta Pearson, 50, artist/homemaker, San Francisco:

A friend of ours, Tracy, was at a wedding once, and Bobby Weir was there. So he was chatting with Bobby, and they had a pair of tie-dye or skull-head skis that had been made. They were the official Grateful Dead skis or something, and Bobby Weir was promoting them. Tracy met him in the bathroom and asked him, "Do you like the skis?" And Bobby said, "Well, frankly, I don't really ski that much." Tracy asked, "Do you think these are gonna be high-grade skis people are gonna want to get because they're so cool, or do you think they're gonna buy 'em so they can put 'em on their wall like some sort of Hard Rock Cafe memorabilia?" And Bobby's response was, "Well, I hope so!"

John Popper, 27, Blues Traveler harmonicist, Princeton, NJ:

A few years ago, I was at the Rock and Roll Hall of Fame when the Dead got inducted, and they asked for me to sit in with them. I met Bobby Weir and he was really nice. The funnest part of that was introducing Gina (personal assistant) to Bob. She freaked out about that one! Playing with Chuck Berry was also really cool. Afterwards, we went up to their big party and hung out. I wanted to see if Bobby had any advice for anything I could do. He looked at me and said, "Are you having fun?" and I said, "Yeah." And he said, "Well, then you're doing it right." Then he went off and fell on the bed with some voluptuous woman. I hung out with Vince Welnick, who was having some sort of laryngitis, trying to get him to make noise with his voice by laughing. It was a fun party.

Steve Eichner, 30, R&R photographer, New York:

During my Grateful Dead period, I started working as road manager with this band in New York called Dreamspeak. My roommate in college, Tom, who turned me on to the Grateful Dead, was Dreamspeak's drummer. They were based around Columbia University because the guitar player went to school there. So we all used to hang out at the Grateful Dead frat house of Columbia called Delta Phi. Dreamspeak was the house band. I met David Graham because he went to school there, and in his freshman year, a couple of my Deadhead friends hooked up with him and brought him into the Dreamspeak scene. He was really into them. So that was how I met David.

I remember before I'd met David or Bill, my college friends and I drove out to San Francisco for my first New Year's Eve show. None of us had tickets, but we all managed to get in. I didn't really know that much about Bill at the time, but in retrospect I remember it was Bill who did this: My friends and I were sitting on the floor in the back of the auditorium. All of a sudden this older guy comes walking through the audience, and a fan stands up right in front of him and says, "Hey! Uncle Bobo!" And Bill grabbed the guy by his shirt collar, pushed him up against the wall, and yelled, "don't you ever fuckin' call me that again, you fuckin' asshole! I'll throw you out of here right now!" The guy was like, "I'm sorry! I'm sorry! I didn't know." *That* was my very first experience with Bill!

One winter after I'd met David, I went on tour with Dreamspeak and we drove all the way to San Francisco, where we got hooked up completely by Bill and David for the Dead's New Year's Eve shows. Backstage passes, stayed at Bill's house, played volleyball with Bill and the BGP (Bill Graham Presents) people. I guess this was 1987, so I'd been seeing the Dead for three years from the other side. I was the guy Bill Graham probably would've hated, the guy who'd break into shows, and now here I was at the other end of everything. I stayed at Bill's house; Bill, David, me, and all the guys in Dreamspeak played volleyball in his backyard. Bill took us around the house and showed us all this wonderful rock-and-roll memorabilia—Janis Joplin's tambourine, and all this really great stuff. Bill was a pretty cool dude. We had a lot of meetings with Bill and Dreamspeak. I remember Bill said, "If you guys want to move to California, I'll manage you. But I can't do anything for you in New York." Unfortunately, Dreamspeak decided to say in New York.

I remember hanging out once with Bill backstage at a Blues Traveler/Spin Doctors show at the Marquee in New York. He was really into Blues Traveler. I watched him when Traveler did one of their classic transitions between songs, and he was blown away. He thought they were a great band.

Sheila Rene, 56, music anthropologist, TX via San Francisco:

y first connection with the Grateful Dead wasn't until after I got into the business working for KSJO radio, in 1977. I interviewed Bob Weir and Mickey Hart. Then a strange thing happened: they stopped giving me interviews. I couldn't understand it. This is a band . . . this is *the* band. Finally, Billy Kreutzmann, backstage one day at a Greek theater show, said, "Sheila, don't you write for *Relix Magazine?*" And I said, "Yes, I do." And he said, "We hate those people. They've ripped us off for

Onstage at Madison Square Garden, 1988 (PHOTO BY STEVE EICHNER)

years." I had no idea! I thought I was on their side. I quit *Relix* the next day.

I went on to have other interviews with Weir. I've never interviewed the Big Man, but I've been in his presence at several dinners at Bill Graham's house—Christmas dinners. I was able to observe and sit around and enjoy the stories that Jerry Garcia would tell, and how he and Bill would relate. Of course, Bill had a lot to do with the Grateful Dead's career early on, and they would fall out from time to time and fight miserably, but there was such a respect between them. Most of the stories came after dinner, back in Bill's room. Even then, Jerry would go off by himself a lot and not be a part of the bigger group. But whenever Bill was around, a lot of talking was going on between them, and I think a tremendous respect for each other.

Perhaps the funniest story I ever heard Bill Graham tell about the Grateful Dead was, during the early days the guards very carefully searched everybody for any kind of drugs, and if you brought in more than one person could handle, they considered you a dealer and they would confiscate them. Bill kept one of those expandable folders—A for Acid, B for Barbiturates, C for Cannabis, D for Dexedrine, et cetera. And then when the folder got full, Bill would call the Grateful Dead, and then he'd call the Jefferson Airplane, and maybe one other band, and give them the code to come see him. Which meant, the first band that got there, got the drugs! It was mostly the Grateful Dead that always made it on time, even though they had to come from Marin. They more than likely got the most drugs from that little collection plate.

One of the holiest women I believe I've ever known was Mountain Girl. I think of her as this wise, old Indian woman. She's always been extremely good to me. I've always considered her the high priestess. When I was backstage, I'd always try and be around her. I didn't care much about "the boys" except musically and when I interviewed them. The last time I saw Mountain Girl, she had brought all her sons to Sacramento to see AC/DC. I about fainted when I saw her there! She was there because AC/DC was her sons' favorite band, so she drove them all up there like a good mom. She's the one everybody looked up to.

Greg Martens, 31, entrepreneur, Portland, ME:

I had some connections with the band through friends of mine in Boston. They would take them out to dinner, so to speak, and made sure they ate well. So I got to meet them a few times. Since I was vending from 1987 to 1981, the whole band knew who the "good apples" were and who the "bad apples" were out in the parking lot. I've always been a good apple because I figured that's good karma.

I know Bob Weir will never forget this. In 1981 in Glens Falls, I was on my first tour. I really wanted to see the band do "Lazy Lightnin'." I got a free ticket from a friend of mine, and he said, "Go up in front and yell 'Lazy Lightnin'' until they play it." In 1981 in Glens Falls beer was about a nickel apiece, and they were about twenty-five ounces. Well, I got shit-faced, I went up front to the stage, the band came out a half hour late, and they all looked shit-faced, they'd all been drinking. The whole first set I was right in front of Bobby, yelling at him, calling him some names, saying, "Fuck you, Bob! Play 'Lazy Lightnin''!" And he came up to the microphone and said, "Uh, we haven't played this song in a long time, but we're gonna do it to shut this guy up," and he points right at me. They started playing it, and he fucked up the words. He looked at me and I started laughing at him. I had my hand over my mouth, pointing at him, laughing at him. Since then, every time I see him, he swears at me in French.

I saw him in a limo once in Springfield in 1985 abut five blocks from the Civic Center. I was once again strolling out of a bar, and this limo pulls up with dark windows, the window comes down, and Bobby sticks his head out and starts swearing at me in French! This happened again in a hotel elevator, and another time in traffic at the Greek Theater. I said, "'Lazy Lightnin''! Glens Falls, '81!"

The whole thing about Jerry for me is that every time I've seen him, I've looked the other way. In a song he wrote called "Liberty" he says, "I look in a puddle and what do I see? The whole damn world staring back at me." I've seen him backstage walk from the stage to his dressing room, and every fuckin' person stops their conversation and stares at him as he walks by. I've had chances to talk to him a lot and I've purposely turned my head the other way. My friend has been on their lighting crew for about five years, and even he's like, "Wow! Jerry said hello to me today." I have total respect for Jerry and his space.

Annie Harlow, 36, green grocer, New England:

For the last show at Winterland, my friend and I, we're early in line, and it was really great. Bill was out there with soup, they had these huge banners draped over the building. It was so beautiful. I was under the Blues for Allah banner. There were these TV people with cameras wanting goodbye interviews, hounding people for stories. I said I might have a story for them, and the guy goes, "Oh, yeah? What is it?" "Well, I got an all-expenses-paid trip to come here." And he thought I was a little rich kid, but I explained my story to him and he asked, "Why did she do it? Why would she want you to come out to California to this concert?" because it was almost baffling back then to really do that. And this is a direct quote from my mother: she said she would rather have her kids be Deadheads than Moonies! That was at a period when Moonies were really blossoming. The TV people ate that up with two spoons and used it on their segment. My friend Steve Brown has it on video, so when I finally met him all these years later, I saw it. I'm a little goober! It was so funny!

My mother thought that we'd be all finished with this Dead stuff by the time we were twenty. Of course, I've just celebrated my twentieth anniversary of seeing Grateful Dead shows!! I met Bill, he was awesome. Winterland was just so magical. It was so puny, it was like seeing them in your living room! It was so good. John Cippolina? Give me a beak! I wanted to take him home with me! Bobby, in "Not Fade Away," was doing these *"Pings!"* I was way up in front, about three people deep. John Belushi! You could see plates of co-caine, you could see these people freaking out, having a major time. The stage was littered with people! It was such a party. New Riders of the Purple Sage, the Blues Brothers, tons of other people . . . and then the Dead. It's New Year's Eve and Bill comes down throwing all these joints.

And then at the end, it really was The End. My brother and I were just about the last people to leave. It was like, how can we leave! We'd been in there for over twelve hours! I went in there at about five in the afternoon and I came out at nine in the morning. They fed us a killer breakfast. It wasn't continental! Bill was styling big time! After that, whenever I'd see Bill at any show, like New Year's at the Oakland Coliseum, he was always very present, and I'd always thank him!

I met the Grateful Dead in 1980. I was working down in Cape Cod doing archaeology. I took a weekend and went up to see them in Augusta, Maine. I was traipsing around, playing Frisbee, just wasting time during the day, and this truck driver came over to me and said, "Here, have a pass!" I said, "Is there anything attached to this, besides the adhesive?" I had too much of a great thing going with the Grateful Dead and didn't want to taint it with some goober. And the guy said, "No! It's yours! It's fine. It's yours. Do whatever!" After making sure there were no strings attached, I got high with him backstage, and then I left with this pass. That was cool. I used the pass! I was right down front with the press photographers. I was actually leaning on the stage! This was when it wasn't as strict as it is now. Then I went backstage, and I was kind of shy. You're totally alone and you don't know anybody. But I checked it out, walked around, went through where the big spread is—all the food and everything. Then I thought, "I don't belong back here, I gotta go back up front." I had a great time, and then after the show, I hooked up with my friends and we were all really psyched. My girlfriend and her boyfriend wanted to go to the Holiday Inn where the Dead were staying. I thought that sounded kind of queer because we'd never thought of doing this before, but then decided to go. Some guy came down and said, "The band would like to invite you upstairs," and it was clear he meant us, but not the guy. The guy couldn't come, so my girlfriend said, "Well, I can't leave him." She regrets it to this very day! She dumped him later!

So I went up by myself! I went into room 254 at the Holiday Inn! The truck driver was up there, and I said, "Hey! Howya doin'!" It was Bobby, Billy, Brent, and there was this guy that was like Jerry's little sidekick, who would come in and out. Jerry was nowhere to be found. They were all talking about this woman downstairs who was way fucked up who'd kind of been tormenting them, like she *had* to sleep with them, she *had* to be with them—real psycho stuff. It was interesting because I got a sense of what was really going on with them. Billy was just about to get married, he was talking about his life, his love, all this stuff. It was kind of awkward, it was kind of a funny situation. They were like, "Oh, so what do you do?" And I said, "Oh, I'm an archaeologist." Then some people came in that were obviously there to just totally schmooze and all that. I hung out up there for a really long time, just hanging. It was normal, unbelievably normal, as a matter of fact! It was not wild, no binging of anything. None of that stereotypical stuff. Drugs weren't even that plentiful.

Then the management requested that people leave because it was late, and I got up to go. I was like, "Okay! See ya! Thanks! Bye!" My friends were nowhere. I'm nowhere! I was like, "Where am I? What am I doing? Fuck!" Then, the truck driver guy asked, "Where are you going?" And I said, "I don't know! My friends aren't here anymore!" and he said I could crash in his room. I thought uh-oh, but it was unbelievably cool. I slept in the same bed with this guy, nothing happened, nothing was meant to happen, he was totally cool. Jerry was in the next room because I could hear him hacking, and in the morning he was right outside the door. I was like, "There's Jerry. He sounds unhealthy." Then in the morning I just said, "Goodbye!" I can't believe I can't remember this guy's name now. That was a really great experience. They were all really nice people, I was not used in any way. I felt like the geek—you do if you don't know how to work that way; you just feel like everybody knows what's going on except you. But it turned out that it was really okay, that it's okay just to be me because that's all everybody else is doing! I remember I felt all right because Brent was so new in the band that I could really relate to him! We were the newcomers! He was like a comrade in that experience.

It was really, really great that it happened, but I didn't go seeking it out.

Bobby and Billy, Cal Expo, 1989 (PHOTO BY STEVE EICHNER)

Trey Allen, 27, R&R caterer, Nashville, TN:

A few years back, I started to work at Shoreline doing catering for BGP (Bill Graham Presents). I helped set up dressing rooms, production stuff. The only close contact I had with the Dead was one time when the Jerry Garcia Band was playing Shoreline, and Jerry at the time was on his big diet. He was wanting something to eat, and I told him what we were serving, and none of it was in accordance with his diet. So, I offered to fix him up some soup and a sandwich, and he said, "Well, how about a cheese sandwich?" And I said, "I'll make you the cheese sandwich, man, but I don't see where cheese fits into your diet. It's a pretty fattening thing there, bro." That was about it. But one thing about doing the dressing room thing is that you always break down the room, and Jerry always has the biggest, fattest roaches in his ashtray, which are always wonderful to smoke.

The weirdest thing I've ever seen was in one of the band member's room where I found a bunch of empty condoms and nitrous poppers. Sometimes I'd find little funny notes from fans to the band and I'd read them. Oh, God! Get a life!

David Gans, 41, radio producer: *Grateful Dead Hour*; author: *Playing in the Band* and *Conversations With the Dead*; San Francisco:

I interviewed Bobby in 1977 for *BAM Magazine*. I went down to Los Angeles and interviewed him. It was cool. He was working on a solo album, *Heaven Help the Fool*. Me and the photographer Ed Perlstein flew down there and went to his hotel in Beverly Hills. John McIntyre introduced us to Bobby. We did this interview, the highlight of which was that Ed somehow persuaded Bob to open a beer bottle with his teeth. He'd heard that he could do that, and Bob obliged us by doing so. Then we all got together and trooped out to Sound City in Van Nuys to listen to some tracks. Ed took pictures of Weir posing on his black Corvette. That was fun. I also interviewed Keith Olsen, who'd produced *Terrapin Station* and was producing this solo album with Weir.

I was meeting one of my heroes, and I made friends with Weir through those experiences and hooked up with him at other times. I went down to L.A. again in February of 1978 when he was debuting his band, the Bob Weir Band, who were touring behind *Heaven Help the Fool*, and that's where Brent Mydland came into the picture, how he got into the Grateful Dead ultimately. I interviewed Weir again at a club down there. I was serious, I was a musician, I was a journalist, and I wanted to understand what was going on. And I think I made a good impression on all of the musicians I interviewed over the course of those years by knowing what I was talking about.

In 1978, Weir was the guy I knew best, and he took care of me at a show at the HaiLai in Miami. Apparently there was some acid floating around, and Weir had gotten dosed. I didn't know that at the time, but he took care of me and sort of parked me on the drum riser, and I stood over by the guy mixing the monitors, Brett Cohen. I hung out with him and watched what he did, and I listened to the band.

I was very surprised in 1981 when I was able to get an interview with Phil because he pretty much notoriously didn't do interviews. But he agreed to do one with me, and we had a really, really great time. I was very ready to deal with him. At one point he sort of stopped himself in the middle of a sentence and said, "Boy, you really have done your homework, haven't you?" I felt like I connected with him very well, and several months later I finished up the interview with him, in the course of which he was talking about all this classical music stuff that he was into, and he said, "You know, you really ought to look at the conductor's scores." And I said, "Hey, man, I'm ready. Show it to me." So on the Fourth of July, 1982, he invited me over to his house and I spent the day. It was like that thing: it was the hip professor that invites you to his house, you smoke a joint with him, and you talk philosophy. Well, this was going to Professor Lesh's house, smoking a joint, and listening to Beethoven while he got out the conductor's scores and showed me all this stuff. He brought out records and conductor's scores, and he showed me all this stuff about Charles Ives, and he played me *Rites of Spring* by Stravinsky, and some Beethoven stuff. I just drank it all in. It was great! He was sharing his enthusiasm for this stuff, and it was just a fabulously great feeling to be learning from him. I was in way over my head, but, boy, I had a great time and I learned a lot. That became the beginning of a creative relationship that I still have with him.

It was just a fairly straightforward suburban house. I would have expected him to live someplace a lot more magical. At that time, Phil was just starting to go out with the woman who became his wife, and he was a different kind of person in those days. The first couple of years that I knew him, there was a lot of partying, and I don't think he was a very happy guy then. After he and Jill settled down together and cleaned up their act and decided to start a family, they started remodeling the house. Now it's a really wonderful, homey house. We connected on a lot of levels, including sarcasm. He was happy to share his knowledge with somebody who was enthusiastic about it and who very clearly appreciated his work. I think it was one of those things where I didn't suck up to him about music, I had opinions about the music, and I had an understanding of how Grateful Dead music works that I wanted to improve, and our tastes were similar enough that, generally speaking, if he thought a concert was good, it was one that I understood was good too. I appreciated his criteria of excellence instead of just being a fan who just loved it all discriminately. I don't think it's possible to be in a relationship with someone who's a real hero without having a certain amount of undue respect. There are other people I know whose dealings with famous people are characterized by pretending they don't take them at all seriously, and dissing them repeatedly. I didn't want to do that. I just wanted to have a good, creative, intellectual relationship with people whose work meant a lot to me. And I did that over the years.

John Perry Barlow, 47, Dead lyricist/cyberspace pioneer, WY:

Bobby and I were bad boys, and we got sent away to the same special school for bad boys at the same time. It was just a prep school in Colorado Springs, Colorado, but they'd acquired some reputation as being able to deal with the smart and incorrigible, which both of us turned out to be. We were both fourteen, I was coming out of Wyoming, and he was coming out of the Peninsula, Atherton, where he was raised.

You run across people in your life where the second you see them, you know they're significant people, and you don't know why. I can't say that I knew my life had turned such a complete fork as it did on meeting Weir, but I can remember the first day of this English class we were both in, and hearing a thumping behind me. I couldn't figure out what it was, it would just go thump, thump, thump, thump, thump. I turned around and there was this gawky kid who had fairly thick, horn-rimmed glasses on, and the most sideways expression I had ever seen. His knee was going up and down at about 120 cycles, and his mouth was kind of hanging open, and he just . . . he did not look fully illuminated, but there was something about him. I just knew that he and I would have a lot to do with each other.

Bobby and I became pretty much immediately one another's best friend at Fountain Valley, and we were very tight, though I think we were forced into it to a certain extent by virtue of being the two singularly unpopular kids in that school. It was hard to tell which one of us was lower on the totem pole. Bobby was always playing music. He'd go into the bathroom where there was a large space lined with ceramic tiling, which would give an echo effect, and he'd sing and play his guitar all the time, and I'd go in and hang out with him and sometimes sing along with him. Music was basically something that Bobby was doing, and that I was participating in in a minor way, and I guess you could say, that's the way it's always been. I always did other things.

Anyway . . . we were tight that year, and at the end of that year, even Fountain Valley decided to give Bobby the boot—for sins that both of us had committed. We hadn't been caught at anything except together, but for some reason they took it out on Weir. They didn't kick me out, and I got indignant at the injustice that was being delivered to him by my not being expelled, so I quit. I was

Peace, love, and pine trees, Squaw Valley, 1991 (PHOTO BY TREY ALLEN)

gonna go to California and live with his family and go to this truly
wacky and also quite wonderful school that he went to next, which
was called Pacific High School. It was ultimately a real seed of the
Haight. A lot of the faculty there became fairly major figures in the
hippie scene shortly thereafter. It was real training camp for what
Bobby became. He came up and worked on my ranch that summer
and helped put up hay. The assumption was, during the time he was
there on the ranch, that we were gonna go to California together
at the end of the year. When it finally came down, I decided there
was something about going off to California and going to this truly
avant-garde kind of place—I just had a funny feeling about my own
ability to handle a complete lack of structure. And I also had a
funny feeling about quitting Fountain Valley. I decided that I was
maybe cutting and running in some sense. So when Bobby had to
go back to California at the end of May, I said goodbye thinking
that he and I were going to see each other in about ten days, and
that we were going to be living in the same room for the next year.
But somewhere in that ten days I changed my mind and I didn't
see Bobby again for three years.

Finally, the Dead came to New York in 1967, and I saw Bobby
again. I went down early to the hotel where they were staying.

There was Weir, and he had hair down to the small of his back. If he had a thousand-yard stare when I first met him, he had a thousand-light-year stare at this point. He was real quiet, much more quiet than he had been, and much more quiet than he is today. It was like the inside of his mind was turning so many revs that there was just nothing moving slow enough to attach on the outside. If it had attached at all, it would've been, "Blrrlrrrrll"! That was what I thought. Lord only knows what was really going on in there, but it was a foreign country to me. I mean, this was my old buddy, and it was like finding your old buddy has been reprogrammed by Moonies or something . . . but not bad. He was just real different. It was hard to tell what his reaction was to anything. His reactions were very abstract. He was also macrobiotic, so he was translucently thin and had that generally translucent macrobiotic I'm-starving-to-death look.

We were glad to see each other. On some level, our relationship never had anything to do with seeing things the same way, it was more something deeper that we felt connected by. Bobby and I went back and forth between having nothing in common and having a lot in common. We'd go into phase shifts on both sides where it would suddenly seem like were practically the same guy and you wouldn't be able to tell us apart on the phone. And then other times, the polarizing filter would move into a perpendicular condition and you couldn't see shit! I just kind of watched the polarizing filters turn around.

Then at about three in the morning, Bobby and I walked back to his hotel, which was on lower Broadway. We went through Washington Square Park. It was really abstract, dreamy, and Weir was in this state. It was like I'd fallen into his mind in some way. There'd always been a really open aperture there, and I had just kind of gotten myself in there. I was in the washing machine of Bobby's mind, bobbing rapidly in the suds!

It was a real hot, sticky night. Bobby had never seen New York before, so in addition to being amazed by the universe, which he so transparently is at all times, he's also amazed by New York! I am too to this day. New York has that thing that attaches itself to the mind of a hick kid. My mouth is still small and round, and my eyes are still big and round after all these years. They were definitely so that night. So . . . Bobby and I sat down underneath the Arch in Washington Square. We're sitting there, *trying* to have a conversation. It was like, "Well, then what happened?" For him to say what happened attaches itself to so much other stuff, it's like a little bit of thread hanging out on the sweater of the universe: you better not pull on it! It's not entirely working on any linear level, but we're kind of liking it anyway. Then, things got extremely linear.

A pale green Falcon came around the corner and came bumping up at the end of Fifth Avenue there, and it was like the car in the circus where all the clowns get out. Suddenly, there are about six or seven tough—I would say Irish—kids from Queens, judging by their accents. They're roaming the Village looking for some action. It goes on to this day, kids from New Jersey or wherever—bridge-and-tunnel people—and they all go in a pack because they're scared of New York. It was a band of those guys, and they're always kind of tricky. Weir doesn't get it at all, and I only mildly get it because, for one thing, I've been subdued by the gentle sloshing of Bobby's mental sphere. They're surrounding us, it's a clear attack posing: "Hey, you a boy or a girl?"—that kind of thing. They were mostly taunting Weir, but my hair was long too. They did the whole routine: "Why ya not in Vietnam? Ya know my brother's in Vietnam. He's about your age. Why ya not in Vietnam? You got somethin' against it? You don't like the war?"

You have to understand, in the context of that time, people who weren't alive then have no sense of the ugliness that was loose in American society. I actually at one point got served a skinned-out lamb's head, lying in a pool of blood, with the eyes still in it, in my own home state. The darkness was on both sides, but it was largely on theirs. They really were in an ugly frame. We weren't that pretty, but they were fucking ugly! They provided by their very presence an energy that was the strongest argument against testosterone I think I'd ever experienced. By this time, Weir and I had both stood up and were preparing to . . . I was just analyzing the situation looking for any options I hadn't previously considered.

Then Weir, out of the blue, came up with the last one that I would've considered; he said, "You know, I sense violence in you guys, and I get that sometimes. You know what I do when I feel that in myself? There's a song that I sing that helps." One of these guys yells, "Yeah? Like what song, hippie asshole?" And Bobby says, "Can you sing with me? It goes like this: 'Ha re ha re, ha re ha re, ha re rama . . .'" He launches into it, and I'm thinking, "Completely from left field. Could work. This might just be the ticket. I'm gonna go along with it." So I start to sing, and a couple of these other

Billy, Bobby, and Mickey playin' Shoreline, California, 1988 (PHOTO BY RICK BEGNEAUD)

guys are thinking, "Wouldn't it be fuckin' funny if we sang along with these freaks!" and they start to sing! They did! They were singing for a little bit. I'm thinking, "Amazing! Amazing! This is the last thing I'd have thought would work." And just at the moment I thought we had it licked, the alpha male of this little troupe suddenly realized that he'd been gulled. He came back around with that wild fury a guy gets when he sees red: "You guys are fuckin' with us!" Then they just pounced. They treated us like animals. We were down. We were all beat up and bloody. It was scary. I wasn't sure if they would kill us or not. I didn't know.

We just sort of staggered back to the hotel. It wasn't bad enough to go to the hospital, but we were both plenty sore the next day.

A while later, I was out in San Francisco and Bobby was sleeping in the central room at 710 Ashbury Street. Neal Cassady would be in there all night awake, throwing his hammer and doing bebop, and Weir would be on this couch in the center of the room with all of his worldly goods down at the end of the couch, often lying there with that look. It was like he was imagining Cassady, who was going a thousand miles an hour. He's making Cassady up; he's the dreamer. It was a wild scene.

A continuous sort of food-related and marijuana-related activity was always going on in the kitchen at 710. Weir was usually in there for long periods of time making this macrobiotic dish of brown paste that he would then eat very slowly. There was always stuff going on in there. It felt like the never-ending lunch.

I've gone on tour with the Dead. I road-managed them on their Fifteenth Anniversary Tour. I'd written a letter before this, sort of Moses come thundering down from the mountain. This was kind of at the height of a heavy drug period in their history. It was not a particularly pleasant phase, and I think if you look across the face of American rock—or entertainment for that matter—1980 was not a particularly attractive year. I was on tour with them at that point. It certainly gave me an opportunity to check my own morality. It was very difficult. It was made all the harder because we had the press on us like a cheap suit. I was dealing with road-managing the Grateful Dead from a cold start, and dealing with all that press as well. The whole thing. The band was very nice to deal with. They were real pussycats. It was difficult for me because I was trying to stay up and hang out with them and get up early in the morning to start making phone calls.

I remember one time Weir got in an automotive duel with somebody down in Mill Valley. We went back and forth: he cut us off, we cut him off . . . it was boys. Guys just get into that thing, "Well, you motherfucker," so we went back and forth and finally pulled over, and he stops, and we all had to get out and yell at each other. This guy looked at Weir real hard and he said, "Wait a second. Aren't you . . . aren't you the drummer for the Starship?" It completely took a lot out of the moment! Talk about going meta! It was really hard to keep track of the original dispute at that point.

With Jerry . . . he and I are in and out of phase. We have times where he's right there and it's really fun. We're not in phase at the moment. I've had lots of experiences with all those guys, and I have independent relationships with each of them.

Weir's little ranch was quite a place. It was goofy! There was a peacock that would attack you if you came out the door and it thought you hadn't seen it. It was bad enough that they had to keep a two-by-four by the door! The horses in the field across the road became rabid! It was a totally hippie kind of, sleeping-on-a-wet-mattress kind of scene. Weir had this Appaloosa hammerhead stud horse that he thought was quite a unit. The whole

place was very sweet in its way, it was kind of a hippie rustifica-
tion program.

Bill Cutler, 47, musician/producer, San Francisco:

$\mathbb{S}$ teven Barncard knew the Grateful Dead and this guy David
Rea, who was putting together a band for this CBS deal.
David wanted to be part of a band, so he was putting this
group Slewfoot together. Apparently Steven gave him a copy of my
tape with my tunes on it. David liked my voice and my tunes, and
he called me up for an audition, and when I got there, another guy
at the audition was Matthew Kelly—the great harmonica player
who'd played with T-Bone Walker, jammed with the Dead, and was
good friends with Weir.

We all hit it off, and we started playing together, and before we
knew it, we'd formed this band Slewfoot. We made this record with
him, some of it was already done, it had a lot of people on it,
Charles Lloyd, Keith Godchaux, tons of others, and I played on
some of the cuts. The band coalesced around the record. Bobby
Weir coproduced it, so that was my first actual meeting with anybody from the Grateful Dead. When I went in to do sessions, he
was the guy. I borrowed his acoustic guitar for the record because I
didn't even have a decent guitar! We were poor, my girlfriend, Judy,
and I. We were living in this little dump with about fourteen other
people. So Bobby took pity on me and loaned me his guitar and
gave me a few electric-guitar lessons, because I was making the transition from acoustic to electric guitar. And we made that record,
which is a great record. It's got so many good people on it, and
Steven Barncard worked on it. It was a wonderful experience.

I guess the first time I met Jerry was at the Matrix. One night I
went to see his very first solo band play—I think Merle Saunders
was in it. I went up to Jerry and I told him I was working on this
record with Bobby, and he said, "Hey. Cool man. What's up? Whad-
dya do?" We had this great little rap, talking about movies and stuff.
We just kind of hit it off. I never thought too much about that, and
then I didn't see him for a while.

Then when Clive Davis got fired from CBS, we had a lot of trouble, because we were kind of under his wing. We were all dropped

Yet another amazing stage design, Greek Theater, California, 1989 (PHOTO
BY RICK BEGNEAUD)

at one time as the new regime came in. Slewfoot just died, and it
left Matthew Kelly, Chris Herald, and myself all just sort of hanging there. So we decided to make a solo record for Matthew Kelly,
just to see what we could do by pulling all our friends together to
kill some time while we decided where we were all gonna go next.
It was a shock to just have this band fall apart. We made one of
the first records at the Record Plant up in Sausalito. Slewfoot was
done there. Matthew wanted to record some of the songs of mine
he'd heard on the original tapes that we didn't do in Slewfoot, but
had gotten me into Slewfoot, like "Riding High" and "Dangerous
Relations." And he and I wrote one together for Matthew called,
"That Good Old Harpoon Magic." He had other friends, like Dave
Torbert of the New Riders, and we all made this record together on
spec. It was a crazy thing that could never happen today. On my
tune, we decided to call up Jerry and Bobby and bring them in to
play on it, and they both said yes!

One day, I walk into the studio, at noon, and there's Jerry tun-
ing up! He's there right at the crack of noon! I walk in and it was
just the two of us. That's when we renewed our friendship. I said,
"Hey, we're incredibly happy to get you on this." And he said,

"Yeah, sure, man. What're the changes? Just show 'em to me." So I sat down, showed him the changes, and he remembered the tune in about five seconds. Then Bobby came in. The two of us played acoustic on it. This was about December of '73 or '75. I sang the lead vocal on it, but years later when it came out on Matt's record, Bobby rerecorded the lead vocal because they wanted Bobby's voice on it. Then we found Robby Hoddinott for those sessions, and that was the first recording he did with anybody from that scene. And we used the local engineers—whoever could make it that day.

The Record Plant, who'd given us all this spec time, were a little bit upset when they found out that our little low-budget project included Mike Bloomfield, Jerry Garcia, Nicky Hopkins, and Bobby Weir! But still, it really was Matthew's album. It sat on the shelf for ten years before anything happened with it. Ten years later, after Matthew had been in Bobby and the Midnights and Kingfish, and I'd been in millions of other bands, we went back and it got finished. I wasn't working on the second phase of it, but my tunes wound up on it when Relix put it out.

So that's how I got to know Jerry Garcia. When Kingfish formed, I wasn't really part of that because Bobby Weir was the lead singer and rhythm-guitar player, and that was the role I filled with those guys. So I started a band. I really wanted a band of my own at that point anyway, and called it Heroes. It had Pat Campbell on bass, who later became part of the Good Ol' Boys with Jerry Garcia, but had nothing to do with Jerry at the time; myself on lead vocals and rhythm guitar; Barry Flast, who later was a part of a lot of those bands and in fact wrote "One Night Stand" that Janis Joplin recorded; and Scotty Quick on lead guitar. Heroes played around from 1974 to 1978, with changes of personnel but the same heart. In 1975, I wanted to record that band. I went to a Jerry Garcia/Merle Saunders show at Keystone Berkeley and popped in backstage with Pat Campbell just to say hello. We were talking about our going into the studio to record some tracks, and Jerry leaned over and said, "Well, aren't I gonna get to play too?" I was like, "You wanna play on this?" He was already in three bands at the time, and he said, "Yeah. I wanna play." I said, "Well, will you rehearse?" because, you know, it's not easy to get the Grateful Dead to rehearse for anything. He said, "Sure! When's rehearsal?" I told him we were going to rehearse at my apartment! I mean, these guys are used to rehearsing in these giant rehearsal halls, but Jerry goes, "Okay." I told him it was on February 1. Never talked to him again, and sure enough, noon on February 1, the night after a gig that he played, up comes Jerry with his banjo and his guitar, up the stairs and into my apartment. We sat down and rehearsed. We had a lot of fun, smoked tons of sinsemilla, learned the tunes, and went in the next day and cut four songs, which I have the two inches for in my bedroom. They have never heard by anyone—not until last year or so, when I got this deal as part of this hip-hop group and David Gans asked me if I'd bring some of this recording with Jerry for his radio show, *The Grateful Dead Hour*. I recently transferred the tapes to fresh tape to preserve them. I'm not sure what I'm going to do with them. They sounded so good when I transferred them that I was thinking about finishing them and putting them out because everyone on those tapes is great. Austin Delone plays keyboards, who's now the guy who has the band for the Bammies every year and also played with Nick Lowe and Elvis Costello; Pat Campbell on bass; Caul Tassy is on drums, a great jazz drummer; I'm playing rhythm guitar and signing; Jerry's playing lead guitar; and Scotty Quick, our regular lead-guitar player at the time, is also playing guitar. The stuff is great. I haven't decided what to do with it because I want to keep it in the spirit of the way it was made then.

We went into Hyde Street Studios, we got spec time, and I popped in with this amazing aggregation of players—not just Jerry, all of them great—and we made these tapes. Somehow, I managed not to get a record deal. It's a miracle! I mean, it got shopped around here and there, but somehow it just didn't happen at the time. But Heroes went on to play quite a few gigs and eventually headlined the Castro Street Fair, and the very first Haight Street Fair in 1978. We had several different lead-guitar players through the years. One of them was a guy named Craig Paulson, who mysteriously died of liver cancer at the age of twenty-eight. Just a very sad thing. He was a great guitar player, it was not a drug-related thing, it was just a bad break. It was a horrible experience. We were on the road with him when he got sick, and we literally had to change the lighting onstage so he wouldn't look yellow. It was very tough, but we loved him, and we played out all our commitments. We had been scheduled to play at the first Haight Street Fair, which Rock Skully was the announcer for, Wavy Gravy, and all those kinds of people. In those days, the Haight Street Fair was right on the corner of Haight and Ashbury—it wasn't down at the end, and it was just humongous when they opened it up with the flatbed trucks and everything.

It was an incredibly exciting event because it was the revitalization of the Haight. Because our guitar player died just before this, and we didn't want to cancel, we had been playing some gigs as the opening act for the reformed Moby Grape, and Jerry Miller offered to step in, much like Jerry Garcia had.

I've been so lucky because at different times in my career some great musician has just shined a spotlight on me . . . this little punk from New York! Voom! Jerry Miller just said, "Hey, I want to play," and of course he refused to rehearse, but he's such a great guitar player. I had to get up in front of about ten thousand people with no rehearsal with the lead-guitar player. Talk about terror! Everybody else on the bill was some well-known star. We got up and played, and we just had an incredible time. Jerry Miller was unbelievable. He was brilliant. We did a song that really meant a lot to me called "Shine a Light" about some friends of ours who died of heroin, and Jerry played a very sensitive solo on it that I'll always remember. I didn't think I'd ever be able to hear any of that stuff, but strangely enough, a Hell's Angel had a cassette deck and was recording it in the street. Somehow the tape fell into my hands. Some Hell's Angel gave it to Karen, the girl who managed our band, and she gave it to me. It's very bad quality because the wind is blowing and it sounds like, "Kwoohwooowooo . . . ," with music in the background. But there it is, the entire set. There were tons of Angels there, and whenever they liked something, instead of clapping, they would rev their bikes! After every song, they're going, "Vrrrrmvrrrmvrrrrm!" It's a great tape. And Jerry Miller, it's the only time he ever played with me, and, boy, I really cherish that.

I went up to Mickey Hart's ranch in Novato for the recording of *Old and in the Way*, the album that Jerry did with my friend Pat Campbell from Heroes. I was invited to those sessions. Mickey had a studio in the barn. I remember Ron Rakow was at the time president of Grateful Dead Records. They were really radical; they had their own label, which was just unheard of. Ron Rakow would sleep on the couch behind me, and every time he heard something he liked, he'd sit up and say, "I like that. I like that," and he'd go back to sleep. Those were wonderful sessions because those guys were terrific. That's the record that became *Pistol Packin' Mama*.

I was a serious songwriter, and a good singer and all that, but it also was the times. People were not so suspicious of each other. Talent found talent all the time. And particularly Jerry. He always amazed me. He had the capacity to be interested in so many things simultaneously. I mean, we would sit and talk for two hours about the process of a blue screen, when special effects were first coming in. We're both big horror-movie/science-fiction freaks. We'd talk about little-known actors like Rondo Hatton, who made five movies in his whole career. Jerry would be the only other guy I'd know who'd be up at five in the morning watching it on the *Late Late Show*. Jerry's always had a tremendous interest in film, and Debbie Koons, the woman he married, is a filmmaker, who I knew way back then. In fact, she was hanging out in the scene. I remember her at the Santa Cruz gig. Those of us who were interested in film, we'd be like another little subculture among the Deadheads. We talked about film as much as we did music. I recall watching a set by Waylon Jennings when he opened for the Grateful Dead, and Jerry and me just sitting backstage fascinated watching him. Jerry and me, two fans of Waylon Jennings! I remember people kept coming up trying to talk to Jerry, and he'd say, "I'm trying to watch Waylon, man! That's Waylon Jennings." This is Jerry Garcia going, "That's Waylon Jennings!" Jerry's a huge star, so I thought, "I better watch this guy, see what's up." And Waylon was great. He was incredible. Jerry turned me on to Waylon Jennings.

Now I'm switching to a different time. This is 1975. February 1, the day before I went into Hyde Street Studios and cut with Jerry a bunch of my tunes. I did this several times with Jerry. One time, we rehearsed at my house. Another time, we rehearsed at Jim Renny's Studio, which was this little eight-track studio, subterranean, out on Judah Street where unknown people came to rehearse. Some of the rehearsal is on David Gans's *Grateful Dead Hour* radio show, some space jamming that's just wild.

We walk in, and I say to them, "I have somebody out in the street waiting for Jerry to direct him in." Jerry arrives with one of his roadies, who brought his little amp in. We're playing downstairs, we're totally secluded in this little downstairs studio. There's nobody around, and we play there for hours. My brother, John, who was becoming an engineer in those days and is now the Dead's soundman, was smart enough to capture the rehearsal on tape in the control room. We never realized he was recording with this little eight-track. We practiced all the tunes we were supposed to, and then we just had a blast jamming out for a long time.

When we were all done playing, we packed up and Jerry was going to have someone bring the car around. We open the door to the studio, and there's a crowd of people on the street that had rec-

Trey Allen (far right) and buddies at Niagara Falls, summer tour, 1990

(PHOTO BY DEADHEAD # 5,333)

ognized the sound of Jerry's guitar! They'd been listening for who knows how long! God knows what they heard: "Fuck you, man! I hate that song. Let's try it this way . . ." We were playing totally thoughtlessly, with absolutely no sense that anyone can hear us, or that these were performances that we'd want anyone to hear, and here's thirty people out in the street! I'll never forget that. It was such a strange thing. Somehow people going by on the street who didn't even know that was a recording studio were listening to a sound they thought might be the Grateful Dead. Jerry's guitar was so distinct that, even though we were doing my tunes, which didn't really sound like the Grateful Dead much, people knew it was him.

That's another thing about Jerry: people had this idea that he's an undisciplined musician. To some degree in the Grateful Dead that's part of what they do—they surprise each other. But when he played with me on any of my tunes—this includes the stuff we recorded at Hyde Street and on Matthew Kelly's record—Jerry always said to me, "Hey, man. What do you want me to play?" and I'd always be dumbfounded that he would say that. "Do you want me to do leads, chords . . .?" I'd say something like, "Okay, you do the first solo." Jerry's a great soloist and all, but his hidden talent to me is as a backup player. He's the greatest coloration player—in other words, just playing little rhythm chinks, backstrokes. He has great time, his innate sense of time is amazing. This is so important, and so many young musicians today don't have a great sense of time because they lean on a drum machine. But in those days, before you recorded everything to a click track, it always felt good if the musicians had good time. Jerry would always say to me, "Man, what's your big rush? Slow it down!" He likes those really slow tempos, and those are very hard to play. Those are much harder to play than fast songs. If you go see his band these days, they play things achingly slow, and then they keep it right there. It's so exciting because the audience is just dying to go faster, but the beat is just so solid.

Jerry taught me to play slow and in the pocket, and he'd play these beautiful backup parts that nobody could believe were Jerry. When I played tapes, people said, "Where's Jerry?" I'd say, "That is Jerry!" Later, when he plays his solo, they go, "Oh my God! It is Jerry," because it isn't till he solos that they recognize his guitar. What I learned from Jerry and Bobby, who's a great rhythm-guitar player, was the sense of how to back people up, how to be a team player, and actually just sit in the pocket with five other guys on a song you've only heard once. Letting the song breathe, giving it space. I learned all of that from Jerry and Bobby. I really did.

I always felt in my personal relationships with various people in that group that we were treated as equals. We always exchanged ideas and felt good about that.

My brother, John, started way back in 1971 with a company that build instruments the Grateful Dead had interest in. He worked with Ron Wickersham, who was one of the early sound engineers who designed things for them. Then he was with a company called Hard Truckers, who built speaker cabinets with Joe Winslow and some of the other guys who were in the crew. Little by little, he got involved. You might have to ask him, but I think he first started working officially for the Grateful Dead when they went to Egypt. He was the advance man. They sent him and he got all the amplifiers through customs and set up the situation, wired up the Pyramids and all that. I guess they were pretty happy with the work he did on that tour, because after that he became one of their guys. He did instrument repair for them, then later he did radio mixes for them because Healy always mixed the house, then he was an engineer on some of the records, like the one Gary Lyons produced, maybe *Go to Heaven*. Then, the first record he ever produced was *In the Dark*. He coproduced that with Jerry, and of course it went platinum in thirteen weeks, which was outrageous for the Grateful Dead, my brother, for everybody!

My brother and I got to know the Dead in a parallel way. He's got a thousand jobs with them.

Herbie Greene, 52, R&R photographer, San Francisco:

For the cover of *In the Dark*, they wanted me to take pictures of their eyes. The whole period was magical in that Garcia almost died but he didn't, hanging around Front Street and talking about failing eyesight and dental care because we're all getting pretty old. It was pretty funny! So I'm working on the portraits at the same time they're working on the album. I'd been taking photographs of them for years, but I didn't assume I could do an album cover for them. This was right around Mardi Gras time in '86 or '87, and while that was going on, they were also formulating the concert tour with Dylan. Bill Graham called me about doing a special picture for it and . . . I got to do that.

Backstage at the Henry J. Kaiser, during and after the shows, we did the pictures of the faces and the eyes, but it didn't work out at all because they wanted to mask out their eyes and just have their eyes sitting in there. It was horrible looking! The next day I did ghost-lighting on it and got them like that. In the meantime, Dylan was supposed to show up for any of the three nights, and of course he didn't show up until the last night, and we did the portraits. He didn't want to be there. The Dead were jumping up and down, and a crowd of people was standing behind me, yelling and screaming. It was a din! It was horrible! You know, you only have a couple of minutes to do these things, because it's all they're gonna sit for. But it all worked out. I did the placement, set up the background, set the chairs out, and shot it.

It was kind of exciting that we did the cover and the Dylan/Dead thing all in the little bit of space. The second night, we were doing more pictures for eyes. Bill Graham was there and we did his—he's the other eye in that album cover shot. So while I'm there doing this, Mickey walks up to me and says, "I want you to take a picture of this for me," and he had this mask on his face that had these

John Popper of Blues Traveler jammin' with Jerry at Bill Graham's Memorial, Golden Gate Park, San Francisco, November 3, 1991 (PHOTO BY DINO PERRUCCI)

collaged eyes. It was done by somebody he knew in some round-about way who'd never been to a Grateful Dead concert before and just kind of wandered in. The synchronicity of that was unbeliev-able because eyes were the theme. It was like this mask was made for it. It was grotesque!

They had recorded the basic tracks at the Marin Civic Center Au-ditorium . . . *in the dark.* So they called the record *In the Dark* and the whole thing had a sinister quality to it. I wanted them to call it *Out of the Dark.* But, at any rate it turned out that the portraits I'd been working on integrated beautifully into the whole concept because they had the black background, they were backlit, and the record-sleeve cover was on a white background. It was really pretty remark-able to me, the way the whole package looked. People either really loved it or hated it, particularly the eye mask. That caused a lot of tension inside the band. Some people really hated it, like the pro-ducer. He thought I was trying to pull something over on him, and in reality I wasn't. People were misinterpreting communication between me and the record company regarding color corrections . . . But anyway, after the whole thing was said and done, it was fantastic.

At the same time this is going on, everybody's gearing up for the Dylan concert. It was an exciting time. The band, of course, had no idea how successful *In the Dark* was going to be. The Dylan thing was taking the most interest. Actually, the best time I ever had in my life surrounding the Grateful Dead and being in the somewhat privileged position I enjoy with them was being able to go to all the Dylan/Dead rehearsals at Front Street Recording. That was remarkable. It went on for a couple of days and it was just plain terrific. I was listening to the rehearsal tapes the other day, and it shows me how good that band is because they were playing all that material unrehearsed and they were playing remarkably well. It was magic because everything worked, click, click, click.

Then, a little bit later, I got to do the Garcia on Broadway stuff for Bill Graham. That was great. My ex-wife worked for Bill Graham in the early days at the Avalon Ballroom, so I knew Bill reasonably well. He had his good points and his bad points, just like everybody else, but his bad was horrible, and his good was fantastic! Anyway, he called one day where I was working and said, "C'mon over. I wanna talk to you about this Garcia show on Broadway." We talked about some ideas of how to do the shot, but nothing specific. He spent at least an hour with me, which to me was like, "Gee, this guy really is paying attention to detail in a way that nobody else would." An hour of Bill's time was worth huge amounts of money, but he spent all this time talking about this Garcia poster in a Vegas sort of way. Then, as I was walking back to work, the magician and the guitar out of the hat dawned on me. And that's what we ended up doing. Then, of course, when the Jerry Garcia Band was at the Greek, backstage, we got two minutes to shoot it. I put Jerry in the clown suit, which I always love doing—putting people in clown suits, with the little cape and everything. I think Garcia was just having a very unpleasant time. But that was the thirty-second run. He did his setup, waited around an hour, and then they came in and sat there for the thirty seconds they give you. I'm not exaggerating the amount of time. You get no time.

I try to get along with everybody. I get along with the band members, the office people, and most of the crew all the time. Garcia is real easy to love. He's not hard. He's a great guy. I hate seeing him doing the stuff he's doing, but that's part of the game. I know Jerry pretty well. There's stuff between us, but we don't talk on the phone every day. I love talking to Mickey, he's always fun to talk to. He's very interesting. He's a fascinating man. I like Mickey a lot because I know him. He doesn't intimidate me at all. I'll say, "I'm listening, Mickey. I'm out there listening. You better not fuck up!" I like Kreutzmann a lot. I like them all a lot. Phil's sort of remote, which is kind of funny for me because I think we'd get along better than we do. And Bobby . . . I like talking to Bob. I'm an old-timer. Everybody knows my name. And we do business.

Ramblin' Jack Elliott, 62, folk musician, San Francisco via Brooklyn:

There was a birthday party for Bob Weir. Seems to me that it took place in a church on the road leading up to his house. I noticed a Cadillac there with Wyoming plates. It said, "Wyoming 1111," and then it had a bumper sticker that said, "East or West, Beef Is Best!" and I thought, "I'm gonna like this guy."

It turned out it was Bob's old friend John Barlow. So that's where I first met Barlow. He had the ever-present black silk scarf around his neck. I don't think he was wearing a cowboy hat, but he had boots. In fact, I've never known him to own a pair of shoes. I've never seen Barlow in anything but cowboy boots and Levi's, and some kind of plain, kind of striped cowboy work shirt. He's a handsome man, a character, with a daring personality. I guess this was around '71 or '72.

The first time I remember meeting Bobby was when Pigpen died. Their manager at that time was an Englishman named Sam Cutler, who was kind of a cockney from London. He spoke with a loud, broad cockney accent. He remembered me from England, and he claimed that I had sung at his birthday party when he was about thirteen years old. I don't remember meeting him in England or being at his birthday party, but he always announced it, every time he introduced me to people. He'd say, "Jack played at my thirteenth birthday pawty, my thirtieth birthday pawty, and my thirty-third birthday pawty." He used to think of me as like Gene Autrey, who'd come over from the United States with a guitar and a cowboy hat when he was a kid. But I don't remember this at all! He says it all the time, so I guess it's true. He always acted like I was his hero or something. I had a friendly relationship with all of those people; they treated me like I was one of them. I went to a lot of Dead concerts back in those times, but when I say a lot, it's not like a Deadhead. When a Deadhead says they've been to a lot of Dead concerts, it means that they've been to 380 concerts. I've been to maybe fifteen or twenty Dead concerts in my whole life.

So there was this birthday party for Sam Cutler. It was his thirtieth birthday, and I'm just meeting Cutler for the first time at this birthday party, which took place at Weir's house. It was also a wake for Pigpen, who'd just died. But then Bob told me this story. He said, "You know, Jack, we met before that party." I said, "Really? I don't know. I don't recall. When was it?" He said, "Well, I was about seventeen years old and someone had told me you had some marijuana for sale and you were playing in Berkeley. I went, and it was just after you'd finished playing." I said, "Oh, you didn't hear my show?" He said, "No, I didn't hear your show, but I was mainly interested in getting some pot from you. And you were putting your guitar away in the case, in the dressing room, and I walked in and said, 'I understand you have some pot for sale?' And you said you didn't have any." Which is very true because I've never sold pot in my life. I've smoked a lot of it, bought some, never sold it. So I said to Bobby, "Gee, that's pretty weird for anybody to even say that because I've never been known to be a salesman of marijuana. I'm a smoker, but I'm not in the business of selling it." He said, "Yeah. Well, you told me you didn't have any and so I left." So naturally I wouldn't remember something like that, I mean, it's not that great a story, but that is the true fact of how we first met. I don't remember it, but Bobby remembers meeting me because I was a name performer at that time and he was just some kid.

I used to stay with Bobby and his wife Franki. Franki had a band of her own. She was tired of living in the shadow of a rock star. She wanted to be a rock star in her own right because she's a Leo. Leo chicks! She played some gigs with me. I was a headline act because I was a name, and she didn't have any, she was just startin' out. She had for her band a couple of Canadian guys called James and the Goodbrothers. So I played a bunch of gigs all that summer with her and between gigs, I'd stay with her and Bobby.

We were a pretty close-knit family. I remember occasions where Bobby was good in the kitchen, and I always enjoyed whatever food they prepared for a party or whatever. I always wanted Bob to show me how you play an electrical guitar. This is of interest to guitar

Yahoo! Cal Expo, 1989 (PHOTO BY
STEVE EICHNER)

players perhaps. But he was never interested in playing his electrical guitar around the house. He preferred to play acoustic and jam with me on his Martin. So we would sit around on the floor and play songs together on Martin guitars. One song we did really well and we were both very fond of was an old Jelly Roll Morton song.

I've got some funny stories about Jerry too. I'm a big fan of Jerry's, but I've never been to Jerry's house, so I can't claim to be a real friend of his, but I love him. We're both Leos. We have the same birthday, August 1. I have a great craving and yearning to someday get to hang out with Jerry in a relaxed home situation and maybe play some. I jammed with him on guitar for about an hour once outdoors at a big party when his assistant married an American Indian guy. That was about five years ago.

Chris Flum, 28, "cool dude," Orinda, CA:

The closest I've ever come to Jerry was within a couple feet at the Ritz Carlton in New York City. With Ramrod. The conversation was something like, "Hey, Jerry. How'ya doin'? Congratulations on the Bammie." I'd been at the Bammies two nights before in San Francisco, and he'd won with David Grisman for Best Album or Best New Something Album. Jerry said, "Thank you. You're the first person that has said that to me."

Another time at a show at Shoreline, I was at the side of the stage, dancing around like the little fool that I am, right in front of the audience. There's dirt, gravel, and a little pickup truck came by carrying stuff up the hill behind the theater, kicking up dust . . . *everywhere*. Next thing I know, somebody grabs me by the back and jerks me. I turn around in a swinging motion, like, "What the fuck is going on here?" and I hit this guy's arms. At the same time I look up, and it's Bill Graham yelling at me because I'm kicking up dust.

At that point, I was totally paranoid, my face turned white, I was like, "Oh, shit!" Luckily, out of the corner of my eye I saw the pickup truck, and I said, "No. It wasn't me. It was that pickup right there." Bill looked over at the pickup and saw it kicking up dust. He grabbed my pass, yanked it, tried to rip it off my neck, and said, "How did you get this?" and he saw Bob Barsotti's name on it and said, "So, you're a friend of Bob's?" I said, "Friend of the Barsottis. Yeah." After he realized it was the truck making all the dust, he kind of knew it was his mistake and introduced himself to me and said, "I want you to meet my son," and took me over to introduce me to David. That was my first meeting with Bill and David Graham, all in one shot.

Stanley Mouse, 55, poster artist extraordinaire, Sonoma, CA:

In 1967, Pigpen and I both had motorcycles. My studio was located in one of the Dead houses on Ashbury Street. He would come by and say, "Let's go riding." He had a bigger bike, and I had a Bultaco dirt bike, so I had quite a time keeping up with him. We didn't talk much; we just rode. I like Pigpen. He gave the band a real gritty sound. Me being from Motown, I liked that.

I haven't seen Jerry for a long time. I saw Bobby at a party in Mill Valley in '94. Last year, Phil's kid went to the same school as my daughters did, and I saw him at one of the gatherings there. He certainly was nice and happy. I've talked with Mickey lately, and I'm doing some projects with Bill's daughter, Stacey. The Grateful Dead, the guys in the band, they are all great guys. They were instrumental in saving my life. For that I do greatly respect them, and I think that the Deadheads will inherit the Earth.

Tom Constanten, 51, pianist/composer, San Francisco:

On tour one time, way back when, American Airlines lost my suitcase. Bless their hearts, they did find it and delivered it to our hotel, Gramercy Park. However, the night I had to go without my clothes, Bob Weir and I went to the East

Village to find clothes. Shopping. It was the hippie-heaven cloth-
ing renaissance. I found a lot of things. I still have a shirt from that
period. It was a good thing too because that night a blizzard hit!

This was around the time we did the Fillmore East and I met
Janis Joplin. It was amazing. She had this reputation, rather well-
deserved, of being "toothy" when she needed to be. Sharp-tongued
and explaining what she didn't like about a certain situation . . .
like when one of her musicians got dosed.

I think Jonathon, our road manager at the time, introduced me
to her. She had the most gentle handshake. It was like lace, hanging. She was totally gentle, sweet, and wonderful. Pigpen's line
about Janis was, "I had my chance." They were kindred spirits in a
manner of speaking, though I think they might have been more like
brother and sister. Pigpen was wonderful. We were roommates on
the road. We lived in a house together in Novato as well. He and
I were probably as close as two heterosexual males can be.

I think the first time I met Billy was in 1962 or 1963. There was
a party at the Chateaux, 838 Santa Cruz Avenue, in Menlo Park.
Which might also be when I first met Garcia. I was in the kitchen
with Phil, his friend Johnny DeCamp Winter, and Lee Adams, who
was the resident African-American guru. And this guy, later identified to me as "Bill," stuck his head in the door and said, "Where's
the head?" And Lee Adams said, "Which one?" because we were all
heads! Jerry sort of recovered and said, "Oh, let's see. There's an upstairs one and a downstairs one . . ."

Bill is probably the one member in the band who I had the least
amount of overlap with, in terms of connections. Although, what
there was of an overlap was fine. I remember him inviting me to
his houseboat in Sausalito one time. We listened to Vivaldi and
Bach and had a great evening talking about what there was about
the music we'd found. What worked, what was attractive . . . There
was another time we were at his place, which was near where I lived
with Pigpen on Seventeenth Street in San Francisco. We smoked
a little something, which I haven't seen since then—we put on the
radio, and it was John Cage. The music just tore it out of those
speakers. Everything else sounded just like a continuation of it. A
nice John Cage moment.

One time after we'd just come off from the road, a DJ I knew at
KTIM woke me up on the phone with the news that Pigpen had
passed on. It was 1973. He was twenty-six. I was not quite awake yet,
and my first thought was—because I'd seen him there days before

when I went to visit him in Corte Madera—my first thought was, "Wow! What an experience! I'll have to call him to ask him what it was like when I see him!" Because that's the sort of stuff he and I would share. There were signs he was on his way out, but they're the kind of signs you probably can't read until you're in your forties or fifties because you haven't seen enough examples of them. He was a fully developed individual. Wonderful man. No one suspected he was going to die.

I've roomed with Bobby a couple of times too. He, Pigpen, and I were the three that were not druggies at a certain particular stretch of time. I had my phases! Bobby was very much into macrobiotics. Of course, according to him, beer and popcorn are macrobiotic!

Bob Rupe, 38, Cracker bassist, Richmond, VA:

The Grateful Dead, obviously, were not hanging out backstage with us when we opened for them. But it was kind of funny: the Dead were all on the side of the stage after we'd finished playing, and they have one of those portable toilets up there for the crew. As we're coming around this corner where these amps and stuff are stacked, the door opens and almost hits us. It's Jerry Garcia coming out! Right? He's halfway out the door and he looks at us and says, "Oh. Hello." And we go, "Hey! Howya doin'!" And he says, "Oh. I'm Jerry," and we're all shaking his hand, and I'm thinking, "You know, there's no sink in that thing, and I'm shaking Jerry Garcia's hand." I can't remember if I was the first guy to shake his hand, you know, so who knows! It was definitely an unusual place to meet him.

Later I caught up with Phil Lesh on one of the drum breakdowns. I saw this thing on television a couple years ago about this charity organization the Dead founded called the REX Foundation, and I didn't even know it existed, so I just asked Phil a couple of questions about it, where I could get some recordings of the material that they're making available through REX. He turned me on to where to hook up through Grateful Dead Productions and who to speak to. He was very helpful, and I think he was also very interested that somebody was asking him about it, because at a Dead show, it's probably not the place where a lot of people would inquire about the REX Foundation.

I didn't make any confessions like, "Hey, man! This is my first show, and wow!" or anything like that. They're just people after all, even though there *are* stuffed dolls of Jerry Garcia available for sale at Woodstock!

Ricky Begneaud, 37, Cajun chef/caterer, Mill Valley, CA:

In the beginning of 1986, I moved to Mill Valley. I was just starting to get my "Louisiana home cooking" catering business together. I was living by myself, and I remember I called a friend of mine in Fort Worth and told him Jorma was playing. He said, "Jorma? You better go!" And I said, "Ah, I don't know. I've never seen Jorma before." He said, "No. You should go."

So, I ended up going to the show, at the Sweetwater in Mill Valley. When I went in, I stood up on my toes and peeked over the crowd because everybody was standing up in front of the stage. I looked over and there was Bobby Weir doing the same thing— standing on his toes, peeking over the crowd. I thought, "Wow. That's interesting," because at this time I was a full-blown Dead-head and it was a pretty cool thing for me to see Weir standing there next to me. I didn't expect it.

Later, there was a break, and I went outside. Weir and I almost bumped into each other as we were leaving. He walked out, he was by himself, and I thought, "Hmm. Okay. I'll say something to him." So I introduced myself and I said, "Do you like Cajun food?" He said, "I love Cajun food." I said, "Well. that's what I do. I cater, I cook Cajun food. If you ever want some Cajun food cooked, I'd love to do it." He asked me for my card, and I started patting myself down looking for it. Of course, I didn't have a card on me! So I told him I'd go to my car and get him one. He said, "Fine. Give it to me later." So I go to my car and I'm thinking to myself, "I don't believe this! I didn't have my card." Anyway, I give one to him later, he sticks it inside his coat pocket, and I'm thinkin', "That's gonna probably be there for winters and winters. He'll never see that card again."

The next afternoon, I get a phone call from Weir! He said, "I'm having this party for Joseph Campbell up at my place. Do you think you can do it?" I said, "Yeah. I think I can do it." He asked me to come up, look at his place, and figure it all out. He gave me direc-

Bill Graham wheelin' it at Cal Expo, 1989 (PHOTO BY STEVE EICHNER)

tions, I hung up the phone, and I thought, "I'm going where? Okay. I'm going up to Weir's house? Why am I goin' again? This is happenin' too fast." All of a sudden, I'm in my car and I'm drivin' up to Weir's. It was one of those rainy, misty days. I'll never forget it. I drove up this big, steep driveway, and I see Weir wavin' from inside this big glass door.

I went in, met his sister Wendy and her friend Joe, and we proceeded to talk about what they wanted from the party. We had some tea, hung out, and we all hit it off. I don't know how it came up, but I remember one thing Weir tellin' me that day. We were talkin' about redwoods, and he said, "You know, redwoods aren't a tree. They're a fern." He's always full of those little tidbits of information.

Around this same time, there was a Valentine's Day–Mardi Gras Grateful Dead run at the Oakland Coliseum. I had a pass, so I went backstage before the first show. I was sitting there drinking a beer, and I remember my friend Lou Tambakos coming up to me and saying, "What're you doin' back here?" And I said, "Drinkin' a beer." He said, "How'd you get back?" I said, "Weir invited me." He said, "You talked to this guy?" I said, "Yeah." He said, "God! You know him better than I do!" I said, "Well, I don't really know him. I just met him."

Anyway, I did Bobby's party, and it was really good. I was excited, but I was pretty subtle about the whole thing. I definitely was nervous. There were about thirty people. I did a big venison roast, which I'd had in my freezer. If I'm not mistaken, we also did a big crawfish étouffée— a really rich, beautiful golden sauce, served over rice. It was really fun. I met a lot of great folks, and Weir and I hit if off. I remember the most embarrassing point of the night: Weir stood up and said, "It's time for dinner. And now, here's the chef, Rick. He's going to tell you all about it." All of a sudden, I got flipped onto the stage! Oh! You don't know! I mean, there I am, in front of almost everyone in the Dead.

I remember the first thing I said to Garcia. I was steaming some boudin, which is Cajun sausage stuffed with pork and rice. Garcia said, "What is that?" I said, "It's boudin," and I lifted one up to show him. He says, "You mean, people eat that stuff?" I said, "Well, *my* people eat that stuff!" He was definitely thrown back, like, what the hell is that shit!

My parents taught me how to cook mostly, and our old black maid, Rita Malveaux. The creativity on top of all that came from my Uncle, Robert Rauschenberg. He taught me that you can just have fun and use ingredients you want. And when you're a chef, you get to go places! Everybody eats, and if you weren't a chef, you probably wouldn't get to go in these places.

Anyway, the meal that night went really well. It was amazing meeting Joseph Campbell. I'd sort of pass in and out of conversations because I was picking up plates and glasses and making sure the food was happening, and all that. I did it by myself. A few of the women there helped me put the food out, clean up, and all that. But as far as the cookin' went, I did it myself. I don't think they'd ever had food that tasted like that. My theory is to season the seasoning before I season it. Lotsa flavor!

After that night, Bobby would call me up and say, "We're rehearsing down at Front Street. You wanna come up and cook?" I'd bring the barbecue pit, or I'd cook a big pot of jambalaya. I remember I got to cook when Dylan was rehearsin' up there. I cooked all this stuff, he walked over to this big spread of food, looked at everything for a minute, dressed in totally black leather. He looked at everything, grabbed a strawberry, ate it, and walked out!

I cooked up at Front Street for a long time. It was hassle free, and cooking is such a social thing. The fire is goin', everybody wanders out by the barbecue, conversations pop up. There's something magical about it, the original campfire thing. I had a lot of fun cooking there. I got to know some great folks. It was one of those things where you just wanna have fun and you want everybody else to have fun around you. I think it's really wantin' to make it fun for everybody, and I think maybe along the wake of that, people caught on that I was all right and that I just wanted to have fun.

That whole scene in Front Street was incredible. I feel lucky. Once you're in, man, it's like the boys' club up there! Words are flying, jokes are flying. It all just happened, really. I didn't plan it this way.

Ever since I met Weir, we've hung out quite a bit.

One summer, Weir went to Colorado and he really got into mountain-bike riding. He came back and bought a brand-new, red mountain bike. I had one already, so one day we were out teaching each other to ride. It's hard riding a mountain bike, it's a lot different than riding on the street.

We're riding, we get halfway up this huge hill on Mt. Tamalpais, and he wants to switch bikes. So we switch bikes. Well, Weir's smaller than me, so I'm riding and it feels like my legs are having to go twice as fast because the seat on the bike is lower. He's also in much better shape than me because he runs all the time. So he hauls ass up to the top of the mountain. He gets all the way up to the top, and I don't even see him. Finally, I spot him way up there, waving his hand. So I get off his bike and I walk up to the top, and he's laughing because on the side of my bike it says, "Sport"! He says, "Look at that! 'Sport'! I love that!" I was wiped out, I was so tired. We hung out a little while, then decided to go down. We got back on our own bikes and started going down. Down is the pleasure, the payoff for the hard work chugging all the way up. You get to coast all the way down.

We were brand-new at this, so we really didn't know how dangerous we were being or how fast we were going. We made it down the fire trail, but then, just above this house, we came onto pavement. We were zipping down, going really fast! I said, "Hey, we should slow down. We're going too fast" Weir said, "You're right. We should slow down." Within the next five seconds, there was a deep manhole cover in the middle of the road. Bobby hit it, and he went over the handlebars. He was on the ground, I slammed on my brakes, I fly off, my bicycle lands on top of him, and then we both flew further. So, about fifteen feet and a lot of scratches later, he looked up at me and asked, "Are you okay?" I said, "I'm okay. Are you okay?" He said, "I think so." I looked at his shoulder and there was a three-inch separation—his shoulder was totally separated and broken. I said, "I don't know how okay you are right now . . ."

I ran down to his house, which wasn't too far, got his girlfriend, got in the car, went back up, and Weir was walking the bikes down the hill. All the wheels were warbled, everything was messed up. I mean, I landed *right* on him! Later, I got the reputation as the guy who broke Weir's collarbone! My stand on that was that Weir was, and still is, totally capable of breaking his own arm without any help from me!

16

Getting It

Cree McCree, 47, writer, New York:

I'm not gonna rearrange my life to go on Dead tour, but I understand what it's like to be inside the Dead's head, and I like it in there, inside all those cranial crevices of multisensory perception. But what matters to me most, as always, is that the music reaches me. Deeply. And the Grateful Dead reach me. Deeply. Period, the end.

Marilyn Welch, 35, artist/photographer, San Francisco:

For me, attending shows is a strengthening, esteem-building, wonderful sharing, encouraging time, which, as time goes by, strengthens my long-term pursuits as an artist. Everybody seems to connect, to encourage the creativity—a validating experience. The subconscious creativity propels many of us. It is this building, this shared strengthening of all our self-esteems, that is the primary interest to me in the Grateful Dead. The power of creativity to heal. To unleash and nourish art. A healing rejuvenation.

Dan Wilson, 49, street artist, Sacramento, CA:

I'll never, ever get the Grateful Dead out of me because they were pretty much a chord that struck me as being something very familiar inside myself. I love their music. I always did. I'll be going to see them again, there's no doubt about that. That's the thing about them: I don't notice a hell of a lot of difference from when I first saw them. I mean, they're really sophisticated now, they can play the shit out of anything. But they were *always* great. They always had that edge that's just a little bit rough, and I really love that. I don't see much of a change that way. I go because I know what I'm gonna hear.

I saw them every time I could for four or five years way back there in the sixties. I probably haven't seen them much more than a dozen times, but every time I have, it's been a peak performance on both ends: theirs and mine!

Steve Brown, 50, filmmaker/Dead's aid-de-campe (1972–77), San Francisco:

Working for the Grateful Dead was one of the better boot camps for being able to deal with reality in a world that's a lot stranger than the reality at the heart of the Grateful Dead. The real world is weirder. To survive being a part of the whole Dead organization gives you a stronger base to deal with a lot of other things.

What it's done for me is kept me interested in alternative styles of living—how I live, what kind of work I do. When you have the experience of working with the Dead, you see what kind of creative envelope you can push as far as the types of work you can do because the Dead are their own thing. Though they have to use some of the same infrastructure as commercial organizations, it's their own personality and attitude in how they deal with things that makes them interesting.

I felt I was a part of the alternative army of workers in this country, as Americans . . . you know, the *real* American spirit. It's something revolutionary, something different than what your forefathers before you did, that it is in fact a new way of doing things. There's a real satisfaction knowing that you cannot only do it that way and

(l to r): Bobby, Shannon O'Leary, John Perry Barlow, the night Bobby disguised himself and checked out the parking-lot scene, Laguna Seca, California, 1988 (PHOTO BY RICK BEGNEAUD)

make it work, but that you can adopt some of the ideas and attitudes that come from it, and help other things evolve by spreading that kind of information, feeling, and attitude to other people in their particular endeavors.

As a teacher, I met students who are looking for an alternative version of the world that their parents had. With their ideas and dreams, kids are on the cusp of entering an evolved world. It's the same kind of thing as with the Dead. It's that edge. It's being out there with a different way of doing things.

With the Grateful Dead, whether or not the experimenting works isn't the thing. The thing is that they're experimenting. *That's* the whole beauty. Out here on the western edge, that tends to be the mentality and motif behind everything. It's a willingness to try out anything: do it your way. Whatever it is, to get the job done, to do it and make sure you're happy doing it. Go for it. It's challenging because a lot of freedom is the hardest palette to work with sometimes. If someone says, "Okay, you've got black, white, and red to work with and that's it," that's manageable. But if someone says, "Well, here's a zillion colors, do it your own way," sometimes the decision thing is hard.

The Dead let people experiment within their own infrastructure and create their own jobs and do their jobs any way they see fit. That kind of approach and consciousness has always been with the band. They're an experimenting entity of ever-evolving ideas.

Caryn Shalita, mid-20s, actress, Los Angeles:

I t's about sharing, giving, respecting your fellow humans, animals, everything. Being a Deadhead isn't about just being into the Dead. You can't just put on a tie-dye shirt and go to a Dead show and consider yourself a Deadhead. It's not even necessarily about the music, it's about a way of living. The music adds to that and helps lead to that freedom, but it goes beyond the music and even beyond the band itself.

Seeing my first show on the East Coast, then seeing West Coast shows since then, the crowds are even more unbelievable out here! It's totally different seeing the Dead in California, maybe because the band feels like they're home. At Bay Area shows, pretty much everyone is always kind. I never feel like I need any kind of protection. The Bay Area is made up of a lot of Deadheads whether they go to see the shows or not. I don't why, but there's a larger concentration in that area of the country of people who want to live a harmonious and kind life.

Of course, there *are* those shows where things go wrong with people and the music. But there's always something that brings me back. It might just be that I'm an idealist, but there's always gonna be somebody nice around me who does something kind to balance out anybody who does something rude or mean. There's definitely been times where I've been more excited about the music than other times, but there's always that feeling of just being around people who all really want to be there.

That's one of the wonderful things about a Dead show: it's not just the music and it's not just about getting dumb, either. It's hard to explain, but there's really a warm, beautiful feeling that goes on between the people. So even though I missed the music, I feel like I was there and still part of this wonderful friendship. I really do enjoy it. It's an inspiration, without a doubt. And it has touched my life in so many ways—outside of the shows too. Sometimes in conversations with friends we'll talk in a line from a song. Or if some inane thing comes up one night, we'll give it a name, like, "designated bummer" (laughs). We just toss that kind of stuff around in conversation, and it's stuff that came out of the Dead experience, and then it flows into our daily lives.

Paul Perme, aka Trinket Guy, 31, Gila Monsters harmonicist, KY:

The Dead are the grandfathers—I hate to use that term—but they're the grandfathers of that extended, experimental, improvisational jam thing. I don't wanna compare or have anybody think that my band is anything like the Grateful Dead, but they kind of started that cruise-off-and-do-it-right-in-front-of-everybody thing. Don't hold back. Pretension is thrown out the window. If they make a mistake, they make it with everybody there with them, therefore *there is no mistake.* That's what's cool about it. And it's cool that they've helped teach other bands that. I can't believe the way people freak out that Jerry changed his shirt, like, "Jerry wore a red shirt in Vegas! He's always worn a brown shirt." Some of that stuff is mind-blowing to me, the phenomenon thing.

The Grateful Dead have really opened my mind to different kinds of music because they touch on every kind. You'll see them play with the great jazz cats, the rock and rollers, African players . . . they touch every aspect of music. Every band that I listen to seems to be a little bit connected to them in some way. They'd be lying if they said they weren't. I mean, even the Rolling Stones probably respect the Dead. Jerry is like Grandpa to a lot of people. The Dead just do it. They don't seem like they're doing it out there for anything else except for the love of doing it.

If I could say something to them? Keep on goin'! Keep on truckin'. I love to see their shows. I hope they don't stop, and when they decide that it is that time, there's a lot of bands who are just gonna keep up their tradition and keep on rollin' and make it fun to go see a show. That's what it is: it's a *show.*

Stuart Wax, 37, music manager, Los Angeles:

I think the Grateful Dead are blessed that they can affect so many people. I remember a show in Maryland and they pulled out "Lucy in the Sky with Diamonds" for the first time as an encore, and everybody just started hugging each other. It was like New Year's Eve. People all over were just hugging each other. It was so beautiful. They're the only band in the world that can really make so many people open up their hearts. It's always the most wonderful thing. Other bands can pull out a song or whatever, but the Dead do something, I mean, when they play, people just *smile!* That's such a gift, to bring so much light into the world. I'm sure a lot of people don't look at it that way, but it's really true.

Unfortunately, the scene can either be looked at through the light or through the dark, and hopefully if enough people see it

Catie Broomhead (middle) with her daughter, Celine (left), and Rachel Clein (PHOTO BY MICHELLE CLEIN)

through the light, then it's a light scene. I've been seeing it that way for over twenty years. When I see a Dead bumper sticker on a car, I really feel like it's family. No other band in the world has that. There's a real kinship in the Jewish world, so I'm covered from all over, because if it's not a Jewish connection, it's a Dead connection! I had a yarmulke with a rose and it said Grateful Dead on it. It's great, because either Deadheads or Jewish people would pick me up and take me home with them, all over the world! That's the greatest thing: I always know that I'm safe. Bill Graham once said that going to a Dead show is like going to the *shvitz*—a steam room for men—because you know nobody in there wants to hurt you. They just want to enjoy the pleasure.

In 1986, I was at a cabala weekend, a *chabad*, studying about mysticism. I had a bottle of vodka and nitrous, and I said, "Who wants to catch a buzz in honor of the Sabbath?" And this guy, Joel Siegel, said, "Wow, I feel like I'm at a Dead show." And we've been best friends ever since. We've been to Russia twice together and have gone through so much.

I'm happy to share all of this because, to me, it's all positive. I mean, the band gets millions of different ideas from different people, and everyone thinks that their idea is the best idea for the Grateful Dead. *I* even get hundreds of proposals just because people think *I'm* connected to the Dead, but my only connection really is my love for them, and my love for what I think they represent in the world. I just hope that they don't lose what they give over to people.

There was this chabad—Jewish outreach group—in Vegas, and the rabbi went to meet with some guy about funding, money for programming—charity. And the guy gave the rabbi a big check. Afterwards, somebody asked the guy how the meeting with the rabbi went, and the guy said he gave the rabbi a big check because he was wearing a Jerry Garcia tie. The rabbi had no idea. It's wild. The Dead don't have a clue about this stuff.

I have forty or fifty people over to my house every weekend for Sabbath, and there are usually twenty or more Deadheads. Especially Grateful Dead Sabbath, the weekend of the seventeenth, people come in from out of town for the shows too, and there's a connection with these people that's an instant bond. With men, with women, with everything—there are no barriers. Once you know you're a Deadhead, you're right in there. You're buddies. You're catching up on old times, and you start talking about, "Oh, yeah, wasn't Boston '77 wonderful!" Some other people are sitting there saying, "What are you talking about?" I always try to explain it: "Look, if you had a favorite club that was only open fifty times a year, but it was your favorite club, wouldn't you want to go hang out at that club as much as you could?" Or if you were a scuba diver, and you got the opportunity to go scuba diving, you'd go. And that's what a Dead show is. It's the family, it's the friends, it's the music. And to me, especially, it's the smiles on the people's faces, the open hearts.

I represent a lot of songwriters. I have cuts on Patti LaBelle and Chaka Khan—all these R & B people. The funny thing is, I only listen to the Grateful Dead!

Gina, 31, Blues Traveler's personal assistant, New York:

I still consider myself a Deadhead. I *love* the Grateful Dead! I'll put on a tape and it's just . . . home. I still think they're a very spiritual band. I remember a personal revelation I had at one of their shows in Hampton, Virginia. I think it was 1987. It was the first time they played "To Lay Me Down" in many, many, many years. It's a beautiful song. I had worked my way up almost to the front of the stage, about fifteen rows back, and I was in a big group of people who all knew each other. I was alone. I'd lost my friends, but I thought, "Fuck it. I'm gonna stand here. I'm not gonna look for them anymore. I'm just gonna enjoy the rest of the show." A lot of good herb was going round, so I thought, "I'm gonna stick right here! This is a good spot!" I felt comfortable.

Right then the Dead started playing "To Lay Me Down," and out of the corner of my eye I saw this huge motorcycle man—he looked like a Hell's Angel—tough, like if you saw him in a dark alley, you'd freak the fuck out! A scary guy, right? And when they went into this song, he looked up toward the sky, eyes closed, and these tears just came rolling down his face. He's sobbing, and I'm watching him, and all these people around me are on their knees. Everyone was just freaking out. The spirit just came out of Jerry into everyone. And for me, it was one of the most amazing experiences I've ever had at a Dead show . . . watching this biker guy with these tears rolling down his face and singing along with the song with his eyes closed, looking up toward the sky.

After the song ended, he turned to me and handed me a joint of really good herb. I took a hit and handed it back to him. He said, "Sister, give me a hug." And I gave him this big huge hug. He said, "Wasn't that the most beautiful thing you ever heard in your life?" And these tears were rolling down his face. To me, it couldn't get any better than that. The song is about dying, surrendering, something like, "To lay me down, if I could be with you one more time, my darling, to lay me down." It's a beautiful song. After the show, I told people about this biker guy crying, and they said, "Don't you realize they haven't played 'To Lay Me Down' in about ten years!" That made it even more amazing. He was all alone, and I was all alone, but I didn't think he saw me watching him. His eyes were closed the whole time, and he just turned to me directly from behind, looked at me, and handed me a joint. It was really wild. A cool moment.

The Grateful Dead made me realize that music could be spiritual and that you can find good in the people around you. That you can open up and not get hurt. And that life can be fun, even when things are down, if you smile and let yourself have fun. I also think they helped me realize that it's okay to love music so much to make it a part of your life. It *is* my life! It's what I do for a living, it's what I do for a hobby.

Chris Flum, 28, "cool dude," Orinda, CA:

I remember one time after a Dead show in New York City, I walked into this bar in the Village and I looked over and this girl looked at me. She was a total babe, incredibly gorgeous. I

Deadettes, Philadelphia, 1986 (PHOTO BY STEVE EICHNER)

said, "What the hell are you looking at?" and she said, "Somebody from Berkeley, California." I said, "What! How did you know that?" There was no way anybody could've ever known I was from Berkeley just by looking at me. I was wearing fairly normal clothes. She said, "I just sensed that you're from Berkeley and that you're a Deadhead." I looked in the mirror to see if anything I had on said "Grateful Dead." Nothing! No tie-dye. I mean, I've been cut up many a times at Dead shows—"Go away, preppie"—because I don't fit the Deadhead image. I couldn't figure out how this girl picked me.

Next thing I know, I'm taking her to the Dead show the next day, and I took her to four Dead shows that week, all at Madison Square Garden. To this day, she's my best friend, and whenever I go to Dead shows when I'm in her neck of the woods or she's in mine, we hang out together.

The Grateful Dead are a great way to meet chicks! "Totally dude!" The best people in the world are Deadheads. Some of the coolest girls in the world are Deadheads, and some of the most gorgeous girls in the world are Deadheads. The most natural, the coolest girls are Deadheads. Plain and simple.

I relate the Grateful Dead thing to northern California. I know it's a worldwide thing, being a Deadhead, but Deadheads are more casual and they're out there to help people, they're always willing to go out of their way, and I relate that to northern California, the way people are to each other. You go down to Los Angeles, people are jerks. They'll be your best friend, but they'll stab you in the back two seconds later. Deadheads tend not to do that. They're nice people. They're happy people.

Would I call myself a Deadhead? That's a good question. I don't know if I could say I'm a Deadhead due to the fact that I don't traditionally run out wearing tie-dyes and I'm not obsessed with the whole thing. I suppose I am, but I hardly own any Grateful Dead tapes. God, I wish I had tons of their music! If I could have tapes of all the shows I've been to, I'd be the happiest camper in the world.

Tom Constanten, 51, pianist/composer, San Francisco:

Back in the sixties, there was a great sense of community, and I think a lot of the energy and the steam, the wind in the sails, of the Grateful Dead phenomenon is from that community: Moby Grape, Charlatans, Big Brother—all of them. They all have their major mismanagement stories. But somehow, grandiose mismanagement didn't sink the Grateful Dead. Maybe because they couldn't do anything but hang together. They had no alternative. Sometimes that can be your saving grace.

It's a bit like when I first started getting comfortable speaking German and Italian. I think what saved me is that there was nobody around who spoke English. It was, "You better find out right now what you've got to say." Once you get that, then you can relax. Taking the step that you're sure you can't. Of course, we fall flat on our faces sometimes! What doesn't kill you makes you stronger . . . all that stuff.

Richard Yaker, 27, futurist engineer/visionary, New York:

Because I was living in the Bay Area, I started reading a lot about hallucinogenics, the whole acid-test era, Kesey, and all that. I was really into that whole scene. I'm not a very verbal person, I'm very math/science oriented, and what I noticed when I read these books and started listening to the Dead's lyrics is that they were all verbalizing things, ideas, and concepts that had run through my head. I thought, "Wow, I've known this my whole life but I never put it into words." They were into various concepts of reality and how the world works. At that point, I liked the Dead's music, but I went more for the *whole* experience . . . the scene thing. As time went on, I got more and more into music, and into *the* music. I don't really remember which Dead show it was, but it hit me: "Wow. *Now* I get it. *Now* the music makes sense to me."

My very first California Dead show, they played "Estimated Prophet," which is all about California. That same show, I had yet to see them do "The Wait" as an encore, and I thought, "Tonight's the night," and then it happened! I kept saying to myself, "Oh, I'm just high. If I was tripping right now, this would've been a religious experience." There are points in the Dead's playing where all of a sudden I think, "Oh, yeah! *That's* what song they're playing!" They just go off somewhere in outer space and then they bring it back to the song. I forgot what they were playing, but I was totally into the music.

I had no idea what the whole Deadhead thing was about. I'd heard them on the radio. I was into classic rock and all that, but I wasn't into music nearly as much as I am now. By the end of that show, I finally understood why people have followed them around all these years and gotten into the whole trip. But I think the whole sixties thing fell apart because not enough people took care of the freedom, understood it, or respected it enough. Everybody's looking for their answer instead of realizing that the answer is within each of us. Somebody can inspire you when you listen to their music and you listen to their lyrics, and you realize, "Wow, this person knows what I'm going through. That's cool that they've been able to ver- balize it. I now realize I have something in common with this per- son."

Ken Fine, aka Kew, 36, organic T-shirt salesman, Liberty, ME:

I believe that when the crowd is really psyched, you get some amazing music out of the band. They start feeding back on everybody's energy, and it's a wonderful energy. I've gone to shows and landed in a mash of people up near the front and not known anybody but really felt close to everybody. That ol' hippie love is in the air! You don't really find it that often, but once I learned how to do it, I can pretty much do it anytime. Grateful Dead shows were definitely the training ground for me. Those magical experiences are just amazing.

For me, I always go to a show with high hopes. Then after the show, I'm always like, "By golly! They did it again!" One of my favorite things to say is, "That's the *best* show I've ever seen!" It's just the *latest* show I've seen! At the Boston Garden in 1994, the ol' geezers pulled off another one! The crowd was psyched up, I was wicked psyched, and the next thing I knew the band was psyched. One of my favorite things is to see Jerry with a big smile on his face!

To the band: Thanks for being friendly. I may not be a friend, but I feel like I could be. That's kind of a nice accessibility. It's all about having fun, which is a good thing to remember. I always respect it when the Dead say, "Hey, do your own thing!" because a lot of people just follow, like disciples, and get a little bit too caught up in it for my taste. That really good energy and that real strong effort the band puts into a show, I think that's a good lesson to those lost people: find something that you're into, that's in your heart, and put some energy into it. It feels good to have other things going when you go to a show, and then for a short period of time you can put an intense amount of energy into being a Deadhead. I was never one who could be a full-time Deadhead. Whatever floats your boat, though. I'm not trying to get down on anyone who's a professional Deadhead.

Annie Myles, 24, music manager, New York:

I don't know that it was necessarily the Grateful Dead, it could've been a different band, but it wasn't. It was them, and they had the crowd of open-minded people who—maybe it was just because they were all drug users—who made the scene on Dead tour, back then, the way I thought the world should be: people being very kind to one another and bartering and just going about their business in a peaceful, clean manner and taking care of each other. Just having good, clean fun. To me, that's what the Grateful Dead were about, even though a lot of it was drug induced and a little crazy and kind of Hunter S. Thompson–ish. It was still good, clean fun. It was the way I chose to do it.

I think for a long time the Grateful Dead provided a safe haven for a lot of people, and an alternative way of living and communicating with one another. When I started getting into it and trying to make money to pay for my tours, we sold a lot of food and jewelry and stuff like that. Stuff that friends had brought back from foreign countries. But really, the only way to make money is to sell drugs, and that's what I wasn't into. It's combining two entities that don't belong together. Most of the people I met who were swinging on tour were getting hard-core and they were getting out of control. I really had no desire to go down with them. The aspirations of a drug dealer, and the desire for cash and a lot of it, and the ramifications of being a drug dealer and having to look over your shoulder all the time whether or not you're secluded within the Grateful Dead community, is just a lifestyle that I never wanted to live. I just didn't want to be looking over my shoulder or be dirty all the time, living my life muling drugs around the country. I'd rather enjoy the music and take it at the level that I wanted to and go elsewhere and find a job. It also got to the point where I grew out of it. I realized there is life beyond Dead tours, and there are only four chords to every song and they're not musical geniuses. But they have an energy about them that is pure. Whatever it is, it attracted me and it kept me there for a long time. I will always be a Deadhead because I love their music and I had so many great times going to Dead shows. But life goes on. I write music, I play guitar, it's fun. I finally found an outlet. And I'm working with Stephani (Warren Haynes's, Allman Brothers guitarist's, girlfriend, a producer/manager), which is most righteous! I like the way things work out. The gods take care of me.

If could say anything to the Dead, it would be: Thank you! Thanks for a good time, man! After working with so many musicians, and being around people who live the lifestyle and actually being on tours and stuff, I realize that my perception of the Grateful Dead when I was younger was much different than it is now. They're a bunch of guys who are making music, and that's about it. I don't think they actually accounted for what was going to happen and the following that was gonna sprout behind them. I don't think they really banked on what they got into! I think the inertia of it all kind of overrode them, and that's cool. They kept up with it, and they kept going. They provided so many different smiles. If I ever met them, I'd just say, "Thank you!" and then I'd talk to them about what they're up to now and who they are and what they're all about. I really don't know much about them as people. You can read what the press prints, but you don't know anybody until you talk to them. The most they've ever done for me is make me laugh and dance and have a good time. They provided a great background for my youth, which was pretty interstellar. I had a good time.

John Popper, 27, Blues Traveler harmonicist, Princeton, NJ:

The Grateful Dead demonstrated on the largest possible terms that you can do anything you care about your way. They had all the success of a band that had to suck the shit out of the assholes of the rock industry, and they never did that. They did it their way, and they did what mattered to them. I think it was not only the way they do business, but their level of integrity in the way they do business that set the pattern for all bands that came after them. Bands like us and Phish are great examples of bands that saw what the Grateful Dead did and saw that anything is possible. The family idea can work. I don't even think the Dead were even trying to do it. They were just going about it the only way they could. I know what that feels like because that's the way we do it. We don't know how to do it professionally, so family is what we require. And it turns out to be a better way to do business. It's smart business. We really see ourselves as a Dead-style band more in the way we do business than the way we sound. Because the ideas are always original when you're talking about music and creativity. But when it comes to functioning in society, it really helps to have a pattern to follow. Even though in the music industry there's no one pattern to follow, there's no way to do it like they did because they lived in a different time than we do. But it's good to have established proof of such fortitude. It really makes you feel not like a total moron to try. No thing in the world lasts. The idea isn't about lasting. The idea is about creating your time. I don't think Blues Traveler has done that yet, and I don't think the Dead have finished doing that. I believe that as long as you're alive and you exist, you're still trying.

Steve Eichner, 30, R&R photographer, New York:

I f I was going to say anything to the Dead, it would be that a lot of times it really feels they're talking right to me. That's sounds cliché, but that's the magic. Whatever they're doing, it's right on, because they're definitely talking to me.

In the beginning, what attracted me to the Dead was the party element, and that's what kept me going back again and again. But after a while, I really got into the music. I started to understand the songs and would analyze the different nights. I also made a lot of friends on tour. It was something I could really identify with. In college, the Fredonia continent always had a keg. No matter what show you were at, if you found someone from Fredonia, you found a keg. And along with the keg were a bunch of people from Fredonia that you knew, and a keg party. Then you were at home at a show. In the parking lot, you knew it was a warm, cozy, friendly scene that you could go back to. If you were in a cold, dark city, it was a place you could go. Or we'd rent hotel rooms together and have these mass sleep jams. There were so many times we'd get rooms in the same hotel. One room would be the tripping room, one would be the eating room, one would be the sleeping room, one would be the sex room. Hopefully you'd wind up in all the rooms by the end of the night. So it was the community of it all that kept me going back.

Annie Harlow, 36, green grocer, New England:

I 'm very grateful that I'm living in the here and now at this time with the Grateful Dead.

Jerry Miller, 51, Moby Grape/Jerry Miller Band, guitarist, San Francisco:

I have admiration for the Dead. I think the Dead know pretty much what they need to know from me. You can't top being the all-time biggest draw of the world. For a bunch of guys from San Francisco, that's pretty good. They've got good spirit, people like them, and they stay true to their fans. That's the reward you get when you hang in there long enough.

David Gans, 41, radio producer: *Grateful Dead Hour;* author: *Playing in the Band* and *Conversations With the Dead;* San Francisco:

I have this theory that eventually you'll end up meeting everybody. In Denver in 1992, I wound up sitting next to this guy I had seen probably at every Dead show I'd ever been to, which by that time was over three hundred. He has this incredibly weathered face, like fifty miles of seriously bad road. I wound up sitting next to him in reserved seats up in the stands, and we got into a bit of a struggle because he thought I was trying to scam his wife's seat. I explained to him I had a seat of my own, but we had one extra person in our party and that person was about to leave. He was kind of obnoxious until he figured out there really wasn't any threat to his real estate. Then he was really fine, and he introduced himself to me: "I'm James Taylor Jones and I've been to nine hundred and seventy-seven Grateful Dead concerts," or words to that effect. It was fun, it was this guy I'd seen a million times. That's happened to me a bunch of times, various people that you see again and again and then you run into them someplace. It's like having this thing in common, this secret society you belong to. There's a thing of running into Deadheads in non-Dead situations, and then there's a thing of running into people at the show who you've seen around forever. And then of course you find out you have six hundred friends in common, you just had never actually been to the same party at the same time. It's wheels within wheels, circles on top of circles. The six-degrees-of-separation thing is way down into the 1½s in the Grateful Dead world because whoever you know knows that other person, and they didn't know that you knew each other, and you didn't know that they knew each other.

The Dead have been a tremendous example to me both in the positive and negative way of how to live and how to be creative. One of the things I've learned about the Grateful Dead over the years is that much of their genius is inadvertent. It's this incredible

combination of the sublime and the lame. It always has been. I think those guys know that on a certain level they've been getting away with murder all this time. And I think on a certain level they don't know how truly brilliant they are. In the gap between those two things, we all fall and stand on one end or another of it. I think that their sense of their own fraudulence makes it hard for them to understand the devotion that they inspire in other people, and sometimes maybe makes them lose sight of their true greatness. I figured out a long time ago that if the audience is going batshit over loud mistakes, then there's not much of an incentive for the band to be better. I think that on a certain level they have been slacking musically for some years. But every time I think that, they turn around and deliver something awesome. They can't consciously make it great and they can't consciously ruin it either. That's what I mean about their genius being inadvertent. They do what they do. I think all of them have ambitions that they realized would never be realized with the Grateful Dead. You're dealing with the incredibly quirky talents of these people, and you're never gonna get exactly what you expected or what you want, but you're always gonna get more than you need.

They've been a tremendous example for me of right livelihood and of instinctual improvisational living. My own music—I like to play music, and I like the thing of playing with people that you trust and trying to invent new stuff as you go. I learned that from them. I also learned to trust myself and my instincts and my standards, and not stand around waiting for anybody to pat me on the head. I have to remind myself of that lesson frequently. It's an amazing thing. The Grateful Dead have provided me with a career and a vast array of life lessons that cannot be discounted.

Timothy Leary, 74, chaos engineer, Los Angeles:

I do a lot of college lecturing, and I always make a point in mentioning the two sacred words that will tell me who's in the audience: "Grateful Dead," and half the crowd just goes crazy! There is a true and, in the best sense of the word, formal, nonhierarchical, nonecclesiastical religion about the Dead.

John Perry Barlow, 47, Dead lyricist/Cyberspace pioneer, WY:

Having the Dead sing my lyrics summons up a lot of reactions. It's very complex, the way I feel about it. I have many emotions, all of them contradictory. I don't actually like my own songs very much, to be honest, and there's always something kind of painful about it. Yet at the same time, if I'm at a concert and they don't sing them, there's something painful about that! I don't feel I've got a way to relate to it as I would like to. I have odd little moments that seem sort of pure; to see something you've written on somebody else's bumper in the middle of nowhere kind of makes you feel there's something that's passing through you . . . it's an honor to have it pass through you. There are moments that arise where fifteen or twenty years after writing a song, suddenly I'll understand what it's about.

I had one of these moments last March with my girlfriend not too long before she died unexpectedly. I had never been in love before that, but I had written about it, I'd thought about it, I'd participated in what I thought was the great collective hallucination on love, the story that we all told, the myth that we had that was important to us in some way. Sometimes stuff would come out that was about that myth, like "Looks Like Rain." I'd never experienced anything like that; it was just there it was and I wrote it down. The Dead started playing that song and I started singing it to my girlfriend, and for the first time in my life, I felt every single aspect of it. It was so appropriate. It was exactly how I felt. It was as if I'd written it to her to sing at that moment. It was so incredible. It was such a pure, perfect moment in my life, in our life.

I'm very grateful for knowing the band and being a part of all this. It had certainly leveraged me in a lot of ways. Even today, where I'm a lot better known because of computer stuff than the Grateful Dead, there is some important element that when I'm going to do a speech or something, and I send out my bio and there's that line in there about how I've written songs for the Grateful Dead, that has a potency especially against the rest of it, that it's opened a lot of things for me. I'm grateful.

I remember one time I asked Garcia, "Why do we have to have these Hell's Angels around all the time? You know, these people are actually committed to darkness, if you think about it." And he said,

"Well, you know, good wouldn't mean very much without evil," which is obvious enough, but there was something about the way he said it at that moment that suddenly made it clear to me in a way it hadn't been before.

This is now so fundamental to my way of looking at everything. The integration of the shadow and the light and the complete seamlessness of both is to me so fundamental to my philosophy. But up to that point, it wasn't really explicitly so. And that's actually sort of a case in point: the reason we had those Angels around was so that I could learn that.

(Excerpts from a letter sent to the Dead, July 21, 1980):

Dear Dead:

I don't know if I have ever been so thoroughly taken by surprise as I was by that job [road-managing for the Dead in 1980]. I've been watching road managers for years and I thought I had it pretty well figured out. And I marched onto the plane right after Pride . . .

I don't feel that I failed you out there exactly, with the exception of Hart's Famous Missing Bag (later recovered). However, given another couple of days on a liquid diet and without sleep, the margin of error would have increased dramatically. That's a hard job. Things happen fast, and you find yourself reacting to events rather than anticipating them. You're also asked to maintain a persona as affable as any social director while, in certain practical areas, dealing with lower life-forms whose extermination would be an act of aesthetic grace.

But I learned a lot, much of which I'm still sorting out. I learned a lot about my own limitations (and capacities). I learned a lot about people I've known for fifteen years. (Having walked in Rifkin's boots for a week, I realized for the first time just how large they are.) A couple of admonitions to road managers, should you ever have the misfortune of losing Rifkin: Never go on the road wearing brand-new boots. I returned here, and after my left boot was surgically removed, I cut off a blister suitable for framing. Secondly, never pretend to be an authority on anything after seventy-hours without sleep.

But seriously, folks.

It occurred to me that the "Grateful Dead" has become a social organism of such complexity that one can no longer determine which parts, or personnel, are indispensable. . . . It's all based on a sense of family, or, to use a more accurate term, a sense of community.

I feel personally committed to you in a way I never have before, and it has a lot to do with what I consider to be your potential in forming and making real new concepts of community. Much of the original sense of that term was lost when America moved out of its hick towns and off the family farm and into corporate suburbia.

I was personally lucky enough to have both a hick town and family farm to go back to, but there are a lot of folks who don't have any home to go back to. They have to find floating communities which are not based on a sense of place. I think the Deadheads (however much their resemblance to Moonies terrifies me) are working on something like this. But it will only be valid for them if the community they behold themselves to be a part of has, at its core, the kind of active interdependency and care which used to characterize every small town in America.

Shit. It's an idea anyway.

Anyway, thanks for another dandy opportunity to find myself. Thanks even more for your assistance and cooperation out there. I expected some obstinance and found none. I'd be honored to do it again for you should I have the time and should Rifkin need it off. I assure you I would come a bit more sternly prepared.

I care.

Love,
The Slightly Rev.
John Perry Barlow

Bill Cutler, 47, musician/producer, San Francisco:

I don't think the Grateful Dead know what we love about them. When I run into people that saw me play fifteen or twenty years ago, they'll talk to me about something that has nothing to do with what I remember. For me, it was the night that the monitors failed, it was the night that I had laryngitis, it was the night that the guy that was supposed to play with came on heroin. That's how I feel about the Dead: I will never forget certain moments, like seeing them play "Uncle John's Band" at Winterland the first time I heard that song. Just the philosophy that was expressed in those songs, and how much it affected how I looked at the world. I wish

Bobby Weir with Cajun chef Rick Begneaud's son, Dylan, Marin County, California, 1990 (PHOTO BY RICK BEGNEAUD)

they would go back to a real concentrated period of song-writing and give us a new batch of songs—not like, Bobby write his song and Jerry write his song and Vince write his song. You've got to let artists do what they want, and I would never presume to tell the Dead what to do, but for me, those records like *American Beauty*, *Workingman's Dead*, and to some degree *In the Dark*, which was the first record my brother produced with them, had a lot of those wonderful songs, where they had played the songs a long time on the road first, and they had gotten that sense of age.

I love the Grateful Dead jamming, and going on trips like "Dark Star." I was so moved by those songs, they meant so much to me, the philosophy in those songs . . . I think about them constantly, in a world where ethics and values have changed so much, and where there's a war on the counterculture. You hear New Gingrich talk about how bad the counterculture was. But the great thing was the values that were instilled in people. The sense of belonging to a tribe, of never polluting anything that was great. Believing in art. The Grateful Dead inspired that in me. Other people did too, but among them, I'd say there's only a handful of musicians I feel that way about: Dylan, the Dead, and a few others. That burst of songs at one point that formed a philosophy, a code that you could live by in a way. I think that the Grateful Dead think that everybody loves them for their spacing out and their freaking out. They've always been embarrassed about their singing. Nowadays, with their little headphones, they sing so much more in tune in everything. But for me, it'll always be hearing them do those great songs when those songs were new and exciting to them: "Truckin'," "Sugar Magnolia," and all of the songs from that period. They've really had a big influence on my life.

Dan O'Neill, 53, cartoonist, San Francisco:

The Grateful Dead just kind of grew like a mushroom. And I think their music is still a primal force to this day. I respect them very much. It's very good music. The melody. They're the keepers of the melody.

I was playing in Ireland a few years ago. There were all these traditional musicians, and then all of a sudden for one whole set they broke into all the music from the sixties. I said, "How come you're playing that music?" and they said, "Well, that's the last time there was melody in American rock and roll. The melody escaped after that."

I have a bunch of sweet memories from back in the sixties, but I'm still having "those" days. I'm having a good time trying to get through this one. I just experience it and keep on goin'. I can't worry about the ones I've already used up! I've got 25,550 days and nights out of life, and I want them all to be nuts! I'm not satisfied with just that period! There's gotta be more trouble out there. The sixties were a good time, and people are still working real hard to keep it going. There's a lot more to life than you might think. Just go get it.

Rachel Clein, 13, student, Marin County, CA:

The Dead are really different from a lot of other bands who try and imitate that era. They just do what they do when they want to. They're not forced and kind of pathetic like a lot of newer bands are these days. I like seeing the Dead. I look forward to shows. And . . . they sell really good carrot cake at Dead shows!

Sheila Rene, 56, music anthropologist, TX via San Francisco:

I think the Grateful Dead have probably lasted so long because of their caring for their audience. Bands try and emulate the closeness they have with their fans. Especially when the Dead started letting everybody tape from a particular place. A lot of bands copied that, as soon as they made it all right to let people come in and tape the show. It was getting taped anyway. Why not give them the best quality? I've always respected the Dead for that. Somehow, everything gets done with the Dead. They say they don't know how to play, they say they don't know how to do this or that, but it always gets done, in spite of themselves.

The last show I saw the Dead do was New Year's, 1990, the last Bill Graham appearance at the Oakland Coliseum. Bill died the next year, so I saw the last flight of Bill Graham at a Grateful Dead show. He came down that year dressed like a Native Indian. He struck Mickey's drums counting down the last seconds of the year. Tribal chief. And that is the grandest thing about the Dead, besides their music, the tribal-ality of it all. I used to go to Days on the Green. Get there at eight o'clock just to watch the tribe come in. That's what the Grateful Dead has: forever tribal members who will come to their call. Should there be a revolution, I would hope the Grateful Dead would just put a call out and everybody would show up.

The Grateful Dead are the only band that still provides that fabulous feeling over and over and over again, and in every town that they've gone to. Everybody remembers something different, but it's a very comfortable place to be, with the Dead.

If I were going to say anything to them, it would be, "Thanks for being yourselves. Keep on keepin' on."

"Afterwards . . ."

Linda Kelly, 33, writer, San Francisco Bay Area:

I feel privileged and honored to have spent time with this great, radiant soul. Thank you Jerry for sharing your music, your wisdom, and your graceful spirit. I will remember you forever and always.

Tom Constanten, 51, pianist/composer, San Francisco:

If I were Gaia—the spirit watching over this planet—and I'd come up with a Jerry Garcia, I'd be going over what I did to see if I could do it again.

Stanley Mouse, 55, poster artist extraordinaire, Sonoma, CA:

A man isn't dead until he's forgotten . . .

Lauren Astra Esley, 20, writer, San Francisco:

The Grateful Dead and its following related a new option for living in American society. Hopefully that lifestyle will not die as did Jerry Garcia. That lifestyle is magical for many, and magic should never be lost.

Sheila Rene, 53, music anthropologist, TX via San Francisco:

I knew that the lifestyle Garcia enjoyed was not healthy, but I didn't care. All the good he did for people more than outweighed the drug problems.

I've interviewed other members in the band, but never Garcia. I was always in awe of his presence and maybe a little scared. Whenever I was in his company, I could only listen to the great stories. He will always be in my heart . . .

Ramblin' Jack Elliott, 62, folk musician, San Francisco via Brooklyn:

I am very sad to lose my friend, Jerry. He uplifted my spirit with his music. I treasure fond memories of times spent playing with him, or listening at concerts. He always had a cheering word for me. He was always in my thoughts.

A giant has left the earth.
Farewell, friend, you are sorely missed. May the angels welcome
you in their midst. You brought joy on Earth.

Bill Cutler, 47, musician/producer, San Francisco:

When I heard about Jerry's death, I thought of what Lyndon Johnson said when JFK was assassinated: "We've suffered a loss that can't be weighed."
My life was changed forever when I met Jerry, played with him, and experienced that kind of an artist. Like all truly great artists, he was generous with his talent, more than anybody I've ever known. I mean, he couldn't wait to do something for you. He was nicknamed Captain Yes because he always said yes when people asked him to do things. Just by working with me in music, he had a tremendous amount to do with my gaining some acceptance here in the San Francisco scene. It was like having a giant light shone on me.

Jerry was a complete product of the twentieth century, born smack in the middle of it, and he influenced the philosophy of millions of people in the second half. There are just a few artists in every century who have done that. Jerry was not a branch on someone else's tree—he was the tree from which branches sprang. That's what was so special about him.

Annie Harlow, 36, green grocer, New England:

Humor. Straight to the core hilarity. That's an encompassing sense I have of my relationship with the Dead and the friends I made along the way.
Thank you for a real good time.

Paul Perme, 31, harmonicist/Gila Monsters, KY:

Thank you, thank you, thank you so much for so many great years, and influencing me and my band. You're gonna influence me forever.

PHOTO BY JANICE BELSON

Rich Yaker, 26, futurist engineer/visionary, Los Angeles:

I met Jerry this past weekend. What? You say Jerry died last Wednesday. I know that, OK? I got to know Jerry this weekend.

I'm someone who did not even consider myself a Deadhead, but I spent the weekend following Jerry's death with a number of people who were close to him personally. Through their stories, laughter, and tears, I got to know Jerry Garcia—the person—better than I had before. I am a bit sad that I came to know what a lovable, humble, spiritual, mischievous rascal Jerry was, too late to experience this for myself, but I am glad that I got to know him. These experiences have made Jerry's death a much more personal experience for me than I had ever thought possible.

Jerry, I think I got the message:

"The wheel is turning . . . You CAN'T go back . . . CAN'T stand still. If the thunder don't get you then the lightnin' will."

Yours Still Traveling Further.

Greg Pearson, 48, computer systems analyst/grand fromage, Berkeley, CA:

The Grateful Dead and Jerry Garcia have been in the foreground and background of my life for the last thirty years. From the revolutionary times of the '60s, through the high life of the '70s, the recession of the '80s and the right-sizing periods of the '90s, they've always been around. Around to provide the entertainment and space where all people were likeable and liked; all music types were appreciated; new friends were made; old friends were feted. Through school, work, girlfriends, kids, a wife and all sorts of other pals, they played the music of my heart and mind to accompany the journey. For me it wasn't just social entertainment; it was family time. I could take any friend with me to the Dead and enjoy both that friend and the Dead. Sort of like my constant companion, for whom I now mourn.

Go in Peace.

Janice Belson, 53, photographer/writer, Los Angeles:

September 1975, I had just finished an incredible three month immersion into the history of pop music. I was the still photographer for the BBC eighteen-hour mucsic documentary, *All You Need Is Love*. As we wrapped the movie, the director of photography said "... Never had a film crew covered so much of the spirit of music history ... but the real magic still had not been filmed or photographed."

I walked into the *Rolling Stone* office and spent several hours talking about my experience on the movie with the editor, Ben Fong-Torres. After a quick phone call, he told me my mission was still on course as the Dead were about to play their first free concert in five years at Golden Gate Park.

I danced with Jerry and the band that memorable afternoon (September 28, 1975). The photos capture for me, the real joy of Jerry. He was a truly divine presence in our lives, giving us all the direct channel to a higher reality.

"And the music never stopped ..."

Thank you dear Jerry.

Steve Brown, 50, filmmaker/Dead's aid-de-camp (1972–1977), San Francisco:

Normally, I watch television in the morning to hear the news, but this morning there was an old '30s movie on. I was watching it mostly for era costuming, cars, set decoration and stuff because I'm making a '30s movie. So I was watching this movie that Wednesday morning, August 9, instead of watching the news.

Around 8:30, I got a call from my partner, who's in Texas doing some location scouting. She asked, "How are you doing?" I said, "Fine. I'm okay." From my answer, it was apparent to her that I didn't know what had happened. She told me a friend had called her from San Francisco to tell her that Jerry had died. So she was the one to tell me, and to hear it from her—a person I've known for fifteen years who's close to me—was kind of nice, because it meant that I didn't have to have the media hit me over the head with it in that kind of cold way. In fact, I had the closest person I know tell me what had happened. I was pretty lucky to hear it that way.

After saying goodbye to her, I decided to unplug the phone in order to not deal

Jerry's memorial, Sunday, August 13, 1995, at Golden Gate Park (PHOTO BY STEVE BROWN)

with it that morning as far as communicating with all the people I knew I'd be communicating with soon about it. I wanted the time really to just be with Jerry. I rummaged around and found some of my favorite Jerry stuff, "Franklin's Tower," "Fire on the Mountain," "Cold Rain and Snow," some good "Aiko." I opened all the doors and windows in the house facing out into the canyon and down to the ocean, and I took my amplifier and cranked it up all 500 watts. I just blasted the canyon, so you could hear it at the beach and you could hear it on top of the mountains. It's the loudest I've ever played music since the twenty-five years I've been living here.

Nobody complained, no police came by, the neighbors didn't bother me. I think they understood. It was kind of my free concert for the whole canyon of Pacifica. It was a nice way to have a healing three hours with Jerry, that release. It was a musical, spiritual scream. I blasted the whole earth. It was the only way I could push through it for myself. I really felt like it was time to scream.

I want to thank Jerry profusely for allowing me to cop a lot of licks off of his personality and attitudes and ways of being, the gentle, kind person that he was, and the friendly, warm, enthusiastic person for life that he was. I borrowed a lot of those personality traits the best I could. I sure as hell can't say I lived up to bein' as good as Jerry Garcia was at 'em, but maybe some of 'em! Jerry was enriched by art, by science, by human nature, by things that he just observed goin' on around him. The comedy of life was pretty much his palette. He was aware of a lot of stuff all the time. I was always impressed with his knowledge and the opinions he had based on a lot of that knowledge.

Having Jerry as a role model has given me, as a result, a very exciting and joyous life. He was a real kind person, a gentle soul. He would do things that other rock artists would not normally do in the way they handled people. Jerry was very friendly and very real.

From "He's Gone" (Garcia/Hunter):

"Goin' where the wind don't blow so strange,
maybe off on some high cold mountain chain . . .

Fletcher Wilson, 33, mountain climber, planted "Steal Your Face" flag on Mt. Everest at 26,000 ft.:

Just as the Tibetans have always called Mt. Everest Sagarmatha, which means Goddess Mother of the Earth, Jerry Garcia will always be the godfather to millions of the Earth's children.

Stuart Wax, 37, music manager, Los Angeles:

Jerry was a vessel of light who brought joy and happiness to hundreds of thousands of people. Unfortunately, the scene around him was turning dark, and rather than fade into the darkness, he decided to go to a place of light.

Ken Fine, 36, organic T-shirt salesman, Liberty, ME:

I happened to be on a business trip in San Francisco when I heard the news of Jerry's death. I wanted to go to the Haight because I heard there were people gathering, but I never got there. I was waiting for the bus too long and got frustrated. So I decided to go do something totally different instead and just forget about everything.

It was weird. I just said "fuck it!" and went with the flow in a totally different direction. I ended up at a club called Bondage-A-Go-Go. I was one of the first ones there, so there was all this room, and I could just flail around like I was at a Dead show! I danced my ass off, which felt great. That's the ultimate, when you get into that energy. But . . . it was nothing like a Dead show. Still, I felt like I was keeping the energy moving, like Jerry would've wanted us to just keep it going and not get stuck.

Anyway, around midnight, I'd had enough of Bondage-A-Go-Go, and I went directly to the Blue Lamp because they had open mike, and I wanted to sing a song for Jerry. I walked in, and there was obviously some Deadhead energy in there. It felt like the old guard, like real San Francisco. It was so subtle, but I noticed a couple of real old classic Grateful Dead T-shirts.

The guy up playing guitar said, "We've lost a good one today, man." Then this other guy came up and started playin' harmonica.

He was the most amazing harmonica player I'd ever heard in my life. Right after that, I got up and joined them with a few others. Then this guy says, "I wanna say a few words. My name is Ramrod. I've been with Jerry and the Grateful Dead for a lot of years." He said he wanted to get back downtown to where it all began to say goodbye, and something like, "We love you and we miss you," and he started playing some songs for Jerry.

It's fitting testimonial that I ran into him here of all places. Just when I thought I was actually moving in a different direction, away from the Dead, I run smack dab into this guy who's been with them since the very beginning.

I'm gonna miss that incredible feeling of all those people together at shows, gettin' that really high vibe, that power of the group consciousness. As a mass gathering, it was incredible, to have that many people focussing all their positive energy and just smiling. It felt like there was a huge beam shooting out the top of the building, like it was gonna blow right off. I always thought it was a fine example of human potential to feel really positive and think grandiose thoughts.

Whenever I saw Jerry smiling and having a good time onstage, it made me think how great the music was and how incredibly generous he was in sharing his gift. How many friggin' shows did that guy play? And he would be up there enjoying himself like it was the best gig of his life. When people tried to pin Jerry down in interviews, like, "What's your philosophy? What's with the Grateful Dead?" Jerry's official recurring statement was "Just have fun!" In one shape or form, that's one of the things he always seemed to be saying.

Michael Mendelson, 41, photographer, San Francisco:

I had thought about it recently, before Jerry died, how grateful I am that I was alive in the same period of time as the Grateful Dead. I was fortunate enough to see them play for twenty-five years.

There are going to be people a hundred or a thousand years from now who will look back on this time in history, and I'm just so thankful and grateful that I was alive in the same time period as the Grateful Dead. I was one of the fortunate ones that got to see them play live.

I finally cried the other day. I'm gonna miss Jerry. I cried for an old friend. It was okay if he was meant to pass on now, but I thought he'd play for another twenty-two years. I just had this number. Anyway, it's not in my hands, that's for sure.

Thank god we have all the wonderful recordings of Jerry. I certainly hope the Dead continue to play, not trying to replace Jerry in any way, but for the sake of the people and the family. For closure.

Dan Wilson, 49, street artist, Sacramento:

Jerry was a human of great intelligence and he spoke his timely thoughts well. He was a leader even if he didn't try to be one. He was a key who turned people, such as myself, to happiness during the '60s, a time when the general outlook continually grew more hopeless and the world was wrapped in negativity.

Jerry was a warrior, but a non-violent sort of person who showed a unique skill for placing his soul and spirit into his music. Millions of us felt that in common.

President Clinton's gentle, accurate, and meaningful words were right on time. He said Jerry was a genius, and later added that he was a genius with a problem. While I agree, I would add that Jerry's contribution lives on through memories and recordings, and his spirited genius is free and doesn't have a problem anymore.

Caryn Shalita, mid-20s, actress, Los Angeles:

I hear the words "Jerry's gone," but for some reason all I can think is, "Gone where?"

As someone who has had many personal psychic occurrences of a bizarre nature (no drugs involved), including seeing the auras of other people and having my own out of body experience, I am sad that Jerry's light may no longer intersect my own in a way that's familiar to me, like it did at a Grateful Dead show, with friends I could catch up with there, surrounded by a warmth that I find sadly lacking in my usual days spent in L.A. I feel sadness for my friends, and friends of my friends, many of whom have lost a person who they considered to be an advisor, a joker, a fun spirit, and a friend they expected to have around for much longer than they did.

But Jerry was nothing if not a seeker of adventure, and I guess in a weird way I have to be happy for him that he found room for himself to grow. I heard he died with a smile on his face. I hope this is true, and that Captain Trips is experiencing Further with all of the joy, intensity and mischievousness he savored during the reality of his last fifty-three years. If there is anything I think people can learn from Jerry and the music of the Grateful Dead, it's that experience is golden, and that experience cannot be limited by definition so easily—sometimes the line where one thing ends and another begins is not that clear. And often, that's the beauty of it.

Chelsey Millikin, R&R manager, San Rafael, CA:

Garcia was a master musician, and for thirty years truly the Pied Piper whose presence will be missed and cannot be replaced.

Annetta Pearson, 50, artist/homemaker, San Francisco:

When the news came, I was shocked by my personal reaction. The grief I felt was as if my mother had died, my husband had disappeared, and a whole busload of my favorite friends had just gone off a cliff.

It was an awesome realization that there were thousands of familiar faces I would never see again.

The party is over. We all knew it would happen one day. That day is now.

Jerry is dead. Long live Jerry.

Steve Eichner, 29, R&R photographer, New York:

Jerry's passing is very, very sad. I'm just glad that he kept on jamming 'til the end. It's what he loved to do.

The Grateful Dead and Dead culture really added a lot to my life. I don't think I'd be the person I am today if I hadn't been a Deadhead in college. I hope the spirit lives on.

Chris Flum, 29, "cool dude," Orinda, CA:

It's not over when the fat man stops singing
the show will go on
We will all see Jerry play again someday
We will all buy our ticket and go
Bill Graham will put on the show
Bobby, Bill, Mickey, Phil, and Vince will be there
jamming with the god with white hair.

Kim Weiskopf, 48, TV writer/producer Married With Children, Los Angeles:

I think many people woke up a bit with the news of Garcia's death. It's now very clear that we are all immortal.

A lot of people may remember Jerry as the white-haired fat man. Not me. I'll always remember him the way he looked back when I used to go see him in the '60s. He was young, full of energy, always smiling, and having a great time.

The day he died, I went home and, I'm embarrassed to say, I ate a whole pint of Ben and Jerry's "Cherry Garcia" frozen yogurt all by myself. Somehow it felt right.

John Popper, Bobby Sheehan, Chan Kinchila, Brendan Hill of Blues Traveler, and their assistant, Gina:

We are deeply saddened and shocked by the news of Jerry Garcia's death. Our sincerest sympathies go out to Jerry's immediate and extended family throughout the world.

We've been influenced by Jerry Garcia and the Grateful Dead, and inspired by the way they put the music and the fans first. We will continue to cherish this philosophy passed on by them and Bill Graham. It is a gift we'll never forget. We, like countless others, will miss him greatly.

Bobby Sheehan, bassist/Blues Traveler, New York:

Jerry Garcia, more than anyone in the music industry or maybe anywhere influenced and helped me in so many different ways, musically and other, that I don't know if I'd be doing what I'm doing today if it hadn't been for him. His death hit me very personally.

My father was a big influence on me and when he died, it was very tragic. I was at a Grateful Dead show the night he died. Then Bill Graham died, and he'd kind of taken on the father figure role in my life. So when he died, another one was gone, but I still had Jerry. And now Jerry's gone. It's a time in my life where it's very strange, and I feel very personal about the things he did for me.

Todd C. Jackson, producer, Marin County:

I lost my father earlier this year to cancer, so I can understand the emptiness and sadness that the Grateful Dead family must feel from Jerry's passing. Although I am only a fan, Jerry almost seemed like a member of the family for my friends and me—the concerts were like family reunions and the music was a brief escape from the pressures of our careers and day-to-day difficulties.

Jerry's kindness, intellect, humor and musicianship can never be replaced, but he leaves behind a timeless legacy of his music and a spirit that will live on in all the Deadheads and in the Grateful Dead itself. I hope the band continues on. There are still so many musical frontiers to explore.

Rick Begneaud, 37, Cajun chef/caterer, Mill Valley, CA:

I had the great pleasure of hanging out with Jerry quite a few times. He was always jolly, cracking jokes, and he was so intelligent. He was so full of knowledge, he knew a lot about everything. No matter what anybody was talking about, he always added something interesting to the conversation. He was great to be around. Yet even to the people closest to him, Jerry always had a real mysterious quality.

I'll always remember the way he'd introduce me to somebody, he'd say, "This is Rick. He's a real nice guy." I was honored to be introduced that way by such a kind and great person.

Jerry did his thing, and now he's left us with a huge community of friends and family. We all have family now because of the Grateful Dead. I wouldn't even be in California if it weren't for them.

I remember the last time I saw Jerry. It was down at the recent Shoreline shows, and I was in the bathroom getting impatient 'coz the line was moving too slow. I banged on the door and Jerry peaked his head out like, "Who the fuck was that?" When he saw it was me, he said, "Oh! It's you. Hey, Rick. How ya doin'? Don't worry about it . . ." I felt really bad, so when I saw him later just before he went onstage to play, I ran over to apologize again. Jerry put his arm around me and said, "Don't worry, Rick. It's okay." Then, as I was walking away from him, he turned and said, "You'll know, Rick. You'll know." I had no idea what he meant.

Now, maybe I do.

Jerry Garcia, radio interview:

I 'd like to disappear gracefully . . .

PHOTO BY KAREN SCHAFF